# SEASONS TO BE CHEERFUL

Dedicated to my girlfriend Tracy Hewitson, who had to endure a lot whilst I was working on this thing and somehow resisted the temptation to bludgeon me to death.

# SEASONS TO BE CHEERFUL
## BRITISH ICE HOCKEY'S ARENA ERA

### LIAM SLUYTER

MAINSTREAM
PUBLISHING
EDINBURGH AND LONDON

First published in Great Britain in 1996 by
MAINSTREAM PUBLISHING COMPANY (EDINBURGH) LTD
7 Albany Street
Edinburgh EH1 3UG

ISBN 1 85158 817 5

A catalogue record for this book is available from the British Library

Typeset in Palatino
Printed and bound in Great Britain by Butler and Tanner Ltd, Frome

# CONTENTS

# ACKNOWLEDGEMENTS

How many names are there on the front of this jacket? One. Just mine. That means everything was my idea, all the good bits, mine. Mine, you hear? Ha ha. All mine. And soon every book in the world will bear my name . . . ha ha ha ha. Oh dear, I feel rather strange . . . I've been under a lot of pressure, I guess . . . Look, to be honest, I could never have done this without the help of some people and, chances are, the only reason you are reading this bit is to see if I've put your name among them, so here goes . . .

Thanks to:
My girlfriend, the long-suffering Tracy Hewitson; my dedicated proof-readers Helen and Anthony Miller, all at Mainstream, especially Bill Campbell and my understanding editor John Beaton; Ogden Entertainment Services, particularly the unstintingly helpful Bernard Eccles; John Lawless, Martin Smith and the rest of the Manchester Storm boys; Julie Oldfield; Lee Pettifer and Orbit International; Mike Smith at PLS Ltd; Andy Yates and the *Manchester Evening News*; Karen Wright Photography; Anthony Beer – what this man does not know about the Cardiff Devils is not worth knowing (nor, frankly, is some of the stuff he does know); Powerplay's Simon Potter; the *Ice Hockey News Review*; Everyone at Sportspages especially David Luxton (but not Dom); Shannon Hope; Stewart Roberts; Tim Dempsey and Paul Fleury; Mark Kuhl, Doug Perkin, Bill Sluyter and John Collett; Rick Fera, Bill Hicks, Thom Yorke and Robyn Hitchcock; and anyone who may have unwittingly inspired me by talking to me about ice hockey sometime. May you all be blessed in every respect. Thanks to you all.

# PREFACE

When Cardiff Devils' Doug McEwan bore down upon the Sheffield Steelers goal during the semi-final shoot-out at the 1995 British Championship, one of the most exciting ice hockey matches ever seen at Wembley was hurtling towards a dramatic climax. An enthralled, capacity arena crowd, not to mention millions watching on *Grandstand*, held their breaths in anticipation as the Devils' all-time leading points scorer took control of the puck and headed goalwards. With the scores level, even after sudden-death overtime, the match had come down to this – a penalty shoot-out. The winners would march on to the final championship match, whilst for the losers the season would come to an abrupt and agonising end. Whilst McEwan may not be a household name in Britain, he was still one of the best players Cardiff had ever had – his nickname there is simply 'God' – and if it came down to one man to save the Devils, most supporters would have plumped for Doug McEwan. He had scored over 300 goals for Cardiff, and now he had to score one more against the Steelers or else the Devils were beaten.

With deft control, McEwan swung in towards the goal and shaped up to flick the puck over the netminder. You'd have put your mortgage on him scoring at that point. At least, that's what sports commentators are traditionally meant to say at such moments. Those of us living in the real world, however, tend to be a bit reticent about gambling our homes on the abilities of sportsmen to score goals at any particular time. A good thing too, because although McEwan was able to get his shot in, Martin McKay, in the Sheffield net, was able to bat the puck away. It was a split second before anyone registered what had happened, but then there was a colossal roar as Sheffield's army of fans exploded with joy and the Steelers players poured over the boards to swarm around the goal in jubilant celebration.

It was all a marked contrast to the previous season's championship when the Devils had meted out a hockey lesson to the upstart Steelers, destroying them 12–1 in the final. For the Steelers, the sweet taste of championship triumph needed only to be rubber-stamped by the subsequent mauling of the Edinburgh Racers in the final the very next day. It was not such a nice moment for the Devils, though, the taste of defeat for them being about as pleasant as one of those funny little burps you sometimes get – you know, the ones where a little dab of vomit inexplicably darts up your throat and you get a really horrid taste in your mouth for some reason. Definitely not a good feeling. They had come within a whisker of defeating Sheffield again and, in all probability, retaining their championship crown, yet even as the Steelers players leapt about, cavorting wildly on the Wembley ice, there was a tangible sense that the balance of power in British ice hockey had shifted inexorably towards the Steelers in what was still only their fourth year.

The 1994–95 season had been a vintage year, and one in which the destination of the Premier Division title had remained in doubt until the final weeks of the season. The Nottingham Panthers had set off at an astonishing pace, unbeaten in their first 21 games, and they had duly collected the first trophy of the season when they beat Cardiff 7–2 in the Benson & Hedges Cup final in Sheffield. The Devils, though, had not been at their best. Notwithstanding an excellent run in the European Cup, they had generally failed to match the intensity of the previous season's campaign and seemed increasingly less likely to repeat their premiership and championship double. Sheffield, on the other hand, after a sluggish start to the season, had managed to build up a head of steam, and as they entered the final couple of months they exuded a quiet confidence.

It was still a case, though, of Nottingham having to lose the title, rather than anyone else winning it from them. They were playing with such fluency and confidence that only a major attack of the jitters could possibly prevent them from taking the title, no matter how well Sheffield had started to play. Unfortunately, just as the season came to the boil, the Panthers did a reasonable impression of a ball of wool as they completely unravelled in the final stages, the final nail in the coffin being gleefully hammered in by a Steelers side that snatched an 8–6 victory in Nottingham on the final weekend of the season. It was, for the Panthers, a desperately disappointing end to the season. Indeed, they managed to lose their last four fixtures, and by the season's end they had slid to third in the table. They then had to pick themselves up and start all over again in the play-offs. Although they managed to scrape through and qualify for the final Wembley weekend, there was now a frailty about them that opponents were able to exploit. The less talented Edinburgh Racers were able to prevent the Panthers – who earlier in the season had beaten them 19–2 – from reaching the final as they took advantage of an injury-weakened side to beat them 11–7. Perhaps it was just as well Nottingham had lost in the semi-final, anyway, because Sheffield were now on a roll, and to lose both the championship and the league to the Steelers would have been so depressing a prospect as to leave the Panthers fans with no alternative but mass suicide.

Instead, it was left to the Racers to try to stop the rise of the Steelers, though the effort of overcoming the Panthers left them with so little in reserve that a repeat performance against Sheffield was about as likely as an Englishman being good at tennis. No great shock to anyone, then, that the Steelers walked the final 7–2. As the three defeated Wembley teams headed north leaving the ever-modest Steelers to reflect on their big-time breakthrough, they must have thought that their worst nightmare had come true. For a couple of seasons it had been evident that they could not hope to match the Sheffield club's off-ice achievements; now it was clear that the gap was beginning to show on ice too. What was more, things were going to get worse before they would get better. Even before the new season had a chance to get under way, some degree of calamity was to befall each of the beaten Wembley teams.

Most dramatic was the complete collapse of the Racers. Traditionally one of Britain's strongest teams, the Murrayfield Racers had run into financial difficulties in the last couple of seasons and at one point they had only been saved from total extinction by a concerted effort to raise much-needed funds by their supporters. As ownership of the club switched from one consortium to another, they were forced to play home matches away from the Murrayfield rink, and for that last season they had to play under the banner of the 'Edinburgh Racers'. To an extent, the success in reaching the championship final was just papering over the cracks as rumours about their ailing financial situation abounded. Indeed, within a few weeks of their Wembley appearance, it was announced that the club would have to relinquish its place in the Premier Division for the 1995–96 season, and instead, drop down into the First Division. All their best players decided to leave, including – horror of horrors for Murrayfield fans Tony Hand – the man thought to be the Elliot Ness of British ice hockey (untouchable, you see . . .).

11

For years, Hand had resisted the lure of richer clubs in order to stay with his beloved Racers, despite the fact that he was often offered obscenely humungous wads of cash because he is undoubtedly the best home-produced player that Britain has ever had. Worse than that though, who should nip in and secure his services? The Sheffield Steelers, of course – which inspired in everyone else the same feelings of resentment as the news that one of the winners of the National Lottery that summer turned out to be a guy who was already a millionaire. Still, at least Edinburgh fans had the consolation of reverting to their traditional 'Murrayfield' tag, which must be akin to finding the favourite watch you thought you had lost forever, the day after having your arm severed in a farming accident.

By comparison, the Panthers must have thought it was their birthday. All they had to grumble about was the fact that they had handed the title on a plate to their most hated rivals, gone belly-up in the championship and then had some of their best players walk out on them during the summer, including imports André Malo and the influential Rick Brebant. Considering how close to glory the Panthers had been, the summer months must have been sobering indeed. As for the Devils, well, surely things couldn't have got any lower than that moment after McEwan's penalty miss, could they? Well yeah, obviously they did. In fact, within minutes of that miss things had got much worse for the Cardiff Devils, as a despondent John Lawless was taken aside by a couple of mysterious gentlemen in suits and, even before he had had time to come to terms with the Devils' loss, been made an offer he couldn't refuse . . .

# BY WAY OF EXPLANATION . . .

In the year I spent writing this book, ice hockey in Manchester went from being something that only a few people cared about, to the hip new sport that everybody was talking about. If you had said one year ago that a game which was usually watched by about 400 diehards could make the phenomenal leap to being watched by over 16,000 people, everyone would have said you were barking mad: almost everyone, that is. One person who wouldn't have said you were a loon was John Lawless, who predicted this exact thing would happen when we talked about it before the season started. Another person who wouldn't have had you locked up was Bill Campbell of Mainstream Publishing. Bill agreed to let me write this book because I had suggested that the sport was on the brink of taking off in this country. The city of Manchester, although it didn't know it yet, was about to get hockey fever, I told him. It would be a story worth following. Whether he actually believed me or not, or was just in a benign mood that day, I don't know, but once I got the go-ahead there was no turning back – I would be following the story of the Manchester Storm from day one. No, scratch that; from *before* day one.

To look at the early history of the Storm, you need to rewind a few years and consider what was happening in Manchester in the late 1980s. In what was a bold attempt to challenge the traditionally held view that London was the only place in Britain that could possibly host such an event, Manchester had decided to make a bid to host the 1996 Olympic Games. Just because 1996 would mark the centenary of the modern Olympics, and Athens, the original host city, was one of the other cities bidding, was no reason to award the games to Greece, they argued. There was more than just sentiment to consider, there were other factors too. The IOC agreed – money, for one – and so they awarded the 1996 games to Atlanta instead. Not knowing when they were beaten, Manchester decided to run again, this time for the 2000 Olympics. It was felt that one of the shortcomings of the original bid had been the lack of adequate facilities in which to hold the games – it was all very well showing off ambitious plans, but if you've actually built something it looks a lot more impressive. With this in mind it was decided, therefore, to show the IOC that Manchester was serious about this Olympic malarky by putting its money where its mouth was and actually building a couple of the state-of-the-art sporting and leisure facilities that had previously only existed on the drawing board. Building began on a new velodrome and a new multi-purpose arena.

As W. P. Kinsella wrote in *Shoeless Joe* (later filmed as *Field of Dreams* with Kevin Costner), 'If you build it, they will come.' At least, that was presumably the idea. When the IOC Committee arrived to look around Manchester and to see the completed velodrome and the arena building site, it was more a case of 'If you build it, they will ignore it and moan about all the rain you get instead'. And so, this time around, the games were awarded to the less meteorologically challenged city of Sydney (and I hope that when the great day arrives, boys, it absolutely pisses it down) and Manchester, once again, was left defeated. Still, at least now the city could boast a spanking new velodrome, albeit with a roof that leaked when it rained; and the massive arena complex by Victoria railway station was nearing completion.

As far as ice hockey goes, this consequence of the failed bids could not have come at a better time. If an arena as vast as Manchester's was going to be a viable proposition, it had to be filled on a weekly basis, and sport was the obvious answer. For ice hockey, it was a case of being in the right place at the right time. Whereas a few years before it had been played out of commercial rinks with capacities of just a couple of thousand, the Sheffield Steelers had recently bounded on to the scene playing out of a 10,000-seat arena. What was more, they were filling the place. It surprised few, therefore, when it was announced that the new arena would also have a resident ice hockey team, the Manchester Storm, the success of the Steelers having established beyond all doubt that such a venture was possible in Britain.

For myself, this was all pant-wettingly exciting. After getting hooked on the sport a few years earlier, and becoming hopelessly attached to the local side, the Trafford Metros, I had once decided to see what all the fuss was about, and went to Sheffield to see the Steelers. Unsurprisingly, since I had been reared on the sport in the less than salubrious surroundings of Altrincham ice rink, I was impressed. To be honest, the sheer spectacle of the sport in a setting like Sheffield's arena blew me away. Imagine the same thing here in Manchester, I had thought. It would be fantastic. Imagine the same thing in Manchester, only twice as big! I was bursting with anticipation of it all.

The book you now have in your hands was conceived in the summer of 1995, when it became clear to me that my beloved Metros were to be somewhat overshadowed by the arrival of this new team, later announced as the Manchester Storm. Rightly or wrongly, I felt that a team led by one of Britain's most famous and successful coaches, playing out of a state-of-the-art multi-million pound 17,000-seat arena, with the most impressive player roster ever assembled in the First Division, might just have a better chance of success than the Metros had, playing out of a rink built 30 years ago out of discarded cinema parts which, off the record, one player described to me as 'a toilet'. It also seemed to me that the Sheffield Steelers' success the previous season – winning the Premier League and British Championship for the first time – would prove to be a watershed for British ice hockey. The sport was, I felt, poised for some exciting changes, what with new big-money teams playing out of even bigger-money arenas, not to mention a new Sky television deal. All things considered, the sport appeared to be on the brink of achieving a level of success and popularity it had not enjoyed since the leisure boom of the '50s. All that was needed now was for some bright spark to write a book about it.

Realising, therefore, that there was a distinct possibility that ice hockey fans would rather eat their own earwax than read about a team they despise, I decided to broaden the scope somewhat.

Rather than concentrating on one team, why not cover the entire sport over the course of a season? At least, that was the plan. As the season progressed, it dawned on me that there was simply too much going on in the sport to cover it all properly, and that I would have to be selective in what I wrote about. For this reason, I'm afraid, this book does not touch upon Great Britain's attempt to qualify for the 1998 Winter Olympics, nor does it cover their solid showing in the World Championship at the end of the season. By the same token, there is little reference to English League hockey – not because it isn't worth writing about, but merely because there wasn't the space to do it justice. Sorry.

What the book does do though, is cover the historic first season of the Manchester Storm, whilst also telling the story of the rest of the 1995–96 season. Steelers fans will no doubt feel that more ink should have been devoted to their team, in light of the magnificent season they were to have, but I would ask them to bear in mind that I wanted this book to appeal to every hockey fan, and although they hogged most of the headlines in the national press they are not featured in as much detail as the Storm. Another thing to bear in mind is that I felt a lot of the people interested in the book would be newcomers to the game and, as a result, I assumed that the reader does not know everything there is to know about the sport. I hope that the more knowledgeable hockey fan will make allowances for this and not get too upset if what I am saying seems blindingly obvious to them. That was my plan. The only thing that remained was to convince a publisher that they should commission a book by someone who had never written anything like it before, about a team that had, at that point, no name, players or fans, playing in a sport that no one knew anything about. Simple. Anyway, now that you know all that, all that remains is for you to turn the page and see what kind of a job I made of it all.

Liam Sluyter
Manchester,
1996.

# 1

# CALM BEFORE THE STORM . . .

After months of intense speculation about Manchester's new ice hockey team, a tiny snippet of information on Ceefax was enough to send excited fans spilling into Sportspages, the specialist sports bookshop, to check if the news was for real. As Sportspages is one of the few places to sell hockey mags through the close season, information-starved hockey junkies find it difficult to stay out of the place. I'd probably be getting severe cold turkey myself if I wasn't working there. Every few minutes, one of them would bound into the shop and say 'John Lawless!' I would usually grin and say back 'Yes. John Lawless!' Then they'd say something along the lines of 'Wow. John Lawless . . .' Brilliant conversationalists, us hockey fans, once we get going.

It was exactly what we had wanted. In retrospect, I guess if you'd asked me who was the best man for the job, I would have said Lawless, but at the time it came as a shock because it never occurred to us that Lawless would ever leave Cardiff. Since the birth of the Devils in 1986, they had won everything: league titles, championships, grand slams, the lot. You name it, they won it – and probably won it the next year, too. They had had the audacity to challenge the side who, previously, had been the giants of the British game, the Durham Wasps, and, in just a few seasons, had swept past them and everyone else into a positon of dominance. Lawless had been with them, first as player, then as coach, since day one. He and the Devils were the best thing to come out of Wales since Shakin' Stevens. And now he belonged to Manchester. In many ways, it was a similar situation to Blackburn Rovers signing Kenny Dalglish a few years ago. It had brought them a great manager, sure, but it also bought instant credibility. It showed the rest of the sport that they meant business, that they were aiming for the top. It also showed that they had a disgusting pile of cash, of course.

Being a highly principled sort of fellow, I had traditionally always rooted for the smaller, poorer teams in whatever sport I followed. If a team was seen to be buying its way to success, that was the green light to go ahead and hate them. I guess most of us do it. It is a terribly British trait, after all, to root for the underdog, be it Frank Bruno or Eddie 'The Eagle' Edwards. We find it easier to slag off the successful than to say 'Well done'. And so the die is cast. If Manchester United, or Wigan, or the Sheffield Steelers fall flat on their faces, the rest of us gloat our heads off. Good thing too, if you ask me. It's part of sport. Part of loving your team is hating another. It's not pretty, but it'd be churlish to deny it. However, all this 'supporting the little team in the face of overwhelming, richer teams' stuff is fine up to a point, but what happens when your team becomes the one with all the money? Well, it's simple, really. You chuck all those principle things out of the window and dash along to the nearest tattoo parlour to get their name proudly splattered across your forehead. Hence, faster than you could say 'Glory-seeking, bandwagon-hoppers', every Trafford Metro fan I knew had suddenly become a fan of the new Manchester Storm instead. They might not have any players at this early stage, or team colours, even a name for that matter, but getting John Lawless aboard was an excellent start and just fine and dandy by us. But why had he left Cardiff ?

Well, there's no great mystery, really. Since helping to found the Devils in 1986, Lawless had taken them from Division Two (Midlands) obscurity to Europa Cup semi-finalists in the space of eight years, but how much further could he possibly take them? Sure, there was a tremendous challenge to be had in taking on the Steelers, now that they had taken Cardiff's crown, but there's also a great challenge to be had in winning the Tour de France on a chopper bike. Like Cardiff before them, Sheffield had taken the sport to the next level in Britain and, clearly, it was going to be very difficult for any team playing out of a 2,500 capacity rink ever to catch up. If the future of the sport lay with big arena teams, as John Lawless felt it did, then the only realistic challenge left open to him was to recreate, if not better, the success of the Steelers somewhere else. He was aware of plans to expand the spectator capacity at Cardiff, but you don't spend over a decade in British ice hockey without realising that for every plan you hear about coming to fruition, there are hundreds that don't. No, a fresh challenge was what was needed. Hardly surprising, therefore, that strange men whispering into his ear about possibilities at the new Manchester arena was music to his ears.

As it happens, a similar offer had been made to Lawless before. The previous December, when it had looked as though the running of the new Manchester franchise would be handled by the same American firm that ran the Trafford Metros, he had been approached and sounded out about the possibilities of taking over a new team. As it turned out, the Mets didn't move into the new building, and instead the arena operators, Ogden Entertainment Services, decided to run the hockey team themselves. Lawless had been intrigued by the possibility of running a team on the kind of scale that Manchester's arena made possible, but, hearing no further, had assumed that everything had fallen through and that he would not be given his chance. Ironic, then, that just as he had reached the low point of semi-final defeat, the men from Ogden had made their move.

'At the time I said that I would think about it for a while, but it took me about a second. I just thought "Yes!" It was perfect timing,' Lawless recalled. For their part, Ogden were pretty pleased too about getting their man.

'The best needs the best,' their Executive Director, Lee Esckilsen proudly intoned, 'and we're absolutely delighted we have been able to work out a deal with him.'

'Ace. Now we'll stuff Blackburn,' added a Mets fan, when he heard the news of the appointment in the shop. All that was needed now, apart from players, was a really cool name for the team.

Everybody coming into the shop seemed to have a suggestion; these included the Manchester Mammoths ('But Manchester hasn't got anything remotely to do with Mammoths . . .'), the Manchester Metros ('Sounds rubbish') and even the Manchester Rapids, a revival of the name used by Manchester's last ice hockey team, who had played before the war. The trouble was that most of the really good names were already taken – the Devils, Flames, Racers etc. – and anyway, the best names were those that reinforced the identity of the place. The 'Sheffield Steelers' is such a perfect name that you can't believe that the English League side previously playing in the city could have been called anything as naff as the 'Sabres'. What is Manchester famous for, we thought? Rain . . .

'The Manchester Storm? Hmm, not much of a name,' was the typical response when we heard it. I wasn't too keen myself, at first, particularly as early reports led me to believe that the 'The' was an integral component of the name. The Manchester Storm. Reminded me of The Status Quo, which is about as cool as an anorak superstore.

'We thought long and hard about what we were trying to achieve here in Manchester,' claimed Lawless in the press release announcing the new name. 'The off-ice competition for public awareness and support, media coverage and the leisure dollar is huge in a city this size, so we decided on a name that is completely different from any other ice hockey team in the UK. And one that hopefully, with a little razzmatazz and of course "lady-luck", will quickly capture the hearts and minds of a new ice hockey marketplace.' What it did to claim the hearts of the Olympic bid committee I don't know. They spent six months playing down the 'rain factor' so as not to discourage a positive perception of the city, and Lawless comes along and calls his team the Storm. Mind you, in fairness to Lawless, 'The Average Level of Precipitation in Manchester Compares Favourably to Sydney in July' was never going to fit on the shirts.

Whilst hockey fans were a little hesitant about the name, journalists were clearly going to love it. 'Storm Brewing in Manchester', 'Storm Warning', 'Storm Set to Break' all appeared in newspapers before the season had even started. Quite clearly, headline writers were finding it a godsend – I look forward to the day when 'Manchester Storm storm up the table' is the headline. The *Manchester Evening News* struck gold when, after a vicious night of thunder and lightning that had kept the whole of Lancashire awake, I was dopey enough to buy a copy because the advertising hoarding had said 'Storm Latest'. A cunning ploy to entice 30p out of my pocket, I'm sure you'll agree. As well as journos, people I spoke to who had no interest in the sport seemed to think it was a good name. It seems as if Lawless was going to have to appeal to people who had never been to a game in their lives, or even thought about it, so this was perhaps a reasonable indication that he had got it right after all.

I soon got used to it. There were much worse names to be found in the sport – the Toronto Sea Slugs, for instance. And once I discovered how close they had come to calling themselves the Manchester Mavericks, I decided things weren't so bad after all. Other possible names turned out to have been the Manchester Lightning and, worryingly, the Manchester Mighty Dogs, but in the event that was too close to the NHL's Mighty Ducks of Anaheim – the team owned by Disney, whose hardened copyright lawyers would have been far more formidable opponents than the team itself could ever be. The Mighty Dogs name was Shannon Hope's idea, Lawless's old team-mate at Cardiff, whose ice hockey design company had done all the logo design for the Storm and would be manufacturing their shirts. 'We had all these great ideas lined up,' he told me. 'We were going to call the arena "the kennel", and the penalty boxes could have been "the pound". I was pushing pretty hard for the Dogs idea, I must admit.' (In the end the rejected Mighty Dogs logo, a Tex Averyesque bulldog in cool dark glasses, turned up as the logo for Shannon Hope's 'Shine Dog Ice Gear' label, where you can see it today.)

Elsewhere, other name changes were very much on the agenda. I've mentioned the Murrayfield Royals already, the artists formally known as the Edinburgh/Murrayfield Racers, but you could also add the Dumfries Vikings, who added the title 'Border' so as to broaden their geographic appeal (does it make the slightest bit of difference, I wonder?), and in the north-east, the Teesside/Cleveland/Billingham Bombers who changed their name practically every period just, so it seemed, for the sheer hell of it. Whilst the Billingham name-changing situation was a long-running joke in the sport, Basingstoke had a name that was just a joke, full stop.

I don't want to shock anyone here, or corrupt innocent youngsters, but someone should have long since pointed out to the management of the Basingstoke Beavers that their nickname was American slang for something that you would be hard pressed to incorporate into a logo without falling foul of the obscenity laws. Whilst I am fully prepared to admit that I am more juvenile in my outlook towards life than most grown-ups, I refuse to believe that I was the only person who, on hearing the name for the first time, associated the Basingstoke Beavers not with industrious, hard-working, amphibious rodents native to Europe and North America, but with, how shall I put this, ladies' front bottoms.

Anyway, after hockey fans in rinks all over the country had subjected the Basingstoke players to predictably unkind abuse regarding the unfortunate connotations of their nickname, the club decided to change it. Apart from the childish sniggers of the crowds, there was also the fact that sponsors are more difficult to attract when you have a comedy name like the Beavers. Whether the main club sponsors, Wella, had any feelings on the matter or not I don't know, but when the club decided to change name and logo they were probably not put out too much. The name Basingstoke Bisons started to appear in the newly drawn-up fixture lists. There was one teeny little problem, though, as pedants were quick to point out. The plural of bison is, well, bison. Not bisons. Still, that little matter sorted out, at least now, when playing badly, the players would only be told that they were playing like a bunch of twits, and not something worse.

Another place where fans woke up one morning to learn that the replica shirts they had bought now bore the wrong name was Whitley. Here, however, the name switch was not a superficial one. The Whitley Warriors were on the move to nearby Newcastle, and so a change in

21

name to the Newcastle Warriors had a reasonable logic to it. Although the first part of the season would still be played at the Hillheads rink in Whitley, the Warriors were set to move into a brand new 9,000-seat arena in Newcastle in December which, incidentally, would also be run by Ogden, as at Manchester. Whilst it was disappointing for some fans that Premier League hockey was leaving Whitley, most accepted that it was a sensible direction for the club to go, and as Newcastle was just down the road they would still be able to watch their team. The Newcastle management were satisfied with the deal, because the move gave them a team with an existing base of support on which to build rather than leaving them having to create one from scratch; and, as the Warriors were a Premiership outfit already, it removed some of the risk involved in forming a brand new team and having to progress through the leagues, as Cardiff, and more recently Sheffield, had done.

Indeed, previously, all new teams had been required to start in the lower divisions and work their way up. However, if the sport was to flourish in big arena settings, new teams would need to be playing at the higher levels as soon as possible. So the rules were changed so as to allow new teams like Manchester to begin at the British Division One level. Although this gives them an advantage, it is a pretty sensible move as investors in arena teams need to get some return quickly, and games between big teams and the lower English League sides tend to be horribly one-sided. No doubt another tempting aspect to the Warriors gaining immediate Premier League status was the knowledge that promotion from the First Division would have been no certainty with the presence of the Manchester Storm, not to mention other capable outfits like Bracknell and Swindon, in that division.

Another team who managed to skip the tedious business of having to win promotion were the Milton Keynes Kings who, despite being relegated at the end of the previous season, were able to gain re-admittance after the Edinburgh Racers had resigned their position in the league, and Peterborough, who had had first refusal, had decided they were inadequately equipped for another Premier Division campaign. At the other end of the scale, the Blackburn Hawks took advantage of the ruling that assures teams with good arenas of at least a First Division place, by being unremittingly crap all season and still retaining their place. And so, as the summer swung into August, give or take the odd team that would inevitably go bust, or change names, or switch towns, this is how the leagues looked at the start of the 1995–96 season:

## British League Premier Division

Basingstoke Bison
Cardiff Devils
Durham Wasps
Fife Flyers
Humberside Hawks

Milton Keynes Kings
Newcastle Warriors
Nottingham Panthers
Sheffield Steelers
Slough Jets

## British League Division One

Billingham Bombers
Blackburn Hawks
Bracknell Bees
Chelmsford Chieftans
Dumfries Border Vikings
Guildford Flames
Manchester Storm

Medway Bears
Murrayfield Royals
Paisley Pirates
Peterborough Pirates
Solihull Barons
Swindon Wildcats
Telford Tigers

(Each team to play against every other side in the division four times, twice at home, twice away. Two points for a win, one for a tie. Top eight teams in Premier play-off at the end of the season for the British Championship. Bottom two play off against top six in the First for promotion/relegation. Or at least, that's the plan . . .)

# 2

# THE PUBLICITY MACHINE

After almost three years of construction, the Nynex arena, Manchester, was opened on time and on budget on 4 July 1995 with one of those ceremonies where a giant key is handed over and everybody claps and smiles while photographers take their pictures and the film crews grab a couple of seconds' footage for the evening news. (I've always wondered who actually makes these giant keys; do you think it is possible to make a living just making stuff like that?) It was a proud moment for all concerned, and not least for me. Although I had nothing whatsoever to do with the construction of the place, I had managed to blag myself an invite to the opening ceremony on the strength of having been commissioned to write this book. Although I had been shown around the arena before, and so was not seeing it for the first time, I was still thrilled to be at the opening. Not only did I get to go on a guided tour of the backstage areas and the executive boxes, most of which are bigger than my flat, but I also got an opportunity to fill my face with free food and beer and share a table with John Lawless, which must have been a joy for him, I'm sure. In years to come I would be able to make everyone else insane with jealousy by boasting how I had been inside the arena long before everyone else. I was outdone, though, when, after raving about the new building to my mates in a pub, a guy outranked me by pointing out that he and some mates had been 'visiting' the place for months: 'It was great, we got away with tons of stuff, steel, cables, the lot.'

The doors were opened to the rest of the public for the first time on 15 July when it was host to a Torvill and Dean performance billed as a farewell, a case of 'Goodbye Torvill and Dean, Hello Arena', which sounded like an excellent deal to me. The arena had not, however, been without its critics. The day after the Torvill and Dean performance, the *Manchester Evening News*, always the first to look for the positive side to any story, ran a front-page item slagging off the new facility. During the performance, the paper pointed out, many people had been so traumatised by vertigo whilst sitting in the upper tier that they had had to leave. Some people had had to wait a while before they were able to get out of the car park and, more sinister still, some of the women's toilets had been blocked! Oh, and a capacity crowd of over 16,000 had smashed the British attendance record, but who wants to read about positive stuff, eh? The first thing that the majority of people in Manchester heard, therefore, about their new arena was that the opening night had been 'a fiasco'. For the thousands of local builders and constructors who had been involved in the project, not to mention Ogden themselves, the criticism stung deeply.

The story was picked up by a couple of national magazines and newspapers, and generally reported along 'disaster waiting to happen' lines. Of course, most of the criticisms were quickly forgotten, particularly once people got to see the place for themselves, but the *Evening News* had certainly got into Ogden's bad books. Let's get things into perspective here. The upper tier of seating at the arena is quite high and fairly steep. This is to give people a good view, which doesn't sound a particularly heinous design flaw to me. If spectators found it uncomfortable sitting up so high, fair enough. This kind of thing happens at every public venue where balconies are used – the balcony at the city's Free Trade Hall for example – but tends not to make the front pages. There are no 'Man in High Seat Horror!' or 'Dizzy Woman Disaster!' headlines. Nor do the delays caused when thousands of people all leave the same place at one time often make the news. Anyone read about how long it takes to get away from Old Trafford after a game recently? The toilet incident was, I admit, pretty horrific, but the thought occurs that the person involved probably had the sense to use one of the other 295 women's toilets instead. Phew, could have been pretty nasty, though, all the same.

In fairness to the *Evening News*, perhaps realising that a blocked loo was not really front-page news they did pull the story in later editions, but the damage had been done. For months after the opening, box-office staff at the arena had to reassure concerned patrons that they wouldn't actually need breathing apparatus in the higher tier. 'But I've heard it's 500 feet up,' one customer complained. A builder I later met who had worked on the arena had told me that the Evening News story had angered a lot of people involved in the project, 'A lot of pride went

into building that place,' he told me 'and it was all Mancs that built it .
Then to have that come out . . .'

However, as far as the ice hockey went, atonement was not too far
away once the paper's sports department got on the case. Despite
previously never having really covered ice hockey in any great depth,
the *MEN* did an excellent job publicising the arrival of the new team
– 'The Iceman Cometh' etc. – and once the season was under way,
they championed the sport by devoting regular column inches to the
team, and frequently carried some excellent pictures from the games.

Indeed, as the new season finally dawned, the Ogden publicity
machine began slowly to roll into action. Alongside the newspaper
coverage there were chances to glimpse John Lawless on telly
proclaiming ice hockey to be the 'best spectator sport in the world', and
there were photo-calls featuring Storm stars posing with Manchester
United players, my own favourite being a shot of Hilton Ruggles and a
shaven-headed Lee Sharpe both grinning madly on the steps of the
arena. An open day was also held when 12,000 people showed up to
meet players from the Storm and the Manchester Giants, the resident
basketball team. This provided Ogden with an opportunity to show off
their new building, and included a competition where people got the
chance to try to score a goal against John Lawless, who was dressed up
as a netminder for the occasion. Ever the good sport, Lawless flailed
around convincingly whilst various youngsters trundled the pucks
past him to the cheers of those watching. Less sportingly, when it came
to his stint, the actual netminder, Colin Downie, stubbornly stopped
every shot that came his way. Whether your opponent is a six foot four
inch Canadian import or a six-year-old from Urmston, it still hurts to
be scored against. Anyway, the open day was deemed to have been a
resounding success, and a great way to introduce the idea of ice hockey
to the denizens of Manchester.

Clearly, the arena had caught the public's imagination, and there
were even signs that the new building was having some impact on the
surrounding area. Most noticeable was the mass of Take That graffiti
that adorned every conceivable surface after the Manc heart-throbs had
played ten nights at the venue, attracting over 140,000 pre-pubescent
girls, many of whom left their phone numbers scratched on to the
concrete paving outside, should any of you be tempted. Of more
tangible advantage to the public was the general smartening up of
many of the buildings in the vicinity. Whilst the adjacent Victoria
station got a bit of a face-lift, the local take-aways went one step further
and renamed themselves things like 'Arena Chippie'. Visitors may also
be charmed to notice that there is even now an 'Arena' porn shop, a

dingy basement importer of adult material that was swift to rename itself. (I only know it's dingy because, in the tradition of true investigative journalism, I had to go in to check. It's not all beer and skittles this book-writing lark, you know.)

Whilst Ogden obviously intended to follow the example of the Sheffield Steelers and sell the sport to an unsuspecting public, they also tried to learn from some of Sheffield's mistakes. When the Sheffield arena opened its doors for the team's first home match in 1991, it attracted a crowd of just 300. (Interestingly, today there are about 4,000 people in Sheffield who claim to have been at that first game.) Realising that this level of support was unlikely to propel the team to national hockey dominance, they started to drum up interest by giving away thousands of complimentary tickets. 'We gave away plenty of free tickets in the early days, but only to carefully targeted groups of people,' explained then general manager Ronnie Wood. 'We wanted youth clubs, sports clubs, business social clubs or any other party to come along. We wanted people to come with their friends, not individuals who might watch one or two games and then not bother.

'The aim was a spirit of togetherness, a party night at the hockey, and we provided more razzmatazz than usual to keep them entertained. It might not have been every hockey fan's cup of tea but we were out to capture a new audience who knew nothing about the history or traditions of the game.'

The strategy, not without its early critics, was vindicated by the fact that Sheffield's average home attendance for that first season was 5,760, a figure especially impressive when you consider it was achieved in the English League where the previous season's attendances had averaged a less-than-mighty 629.

So Ogden also gave away thousands of tickets, and chief sponsors, Allsports, gave out tickets for the first few games to customers spending more than ten pounds. Sportspages, an obvious place to hand out some of the free tickets, were inundated with people coming into the shop after some freebies. In an effort to attract kids, who would have to drag their parents along as a consequence, schools were also targeted. For those too old to be given a ticket by their teacher, or too unhip to know about Sportspages (I'm on an extra bonus from my boss at Sportspages, by the way, if I can fit in more than 20 gratuitous remarks about the shop during the course of the book), they could, of course, just buy a ticket instead. These were the cheapest in Britain, with adult tickets costing just £5, and a child's seat only £1 ('Quid-a-Kid'). Ogden also took the unusual step of advertising the first game, a Benson & Hedges Cup match against division rivals the Telford Tigers, in the hockey press. In order to attract as many fans from all over the country as possible, admission to this first game would be just £1 for supporters of any other team, so long as they wore a replica shirt to the game or showed their membership cards. As the game was on a Friday night, the Storm could not be accused of trying to poach other team's fans, and a gala opening night for everyone connected with the sport was planned. It was, as they say, all about putting bums on seats.

Amidst all the excitement concerning the opening of the arena, there was the small matter of actually having a team to play there. Lawless was starting from scratch, but at least had the pick of the old Trafford Metros players. 'When I first came here, I wasn't sure how strong Division One would be. I was recommended a good three or four players – David Smith was top of the list as far as the Trafford players were concerned. Then you had Colin Downie, a solid Division One goalie, and Paul Fleury, plus a lot of potential players – not just to make the numbers up, but to be given an opportunity to be a part of this.' As a result, Alan Hough and Nick Crawley got the chance to sign for the Storm, and Tim Dempsey was signed alongside the Mets' Ged Smith as temporary cover. The first person to agree to join the fledgling club, though, had been the Cardiff Devils' import forward, Hilton Ruggles.

When Lawless left Cardiff, there had been much speculation that half his team would follow him, but in the event there was to be no mass exodus. Only Ruggles and young defenceman James Manson signed up for the Storm, and Manson only joined on loan. Lawless had attempted to woo the Devils' Shannon Hope along to see if he could star in a Storm shirt and not just make them, but the GB captain felt obliged to stay in South Wales because of his business interests. The Cardiff connection did come in to play with the signing of import Steve Cadieux. Although Cadieux had recently been playing in Switzerland, Lawless knew him from the year he had spent in Wales a few seasons before. The squad was starting to take shape. Hilton had been the easiest to sign. 'He didn't need any convincing,' Lawless told me, but other players he talked to were less keen.

'A lot of players I was negotiating with, I felt were looking short-term – "How much do I get this year?" We didn't have a huge budget compared to some others, because it was a step into the unknown, but I said, "We'll look after you – you won't be worse off, but potentially, you'll be way better off,"' Lawless explained. 'As a player, you've got to take care of yourself, but you don't get greedy. I felt some of the players I talked to just thought, "What's in it for me right now?" I was saying to players, "See your future – look at this place." But some players would uhm and ahh and then I'd let fate take its course, think,

"Well, you missed the boat." But we got the right players in the end.'

These included veteran Daryl Lipsey from Swindon, quickly installed as John's right-hand man, and Great Britain and Peterborough defenceman Jeff Lindsay, who was made club captain. British defenceman Simon Ferry was prised away from Telford, for what was purported to be a record transfer fee, and after Ruggles and Cadieux, the third import slot went to Lindsay's Peterborough team-mate, Dale Jago. (Nottingham's Paul Adey was another target, but after Panthers' coach Mike Blaisdell had lost out to the Storm in the bid to sign Lindsay, he was determined to hang on to him, and with the promise of a testimonial, Adey was persuaded to re-sign.) According to Lawless, the idea was to assemble a squad capable of achieving promotion in the first season – essential if the Storm were going to establish themselves – but which would also, after a year playing together, be good enough to survive in the Premier Division.

The Storm were invited to take part in the early-season Benson & Hedges Cup, a tournament open to all Premier Division outfits and the leading First Division sides. They decided to warm up with the inaugural Milton Keynes Invitation Tournament, a two-day event involving four teams played at, surprisingly, Milton Keynes. When I saw who the other two invited teams were I was slightly taken aback at Lawless's apparent confidence; still, he obviously knew what he was doing.

'I see you're going for this tournament in Milton Keynes,' I said to John at the arena opening ceremony, by way of cheerful conversation.

'Yeah, it'll be a good warm-up for us, though I don't know who the other teams are going to be,' he replied.

I paused a second, not sure if I should be the person to break the news to him. What the hell.

'It's Sheffield and Nottingham,' I said, somewhat apologetically. He paused a second then smiled.

'Should be interesting, then.'

'Baptism of Fire' declared the *Evening News*. Well, I hadn't really expected them to beat Sheffield anyway (3–11 defeat); nor Nottingham, for that matter (3–9). Still, at least they beat Milton Keynes (9–6). One out of three ain't bad. It was enough to dissuade me from slapping a huge pile of cash on the Storm to win the B&H Cup, though. After the Milton Keynes event, Lawless was quoted as finding the tournament 'a little bit demoralising'. It was clear, even at this stage, that there was a burden of expectancy on his new team to perform but, having said that, losing to Sheffield and Nottingham was no disgrace, even if it did show

how much work was going to be needed before the Storm could take their place among Britain's top sides. Another thing to note during the tournament had been the Steelers fans getting behind the Storm after the initial game and effectively being their supporters for the event. Perhaps, after years of enduring bitter criticisms from hockey fans all over the country because of their money and size, they felt a certain kinship with Manchester, who were presumably destined for a similar fate; or maybe it was just the innate love of the underdog I was talking about earlier; or maybe it was because Manchester were playing the Panthers, the team they hate most out of any in our solar system. Anyway, something akin to a bond between the hoards of Steelers fans and the Storm seemed to have been established and it was no surprise to learn later that hundreds of fans from Sheffield planned to make the journey across the Pennines for the historic opener against Telford.

In previous years, my experience of the B&H Cup had not been particularly sanguine. For the Trafford Metros, the GBH Cup would have been a more apt description, as the tournament had merely allowed me the opportunity to witness Trafford beaten up by larger, more skilful opponents. Especially painful had been one night at Humberside where the Hawks had done a savage job of dismantling my early-season optimism by drubbing Trafford 13–0. Character-building though such events no doubt are, I was somewhat relieved to think that such humiliation was unlikely to happen again with a team of the Storm's calibre. Before the Manchester public could get a glimpse of their new hockey team at the Nynex, however, Manchester faced four fixtures away from home in the group stages of the B&H Cup, including a 'home' game switched to Milton Keynes because home ice at the arena was unavailable due to the installation of a giant scoreboard. This prolonged delay to the opening home game proved to be a blessing in disguise. 'Before, we couldn't wait to get started at home,' Daryl Lipsey told me, 'but now we're almost there, there's so much to do.'

Indeed there was. The Storm's first ever competitive match, away to Telford, produced a 6–4 defeat. A disappointment, certainly, but there were mitigating circumstances. Ferry had been unlucky enough to dislocate his shoulder at the pre-season event at Milton Keynes and, much to Lawless's chagrin, it was revealed that Dale Jago would have to miss the first few games of the season as a result of a suspension incurred at the tail end of the previous campaign. On top of this, Jeff Lindsay and Steve Cadieux were involved in roller-hockey play-offs in the States and wouldn't be joining the Storm until their teams had been knocked out. As luck would have it, both their sides enjoyed good runs in the play-offs – great for them, as play-off time is when the players earn the big money, but exasperating for Lawless. In the light of all this, Lawless had had to come out of retirement for this first game and, indeed, had scored the historic first goal, but it had not been enough to avoid fellow promotion candidates Telford from gaining a useful win. A defeat then, but an understandable one, we felt, with so many players missing.

Next came the 'home' game at Milton Keynes, so far the only team to have been beaten by the Storm. The result? 11–9 to the Kings. In the light of this, progress from the group looked pretty unlikely, but Storm fans took some comfort from the fact that the roller-hockey season had ended and the cavalry, in the shape of the long-awaited duo Cadieux and Lindsay, was finally arriving. It was at this point, however, that the phrase about 'counting your chickens' seemed sadly apposite. Lindsay was on his way, thankfully, but Mr Cadieux wasn't. At the ripe old age of 25, he had decided to hang up his skates and live in LA with his girlfriend. Earlier, because I had known nothing about him, I had asked Lawless what kind of a player Cadieux was. He had felt that, during his previous spell in Britain, he had not been all he could have been because he was too young. 'Since then, though,' Lawless added, 'he's matured.' What neither of us realised at the time was that Cadieux had matured so much that he had apparently reached retirement age.

Still, at least Cadieux had been thoughtful enough to give plenty of notice, making his announcement when Hilton Ruggles phoned him up to tell him which flight to get on. I mean, he could have had them waiting around at the airport, which would have been really inconvenient. Ah, well, no chance to get another import at such short notice, so best to soldier on. The important thing now was to gain some good experience before the home opener on the trips to the two Premier Division sides the Storm had been drawn against, the Durham Wasps and, firstly, the Humberside Hawks, the scene of my 13–0 worst-moment-in-hockey nightmare . . .

# 3

# OPENING NIGHT NERVES

One of the worst things about waking up one morning to discover that you are a hockey junkie is the realisation of all that suffering you will be put through. Not just the agonies of defeat or the humiliation you endure when you tell someone you're a fan of ice hockey and they look at you as if you've just told them you're into squirrel-baiting, but the day-to-day aggravation involved in following an ice hockey team; for instance, the away matches. Unless you actually go to a game, how do you find out the result? Waiting a couple of days for the results to appear in a newspaper is not a realistic option – how can you consider yourself a supporter if you allow more than three hours to pass before learning the score? You can ring one of the phone lines available to find out, but there is something particularly galling about hearing that your team has lost and paying for the privilege. ('We lost 13–2!?' 'Yes. That will be £4.87 please.') There is the radio, but the chances of finding out the result from that tends to be fairly remote, so we come to the old reliable television. Not the channels themselves, of course; I mean, ice hockey scores on the news? Are you insane? No, I refer to that old chum Teletext, or Ceefax. The problems with these are that firstly, you have to wait ages before they actually put the results up, and secondly, on my battered old telly at least, when they do finally appear, you get something that looks like this:

BRITISH PREMIER DIVISION
BASIN 6oKE  4-5 CARDIFF
FIFE 6-SH FFI D
MIL4ON .K.4-7
SlOUGH  –  2HUMBEYGHDE
WHITLEY 8-6 @@@@AM444

This falls slightly short of a definitive results round-up. Eventually, things sort themselves out and the proper results appear, but because of the earlier glitches, the thought that the results you are now reading might still be wrong refuses to go away. I know for a fact that at least one result appearing last year was incorrect; after I'd made a tit of myself slagging off Trafford for not even being able to beat a Billingham side whose players had all left, I was informed that, in fact, they had. Bloody Teletext! Anyway, it was against this backdrop of potential mis-information that I tracked down how Manchester had fared against Humberside.

Punching in the numbers for the scores on Ceefax on that fateful Sunday evening I felt the little rush of anxiety we all feel when we know we are about to learn the outcome of something we have been worrying about for some time. As the little numbers at the top of the Teletext screen spun their way slowly to the relevant page, it gave me time to prepare myself for what I was sure would be a defeat. I've always sworn by unfettered pessimism when it comes to these things. If you prepare yourself for a bad outcome, the worst thing that can happen is for you to be proved right; who knows, maybe you'll even be pleasantly surprised. Optimism, on the other hand, is a dangerous state of mind for the sports fan. Like life itself, sport can be very cruel. A defeat, then, I was sure (daring fate to prove me wrong and provide an unexpected win; it doesn't happen often but when it does it is very sweet). My eyes scanned the screen, looking for the news . . .

It was an obscene sight. The disturbing thing was that, glancing at the other scores on display, everything appeared to be in order. There was no reason, apart from wishful thinking, to believe that Ceefax had thrown a wobbler.

'Humberside Hawks 22–3 Manchester Storm.'

22–3! OK, I had expected them to lose, but 22–3? That wasn't a hockey scoreline, it was a time of day. After a troubled night's sleep (22–3!) I got up and went to work. My workmates bravely masked their deep feelings of commiseration by pretending to be completely indifferent when I told them the score. I was still in shock.

'I mean, maybe the score was wrong,' I reasoned.

'Yeah, perhaps they won 22–23.' One of my colleagues chirped. Even I couldn't accept self-delusion on that scale. There was no doubt about it. They had been stuffed. The words 'laughing' and 'stock' popped into mind. Perhaps I could write a book about figure skating instead.

'The worst moment of my hockey career' was how Lawless described it. Since at Cardiff a draw had been calamitous enough, it was probably no exaggeration on Lawless's part. Changes needed to be

34

made. Unless improvement was forthcoming, Lawless added, he was quite prepared to clear out the whole squad and start again. Another performance like the Humberside débâcle and they would be out. Blimey, we thought; on to Durham, then. This time things were different. This time they held out for 17 and a half minutes before Durham scored – an improvement on the 41 seconds they had lasted against Humberside – but then things went downhill, with Durham scoring another nine unanswered before Ruggles ruined the Wasps' shut-out ambitions; 11–1, the final score.

Time for the home opener. Fearful of what kind of scoreline would result, we made our way to the Manchester Nynex arena for the historic first game. No one knew what kind of crowd to expect; after recent results I felt that 6,000 would be a good start, but what became clear from the onset was that Mancunians were in short supply. As we approached the stadium we noticed support had come from all over the country. Most obvious, as they always are, were the Steelers fans. They arrived by the coachload with their rattles and drums, and throughout this first game, the night was to be punctuated by choruses of 'Steelers!' There were also plenty of people wearing Swindon Wildcats shirts. Daryl Lipsey, a great favourite in Swindon after spending nine seasons in Wiltshire, found that his every move was to be applauded warmly by the Wildcats contingent, which was sporting of them, considering how the Storm were now one of their main rivals. By the same token, well-wishers from Cardiff arrived in numbers to say hello to Lawless – and to Ruggles and Mason as well, I guess. Warriors fans came down from Whitley, possibly to get some kind of sneak preview about what life in a new arena was going to be like for them, and Telford fans arrived because, well, it was their team Manchester was playing, after all.

Indeed, amid all the excitement it was easy to forget that a match was due to be played. By face-off time the entire bottom tier of the building had filled with expectant hockey fans, with more fans still queuing outside. More than 6,000 after all, I thought. It was announced that the face-off would be put back a few moments in order to allow everyone in in time to see the start. To keep everyone entertained, the public address system pumped out the obligatory rock anthems, and the giant video screens on the scoreboard were used to show pictures of various members of the audience. Cheesy though such sub-candid camera antics may seem, they were actually very entertaining. Typically, the camera would home in on someone reading their programme, or picking their nose, then the announcer would cheerfully say something along the lines of, 'You. Yes, you. Go on. Give us a wave.' At which point the unsuspecting prey would glance up and see a 50-foot image of him or herself looking gormless being beamed live to everyone in the building. Mortified, the person would then shriek with embarrassment, go lobster-red and cover their faces in horror. Needless to say, it made compelling viewing. When not being used to torture various members of the audience, the screen showed commercials. During the match it showed replays of the action. If everyone was impressed by the arena up to this point, the best was yet to come.

Suddenly, the lights dimmed, and the noisy chatter of the audience gave way to excited cheering. Searchlights danced around the arena as the announcer read out the names of the Telford players, each bounding on to the ice in turn. Then a pause, the screen went blank and a hush fell upon the audience. The dramatic, staccato introduction to Dire Straits' 'Private Investigations' boomed out as, one by one, letters appeared on the scoreboard, forming a message welcoming us all to the arena. As the excitement grew, the scene on the scoreboard changed again, to an aerial view of the arena itself. With a tumultuous rumble of thunder, and a shattering crash, the Storm logo, which had now taken on a sinister, menacing air, spun around above the image of the arena. Lightning bolts cascaded from above, the logo illuminated by their incandescent brilliance. The effect was spellbinding, gasps from the audience clearly audible; the scene shifted again.

This time the image was of an ice rink. The camera prowls around the surface, showing a Storm player on the ice. The camera speeds up, crashing around the rink as the Storm players pound their opponents into the boards, the noise at this point thunderous. Suddenly, amid the smoke on the screen, a Storm player appears right in front of us. In slow motion he takes a slapshot straight at us. The puck hurtles towards the screen; in an instant, the viewpoint is suddenly from that of the puck itself, heading towards a netminder. Like an Exocet, it tears towards the goal; the netminder throws up his glove to catch it but, before we can catch our breath, the netminder's mask mutates before our eyes into the Storm logo, the music an insane cacophany. The effect was awesome. The audience cheered, as dry ice rose from the tunnel and the announcer, by now almost hysterical, brought everything to a climax. 'Ladies and gentlemen, let's raise the roof for the MANCHESTER . . . STORM!' The building almost shook with excitement as the players took the ice, their images emblazoned in turn on to the giant screens above. The noise was deafening. I cannot remember the last time I was this excited. The introductions ended, the players lined up on the bluelines. The audience had been cranked up as far as they would go. And then they had to go and spoil it all. 'Ladies and gentlemen, please be upstanding for the national anthem.'

Ice hockey thrives on atmosphere, and at the Nynex arena the atmosphere was superb, but broken by observing some naff tradition. At every ice hockey match I have ever been to, the national anthem has been played before the start. In North America, anthems are still played at the drop of a hat. In the US people are so brainwashed by their national anthem that once, at the end of an Atlanta Falcons game, the scoreboard accidently flashed up the message 'Please rise for the playing of the National Anthem' instead of 'Thank you for coming to the game,' and everyone in the stadium stopped filing out and stood awkwardly to attention for several minutes until someone realised and put the right message up. In Britain we are an older nation, and our feelings towards the anthem are more ambiguous. Most people only rise to attention in the first place because they are compelled to out of an acute sense of embarrassment. Ice hockey is, first and foremost, a source of entertainment, but do they play the national anthem before every football match, or at the cinema, or anywhere at all apart from the last night of the Proms? For a big game, a cup final or an international when both anthems are played, fair enough, it creates a sense of occasion for what is a rare event; but week in week out, why play the national anthem every time Medway play Guildford? Anyone else out there who feels the same as I do should make their feelings known to the rink managers. It is time, I feel, for us to sit down and be counted.

The hiatus quickly forgotten, we settled down to watch the game. The referee called the two centres together for the face-off. This was it. Ice hockey had returned to Manchester. The puck was dropped, a whirl of blades and sticks, and we were off. After a build-up like that, national anthem notwithstanding, it was always going to be difficult for the match to live up to everyone's expectations. In the event, although far from a classic, it wasn't all that bad. A little scrappy, certainly, but with Manchester nervous about finally playing at this new monster rink of theirs, and Telford determined to poop the party, this was perhaps understandable. However, 2.49 into the game, the moment we had all been waiting for arrived. Hilton Ruggles broke clear. As the defencemen furiously backpedalled, Ruggles, with his natural goalscorer's instinct, bore down on Dave Graham in the Tigers' goal. He faked to his left, drew the puck to the right, and slotted it home. It was one of the sweetest moments any hockey fan in Manchester had ever known. It was, I felt, a moment of poetry. After all the waiting, after all the setbacks, the Storm had finally arrived. Pity that Telford had to go and spoil things by scoring the equaliser almost immediately.

With no further scoring in the first period, those members of the crowd who had nipped out during the interval to buy tacos, beer and burgers, and were late returning to their seats, were somewhat bemused to see that they had missed three goals, all scored within a few minutes of the restart. Claude Dumas, formerly at Trafford, grabbed a goal for the visitors in between a brace from Dale Jago. By this stage, though, I had some explaining to do. After the Milton Keynes tournament, where I had felt that the Steelers and the Storm had developed some degree of solidarity, I had been busy telling the mates I had managed to drag along to this historic opener that, not only would thousands of fans be arriving from Sheffield, but that furthermore, they would all be on Manchester's side. However, after each Telford goal had been greeted with a colossal roar from the Sheffield contingent, my friends were questioning my earlier judgement. They had a point, I admitted. It had become evident that the bulk of the Sheffield fans there were supporting the Tigers.

Such treachery seemed inexplicable at first, but then I noticed a trend amongst the differing allegiances of the various groups of supporters. The Telford fans were there to support the Tigers (I must concede that there was a reasonable degree of logic in this, unfortunate though it seemed to me at the time) whereas the Cardiff fans seemed to be rooting for Lawless's boys because, well, they still loved him, after all, and likewise the Wildcats with Lipsey. So perhaps the Steelers were behind the Tigers because of one of the players. Checking the programme I recalled that Dumas had had a brief spell at Sheffield. However, this didn't seem to be the most compelling of reasons to wish defeat upon the Storm. Then I noticed a cheer whenever the Tigers' Rob Wilson was on the puck. Of course. Wilson had been with the Steelers last season, helping them to that championship, and, indeed, would be back on loan to Sheffield for the duration of their Europa Cup campaign. Even so, I felt it was a bit mean for them to turn up on Manchester's big day and root for the opposition; perhaps the old Yorks/Lancs rivalry was rearing its head. Whatever the reason, they certainly didn't hold back when it was Wilson who netted Telford's equaliser on the powerplay. One day, they would rue this betrayal.

With the score delicately balanced at 3–3, it was clear that everyone was enjoying the match. The in-game presentation was easily the most impressive I had ever seen with the giant scoreboard being used to display film clips and animated sequences to complement the action. For instance, whenever a Telford player was sent to the sin-bin, Arnold

Schwarzenegger would pop up on screen to send them off with a 'Hasta la vista, baby'. And whenever it was a Storm guy who had fallen foul of the rules he popped up with 'I'll be back'. Needless to say, the crowd loved it. With the bulk of the Mancunians in attendance presumably watching their first ever ice hockey match, it was up to the fans of the other teams to provide the bulk of the atmosphere. It was here, I must admit, that the Steelers fans came into their own.

Despite their inexcusable tendency to cheer Telford goals, they really got the rest of the crowd going, including the inevitable Mexican wave, later embarrassingly dubbed 'The Manchester Wave'. Besides, they obviously weren't all that bothered about who was going to win this match as they kept the volume up even when Martin Stokes notched a couple for the Storm to put them two up going into the third period. My hopes that this would inspire Manchester on to greater heights in the final section proved unfounded when the Tigers drew level within two minutes of the restart. David Smith put the Storm back in front with quarter of an hour to go with a superb drive to the net, only for Simon Leach to grab his second of the night to level the score at six apiece. The final moments were filled with breathless, end-to-end charges, but at the final hooter no one had quite produced enough to steal victory. And that, as they say, was that. The Storm had arrived.

Filing out of the arena that night, the most tangible emotion among Storm supporters was one of relief. Not only had they survived the night without enduring another drubbing, but the attendance, announced shortly before the end of the game, of 10,034 was just 16 short of Sheffield's modern-day record, and was massively encouraging. Certainly, the bulk of this crowd had been composed of supporters of other teams, but the excitement generated on this first night had been enough to hook those débutant Mancunians there. Like Arnie, they would be back.

# 4

# REALITY BITES

The 1995–96 season had started in earnest with the Benson & Hedges Cup tournament, a competition traditionally known as the Autumn Cup – probably because it is played in the autumn, although I'm only guessing. The competition starts with a round-robin series of games, after which the top two teams in each group qualify for the two-legged knock-out stages. The final, which is played as a single match, has in recent years been played at the Sheffield arena, which is a great venue when you consider the capacity, but slightly flawed when you consider that the Steelers are bound to end up playing in it sooner or later. (Last season, callers to the Sheffield box-office who wanted to buy tickets for the final were presumptuously asked if they wanted to sit at the Steelers' end or not. Needless to say, they got beaten in the semi-final by Cardiff. Ha!)

Although the Cup is contested primarily by the big boys of the Premier, some of the First Division sides are invited along. Usually, this means that the Premier Division sides get to warm up for the start of the league campaign by pasting their hapless First Division chums, getting their eye in, as it were, whilst the First Division sides (un)lucky enough to blag a place find that, gate money apart, the whole experience is one of damage limitation. Whilst a run-out against tough opposition may be good for testing mettle, it is unlikely to do much for morale if you get stuffed 22–3 – not that that would ever happen, of course. In the event, the group stages went pretty much according to plan, with Premier sides coming out above the First Division ones in every group, although with 10 Premier teams contesting eight quarter-final places, Milton Keynes and Slough were squeezed out. This is how the groups finished:

| Group A | P | W | L | D | Gls | Pts |
|---|---|---|---|---|---|---|
| Fife Flyers | 8 | 7 | 1 | 0 | 72-38 | 14 |
| Newcastle | 8 | 4 | 2 | 2 | 76-46 | 10 |
| Blackburn Hawns | 8 | 4 | 4 | 0 | 59-63 | 8 |
| Paisley Pirates | 8 | 3 | 3 | 2 | 64-51 | 8 |
| Murrayfield Royals | 8 | 0 | 0 | 8 | 25-98 | 0 |

| Group B | P | W | L | D | Gls | Pts |
|---|---|---|---|---|---|---|
| Durham W. | 8 | 8 | 0 | 0 | 66-20 | 16 |
| Humberside | 8 | 5 | 2 | 1 | 74-37 | 11 |
| Milton Keynes Kings | 8 | 2 | 5 | 1 | 56-61 | 5 |
| Telford Tigers | 8 | 2 | 5 | 1 | 38-78 | 5 |
| Manchester Storm | 8 | 1 | 6 | 1 | 38-76 | |

| Group C | P | W | L | D | Gls | Pts |
|---|---|---|---|---|---|---|
| Sheffield Steelers | 8 | 7 | 1 | 0 | 81-26 | 14 |
| Nottingham Panthers | 8 | 7 | 1 | 0 | 67-21 | 14 |
| Guildford Flames | 8 | 2 | 5 | 1 | 42-63 | 5 |
| Swindon Wildcats | 8 | 2 | 6 | 0 | 40-73 | 4 |
| Peterborough Pirates | 8 | 1 | 6 | 1 | 31-78 | 3 |

| Group D | P | W | L | D | Gls | Pts |
|---|---|---|---|---|---|---|
| Cardiff Devils | 8 | 7 | 0 | 1 | 74-24 | 15 |
| Basingstoke Bison | 8 | 4 | 2 | 2 | 41-34 | 1 |
| Slough Jets | 8 | 4 | 3 | 1 | 55-44 | 9 |
| Bracknell Bees | 8 | 2 | 6 | 0 | 38-67 | 4 |
| Medway Bears | 8 | 1 | 7 | 0 | 22-61 | 2 |

Before the tournament started, I asked John Lawless whether he looked at the B&H Cup as good match practice before the serious business of the league began. 'Oh no. We intend to win it,' he had replied. Foolishly, at the time I believed him. Way to go, John! But in retrospect, I put the remark down to bravado. The Storm had no chance of winning the group let alone the tournament, and in the end the Storm finished bottom of their group, prompting naff journalists to suggest that the Storm in the B&H Cup had looked more like a storm in a teacup. Having said that, they did gain the satisfaction of their first competitive victory, when they repeated their pre-season feat of winning at Milton Keynes, and that alone was something to build upon, particularly when you consider how rarelyFirst Division sides beat their Premier Division brothers, let alone away from home.

Other instances of Premier Division 'giant-killing' came at Telford, who also beat Milton Keynes, Blackburn, who beat Fife, and Bracknell who chalked up a five goal shut-out over Basingstoke. Generally, though, the odd victory over Premier opposition counted for little as there was no chance that any of the First Division sides would outstay their welcome and actually qualify for the next round. Most of the attention, therefore, was focused on the performances of the Premier Division clubs. Top honours went to Humberside and Cardiff, neither of whom lost a game, but there were also some fun and games in Group C, where Sheffield and Nottingham were thrust into combat. With both sides winning all their other games in the group, qualification was never going to be in doubt, but an early victory in the head-to-head contests for either side could provide a useful psychological edge in the weeks to come. In the event, both contests were low-scoring, keenly fought games. The first game, at Sheffield, saw Nottingham gain a surprise 4–3 win, the Steelers' first defeat of the season, but Sheffield then returned the favour when they won 2–1 in Nottingham. Honours even for now.

The draw for the quarter-finals, arranged this year on a geographical basis so as to reduce travelling costs for the two sides, was as follows:

| | | |
|---|---|---|
| Cardiff Devils | v | Sheffield Steelers |
| Basingstoke Bison | v | Nottingham Panthers |
| Fife Flyers | v | Newcastle Warriors |
| Humberside Hawks | v | Durham Wasps |

The pick of the ties was undoubtedly the repeat of the previous year's semi-final, Sheffield v Cardiff, which Cardiff had won 12–8, on aggregate, but the draw as a whole came under criticism. Because the group winners had not been seeded, the games involving Fife and Newcastle, and Humberside and Durham, were repeats of games already played in the tournament. Apart from being a little boring for the fans, this meant that actually winning the group gave no advantage whatsoever over coming second; a curious way to run things.

Whilst all this had been going on, the little brother to the B&H Cup, the Autumn Trophy, had got under way too. (Nice to see the traditional title of 'Autumn' live on in some form, although last year they didn't get round to finishing the competition until February.) This was a tournament open to the teams who had not been invited to play in the B&H Cup. This year, that meant only four teams were taking part, so it is unlikely that anyone booked the open-topped bus and civic reception in case they won it. For the record, the group ended like this:

Autumn Trophy Group Standings

|                           | GP | W | L | D | GF | GA | Pts |
|---------------------------|----|---|---|---|----|----|-----|
| Chelmsford Chieftains     | 6  | 5 | 0 | 1 | 65 | 29 | 11  |
| Dumfries Border Vikings   | 6  | 4 | 1 | 1 | 58 | 28 | 9   |
| Solihull Barons           | 6  | 2 | 4 | 0 | 41 | 56 | 4   |
| Billingham Bombers        | 6  | 0 | 6 | 0 | 20 | 71 | 0   |

The top two sides, Dumfries and Chelmsford, qualified for the two-legged final. This, however, proved to be one of the saddest games of the season. Dumfries, sensing that this was a good chance to win their first ever piece of silverware, were fired up for the contest, especially since Chelmsford had had the better of the group games. The Chieftains, on the other hand, stricken with injuries and unable to organise a full squad for the game at short notice, were able to fly up only nine players for the first leg, none of whom were netminders. By the time they had managed to recruit some guest players, including Ayr's Under-19s goalie, David Kennedy, who had never played a senior game in his life, the omens were not good. Predictions that the Chieftains were in for a torrid 60 minutes proved to be wide of the mark, though. In the event, it was only torrid for 45 minutes, by which time Chelmsford had lost so many players through penalties that they were unable to continue. A shame really, because with the score poised at 23–0 to Dumfries, the game could have gone either way . . .

The BIHA decided not to bother with a return leg and awarded the trophy to Dumfries who, presumably, had felt confident that they would have held Chelmsford to a 22-goal lead in the second leg, anyway.

'To lift a trophy is nice,' said the Vikings' Steve Marshall. 'We think the BIHA decision is a fair one, but we can't help having a bad taste in our mouths. Chelmsford reduced it [the final] to a pantomime.' The Chieftains, however, were dismayed at the decision, and somewhat bitter about the whole event. Not only had they forked out money on flying players up to Dumfries, and now found that they would get no chance to recoup some of the losses with gate receipts from the return leg, but they also felt horribly guilty for exposing young David Kennedy to the trauma of facing 85 shots in his first ever game. Still, at least Dumfries got to parade their first ever piece of silverware at their next league fixture – against Chelmsford. For the Chieftains, the only consolation from the whole saga came a few days later when, indignant at the suggestion in the Peterborough programme that they had deliberately tried to get the game abandoned in order to avoid further humiliation, they exacted some degree of revenge by beating the Pirates 8–7 in a league match.

The start of their First Division campaign had seen John Lawless make a few early changes to the Manchester Storm roster, with ex-Metro Tim Dempsey relocating to Germany for a year to pursue his academic studies, and two other old Trafford players, Ged Smith and Paul Fleury, being released. Whilst Ged Smith had generally been seen as just helping out the Storm until more players arrived, Fleury's departure was more of a surprise. Lawless had taken advantage of the British passport holder ruling to beef up his squad, adding a couple of forwards in 19-year-old Stefan Barton and 24-year-old Martin Smith, who had started the previous season as an import with the Trafford Metros. At the same time, he added defenceman Steve Barnes who, strangely enough, had just finished playing for another Storm, Toledo in the States. Suddenly there was no room for Fleury, who up to that point had struggled with his form. Some observers felt that Fleury's lack of form was less of a factor than his lack of Canadian accent.

'He is a victim of the rule changes,' conceded Lawless. 'Originally I didn't plan to bring in these extra guys but I decided I had to aim higher than I originally had done.'

Fleury was philosophical about it all.

'I'm sick about it, although I guessed it might happen after the rule changes allowing more imports in. Though I didn't think it would happen so quickly . . . I was one of the highest-paid Brits so I guess it was obvious I would be first to go.'

It was a shame for Fleury, who on his day is one of the more skilful British players in the league, but it was also an indication of the high stakes the Storm were dealing with even this early in the season.

'I'm sure Paul will get hooked up with another team in the First Division. He might even come back to haunt me,' said Lawless just before Fleury signed with division rivals the Blackburn Hawks.

Of the three new arrivals, Martin Smith made the most immediate impact, linking up well with Hilton Ruggles on the first line and, after scoring on his debut in the win against Milton Keynes in the B&H Cup, he started to rack up the points in the league. There was still a vacant import slot left for Lawless to fill, but with early league games not proving too difficult for the Storm, the sense of urgency was not too great.

Whilst the Manchester Storm had been taking part in the B&H Cup (or should that be 'taken apart in the B&H Cup'?) some of the other First Division clubs were well into their league programme. The early pacesetters were Paisley and Dumfries, who took turns early on to lead the division. The success of the Paisley Pirates, who had been the surprise team of the previous season, was not so unexpected this time around, but Dumfries, who were playing only their third season, even surprised themselves when they started so brightly, topping the table after their first eight games. Much of this success was attributed to some useful signings Dumfries had made during the close season, notably the trio of Pentland, Lamb and Hanson from the beleaguered Murrayfield side, with Hanson, a former GB netminder, proving to be the pick of the bunch. Their first big test of the new campaign came on the first day of October when Dumfries visited the Nynex for the first-ever league match to be played in Manchester. A crowd of 4,880 turned out to see the Vikings face a Storm side determined to put the frustrations of the B&H Cup behind them. Dale Jago, fast emerging as the Storm's key player, put the home side ahead in the first period. After Dean Richards had equalised and David Smith had restored the Storm's lead, Manchester's other Smith, new signing Martin, put them 3–1 up. From then on the game was never in doubt. By the time Ruggles had notched his first league goal in the third period, the Storm were already assured of their first-ever league win, 6–2 the final score. After such an arduous B&H Cup campaign the win was sweetly satisfying for the Storm.

At the other end of the table, four sides had already become embroiled in the massive struggle to assert themselves as the worst side in the British League. That Murrayfield should be one of the stragglers surprised no one. Losing all your top players, resigning your place in the Premier League, flirting yet again with total financial ruin and then sacking your player-coach before he had even played his first game of the season is hardly what you would call 'ideal preparation'. Having said that, I can't help but hold a sneaking regard for the coach concerned, Len Giacalone. Just what kind of coach was he to get himself sacked 11 days into the job, apparently because he was so poor in practice? Sadly, we may never now know. A great loss to the game, surely. Still, it was not all doom and gloom for Royals fans. The Murrayfield club management bravely decided to go with youth for the forthcoming season – not that they had a lot of choice, I'll admit, but it meant that they were icing a team with players whose average age was just 20 years old. Obviously, this was going to result in a lot of losses, but it would probably be good experience for these young players, some of whom would emerge all the stronger at the end of the season. In theory, anyway.

Another side you'd expect to find in the box marked 'struggling no-hopers' in the metaphoric hockey jumble sale, were the Billingham

Bombers. Originally formed in 1973, the Bombers had enjoyed a chequered history, not to mention that series of dubious and bewildering name changes. As recently as the 1992–93 season, they had been a decent Premier League side. In 1993–94, however, they had a miserable season, winning just five games out of 44. Inevitably, they faced a relegation play-off and, equally inevitably, they fared poorly, being relegated with barely a struggle. Determined to make a speedy return, they began the 1994–5 season with a formidable squad, but a series of injuries, not to mention defender Mark Pallister's failed drug test, followed by catastrophic cash-flow problems, did not augur well. By the time the Bombers had suffered the ignominy of having to ask a local journalist who had travelled down to Medway with them to lace up his skates and play, so short were they of players, the writing was on the wall. They resigned from the league in January. This season, there had been a fair degree of uncertainty about whether or not they would be able to ice any kind of side at all. In the end, though, they were just about able to confirm their place, but given their experiences the previous season, they wisely decided to start again on a more modest scale. Given all this, no one, least of all their loyal, albeit small, support, expected Billingham to be any good. Just surviving this season would be a success in many respects. And they were right. They weren't any good.

The match between Murrayfield and Billingham on 21 October, therefore, was eagerly anticipated by both clubs. It was a chance, after all, for one of them to win a game – they had survived 29 games without a win between them up to this point in the season. What's more, with that elusive first victory in the offing, they served up a corker. To the delight of the home Royals fans, who had had to endure some of their players walking out on them a few weeks before, the Murrayfield side had grabbed an 8–4 lead just before the end of the second period. Then, to their horror, they watched as the Bombers slowly clambered back into the game, tying things up at eight apiece with just under two minutes remaining. The Bombers, now revitalised, then had to decide whether to go for the win, or hang on for a share of the points. Throwing caution to the wind, they went for it. Big mistake. Murrayfield scored in the last minute. A 9–8 win for the Royals. 'The gamble never paid off and we lost,' admitted Bombers captain Stephen Johnson. 'It was the kind of thing that leaves you absolutely devastated.' Cruel sometimes, ice hockey.

While Billingham and Murrayfield were battling it out to see who was bottom dog, another couple of contenders for the throne emerged.

After a solitary early victory in Billingham, the Solihull Barons set about losing every game with admirable vigour, not winning again until late October when they met Murrayfield. Traditionally, Solihull is one of the hardest places to go and win. This is due not so much to the prowess of the Barons players as to the intimidating atmosphere generated by the fans at the Hobs Moat Road rink. This hospitality seems to extend to the visiting fans, too. Whenever you meet and talk to ice hockey fans in this country you'll find the 'Solihull-as-horrible-unfriendly-dump' doctrine is almost universally accepted. I don't wish to be unkind to Barons supporters here. After all, they get behind their team with a passion that many other clubs would envy, but having said that, they are hockey's answer to Millwall. This season, though, the Barons were forced to play a weakened side, consisting mainly of youngsters, and with player-coach Dave Graham leaving the club in October, it was no surprise that the defeats kept coming, and no surprise that everyone else felt little in the way of sympathy for them.

By comparison, sympathy was felt for the plight of the Peterborough Pirates who, clearly influenced by the example set by Murrayfield, had trodden the path of 'Premiership side to Division One whipping boys in one easy stride'. After passing up the chance to retain their Premier Division place when Murrayfield resigned, the Pirates felt that consolidation was likely to be the important thing in the 1995–96 season. Ideally, they would have liked another shot at the Premier Division, especially as they were so unlucky to be relegated in the first place. Promotion rivals Slough had been allowed the advantage of facing off in their final play-off game an hour later than the Pirates, and therefore went into the final period knowing exactly how many more goals they were going to need. They got the crucial goal with just seconds to spare. However, by the time the possible reprieve arrived, most of Peterborough's top players had already signed with other clubs, Jeff Lindsay and Dale Jago going to Manchester, and Player of the Year centre Randy Smith signing for Cardiff, among others. The Pirates knew that they had no chance of survival in the Premier and so, wisely, resigned themselves to a season scrapping in the First.

To begin with, things weren't too bad, indeed, they won both their opening fixtures (mind you, these were against Billingham and Solihull) but then things started to go wrong for the Pirates. One of their imports, Igor Slivinsky, was denied a work permit, so the Pirates now had to find another import from somewhere, and then, when they got one, Canadian Al Latreille, he injured himself in only his third game. With Peterborough unable to afford any of the Canadian-Brits on offer, they were left woefully short of cover. As a backdrop to all this, there continued to be rumours concerning the financial stability of the club and the Peterborough rink – a problem that had been dogging the Pirates for some time. Hardly surprising that they started to rack up the defeats, too.

By the middle of October, then, the First Division was headed by Dumfries and Paisley, with Telford and Blackburn in the chasing pack. Although Manchester got off to a winning start, the other teams had played more games, so they initially hovered in a mid-table position, but even at this early stage, it was clear that a long season was in store for Billingham, Murrayfield, Solihull and Peterborough. The Premier Division had only just started up by this point, so it was too early to be filling in any report cards, and besides, there was still some unfinished business in the B&H Cup to attend to.

# 5

# A THRONG FOR EUROPE

As newly crowned champions of the British game, the Sheffield Steelers fans had much to be pleased about. That the Steelers had achieved a great deal in a relatively short period of time was, of course, immensely satisfying. That they had paved the way for other 'arena' teams was, also, a job well done. That they could spend the forthcoming season taunting Panthers fans with cries of 'Champions!' was wholly splendid, but the fact that they had also, in winning the Premier League, qualified for the European Cup, was news that inspired greater excitement amongst Sheffield travel agents than amongst the fans themselves. Sure, it would be a nice trip to wherever it was they were supposed to be playing, and an ideal chance to see whoever it was they had been drawn against, but as regards the event representing the pinnacle of the Steelers' achievements, well, it would be a fun weekend, sure, but not much else.

Although parallels with the European Cup in football are obvious, the ice hockey equivalent is, in truth, far removed. The tournament was inaugurated in 1965 but Britain didn't start providing cannon fodder for the other teams until 1983 when, after the sport in Britain had all but died out in the '60s and '70s, the modern era of the game began. In the 12 seasons since then, British sides had competed on 30 occasions against foreign opposition, and come out victorious just five times. Traditionally, things would go like this: British club qualifies for the European Cup. British club spends thousands of pounds flying out to somewhere no one has heard of. British club gets drubbed by teams no one has heard of. British club comes home. No one cares who wins the tournament. Be honest, how many winners can you name? Of course, you could argue that this attitude is really only prevalent in Britain, that our traditional poor showing in the event stops us celebrating it as the festival of Europe's finest that it is. You'd be dead right. In the past, we've not been very good in it and not very bothered about it.

Surely, though, in the future, things will be different. As the British game gains in popularity, Johnny Foreigner is just asking to be put in his place by the plucky British. I asked John Lawless whether his plans for the Storm included an assault on Europe. Since they had the finest arena in Europe, how about a crack at the finest teams?

'No, I don't think so,' he shrugged. 'The trouble with playing in Europe is that people here don't know who these [the European] players are. All the stars play in the NHL, so while these guys are still world-class, they mean nothing to the public. Personally, I'd rather be playing domestic games where it means something. And anyway, they're simply better than us.'

He had a point. Even if ice hockey was ever able to establish itself fully in Britain, could we ever realistically hope to produce the home-grown talent to compete with the Europeans? (The answer is no, by the way.)

In the last couple of seasons, though, a strange trend seems to have emerged – British sides actually winning games. The previous season, Cardiff had become the first British side to win a quarter-final group. Facing two tough sides, from Kiev and Kazakhstan, they astonishingly beat both.

'I just told the guys to ice it,' John Lawless told me. 'Every time you get the puck, just bang it into the corners. It wasn't pretty, but I knew that if we tried to outplay them we'd get beaten.'

This sage piece of advice was perhaps instrumental in the Devils pulling off an heroic 6–2 victory over Sokol Kiev, and then squeezing past Torpedo Ust-Kamenogorsk 4–3. It was a remarkable and highly disciplined performance from Cardiff, especially given the fact that they went out with a 14 year-old in goal, Stevie Lyle, who to the amazement of the opposition, and the great interest of the foreign scouts, performed heroics in the Devils goal. Defeat against the less-fancied home side from Tilburg in the end counted for nothing as the Devils clinched top spot and qualified for the semi-finals stage in Minsk, Belarus. For John Lawless, the games had been massively satisfying. 'Our whole game plan was based on the three Ds – Defence, Discipline and Desire. Now we can add the fourth D – Delight!' he was quoted as saying at the time.

Anyone who thought that Cardiff were getting a little too big for their skates probably felt a little smug when they saw what happened to the Devils on their return to the tournament, a month later. 'We had earned a lot of respect from the other teams for having beaten the Russian sides, and we thought, well, let's show them we can play hockey too, and we got found out,' admitted Lawless. The first game, against Dukla Trencin, was a sobering experience – they got hammered. After the 13–2 defeat, some of the Cardiff fans and players decided to visit a local restaurant, where they could more comfortably reflect on the evening's humiliation. Any chance that they might have had to wallow in self-pity was scuppered when they discovered a dead man slumped in a corner. The unfortunate fellow had, apparently, died an hour previously – no one is entirely sure what of – and it was a further hour before anyone could be bothered to remove him, although someone did nip in and whip off his shoes and socks. Unsettling though the evening was, the players felt that it had, at least, given them some sense of perspective. They still had their shoes and socks, after all. After a start like that, it was no surprise that the Devils were slightly off their game, and after two further big defeats, 14–0 against Minsk and 13–1 to Feldkirch, they were simply glad to get out of Belarus still alive.

Given this history, you can understand why the Steelers had hoped to stage their qualifying group in Sheffield. Not only would home advantage give them a great chance of progressing through to the later stages, it might also mean they could enjoy a post-game meal without worrying if it was poisonous. Besides, it would not be the first time a qualifying group had been played on British soil; in 1992 Durham got to play their group in Blackburn, finishing third. With Sheffield enjoying the added advantage of playing in their own rink it was generally felt that this would represent the best chance yet of a British side making an impact on the European stage. In the event, it was found that the dates set for the quarter-final groups clashed with an event already booked at the Sheffield arena, so the Steelers faced a trip to Tilburg, in Holland, the scene of Cardiff's triumph the previous year.

The mechanics of the European Cup are such that in order for a British team to triumph, they would have to battle their way through three qualifying groups against increasingly tough opposition before reaching the final. In other words, the Steelers had absolutely no chance of winning, but qualification from the initial group was not beyond the realms of possibility. The Steelers were drawn into Group D, which looked like this:

European Cup Quarter-final
Group D (Tilburg, Netherlands, 6–8 October 1995)
Tilburg Trappers (Netherlands)
Sheffield Steelers
Olimpija Herz (Slovenia)
Txuri Urdin (Spain)

Should the Steelers win their group they would get the chance to play against top sides from the Czech Republic, France and Poland. It was felt that the weakest side in the group would be the Spanish champions, who themselves had had to win a qualifying tie before getting to this early stage, whilst the toughest game was likely to be against the Slovenians. An outside chance of qualification lay in the possibility of finishing in second place with a better record than any of the other three second-placed teams in the other groups. This came about because one of the seeded teams from the next stage, Latvian side Pardaugava, had to withdraw at late notice due to going bust. (Do you see what I meant earlier about no one having heard of any of these sides?)

Friday 6 October was the date of Sheffield's first foray into Europe. Hundreds of Steelers fans decided to make the trip across the Channel, many taking time off work to do so. Once there, they set about making their presence felt with their drums, trumpets and horns making a noise almost as loud as the special 'Steelers into Europe' gear they were wearing. For the Dutch, it must have been a fearsome sight. When Sheffield had claimed, during their bid to host the event, that they had a big supporters club, the largest in Europe, many on the continent were sceptical, particularly when you consider that the game is in decline in many parts of Europe, not least in Holland. As a result, it was probably hard to tell who was the more satisfied with such an impressive turn-out from Sheffield, the Steelers organisation, who felt that such a showing could only strengthen their claim to host subsequent events, or the financially strapped Tilburg side, who found their coffers considerably boosted after the weekend. This support, it was widely felt, would be a significant factor for the Steelers, as few supporters of the other visiting teams would be making the journey, possibly giving the Steelers the edge they would need. The opening game was against Tilburg, which the Steelers had to win if they hoped to qualify. On paper, this didn't look like it would be beyond the Steelers but on home ice Tilburg, too, were confident.

Before either side had the opportunity to show how they could play, however, Olimpija Herz decided to put on a little show of their own. Facing Txuri Urdin they decided that a good mauling was in order, and hammered 17 goals past the Spanish champions. It wasn't a complete rout, though. They were careless enough to concede a couple of goals along the way. For those watching, the implications of this opener were clear: Olimpija were a very dangerous outfit, excellent skaters and more than equipped to punish mistakes. Txuri, on the other hand, were rubbish. This made the game with Tilburg all the more vital. Assuming that Txuri would happily capitulate to anyone who could be bothered to fire a few pucks at them, it meant that Sheffield would probably have to beat both Tilburg and Olimpija to qualify. The good news for the Steelers was that the influential Steve Nemeth had sufficiently recovered from an elbow injury to play, much to the chagrin of the television crews present who had just told everyone watching that he was unable to. The game itself was expected to be tight. Sheffield had to be patient and disciplined, it was felt, if they were to get the result they were looking for. Once the game was under way, however, they quickly ran into trouble. They had fallen into the trap that all British sides succumb to – drawing far too many penalties. Why is this? I'm sure you are all asking. Well, time for a bit of sociology, I think.

Although arguments about the origins of ice hockey still persist, there is little doubt that hockey as we know it today has its origins in Canada. There are, I suppose, two things that everyone knows about Canada: it is very big, and it is appallingly cold. When early European settlers arrived in Canada they wanted a game that could be played on ice. There were two reasons for this. Firstly, the settlers felt that such an activity would be like confronting nature head on, proving that man's spirit had conquered the frozen waste – an act of defiance, if you will, against the cruelties of life. Secondly, it would help keep them warm with the added bonus that it would give them the perfect excuse to batter each other's brains out while they were doing it. Their initial idea was to play lacrosse on ice. The trouble with this was that it was very difficult to play and, furthermore, insanely dangerous. Realising that the entire male population of the new colony would be wiped out in a fortnight if they continued to play such a game, they decided to think again.

The new game came to be known as ice hockey. As so many of the settlers came from Britain and France, both rugby-playing nations, it was perhaps no surprise that many of the rules were developed from that sport. For instance, to begin with, you could only pass backwards in ice hockey, as in rugby, which helps explain why the goals are set a few feet in from the perimeter, the idea being to skate to the end of the rink and then pass back for a team-mate to score. As well as the rules owing something to rugby, the style of play itself was influenced by the older game. Ice hockey became very physical. Sure, there was a lot of skill involved, but an ability to play well at ice hockey and still have your own teeth became a rare thing indeed.

Whilst the Canadian game evolved into a very tough and rugged sport, the game in Europe developed on a slightly different tack. Although the game and its rules were quickly adopted in the colder European countries like Sweden, Finland and Russia, it developed independently of the game in Canada. Here, there was no history of rugby playing, just football. (Admittedly, football was played in Britain and France at this time too, but the people who colonised Canada came from 'rugger' backgrounds, rather than nasty, working-class football-dominated backgrounds.) With football as the most obvious influence on ice hockey in Northern Europe, the game developed along different lines. Here, passing and movement were seen as the keys, rather than strength and brute force. But what has all this got to do with the Steelers?

Well, as fans of other British teams have often been quick to point out, Sheffield have a lot of Canadians in their team. It is, perhaps, no surprise, then, that when they come up against European officials, they find every infraction called, many of which would go unpenalised in their own league. Not that this problem is confined to Sheffield. Every time a British side enters Europe much the same thing tends to happen, even if they don't have a roster stacked with Canadians. The trouble is that because British ice hockey has always been dominated by Canadians, we tend to play a very physical, dump-and-chase style of hockey like they do. As I said earlier, teams on the continent have their own style. They use Canadians as imports, too, but generally these other countries have enough home-grown talent to develop their own style of play, rather than just aping the Canadian one. When you add all this to the fact that Sheffield were playing their first ever game in the European Cup here in Tilburg, it was no surprise that they ended up playing half the game shorthanded.

The first period of the game against the Trappers was one where the Steelers were desperately trying to survive one Tilburg powerplay after another. Even with netminder Martin McKay in outstanding form, everyone watching felt that the first goal could not be too far away. Finally, at 6.27 into the first, the inevitable powerplay goal arrived. The thing was, it was Sheffield who scored it. After doggedly hanging on as Tilburg had lurched from one powerplay opportunity to another, Sheffield had scored on their very first powerplay, a Ron Shudra slapshot finding its way through a crowd of players to put Sheffield one-up. It was clearly a demoralising blow for the Dutch, who had been the better side up to that point. At the end of the first period the game statistics showed Sheffield 1–0 ahead on goals, and about eight ahead on penalties.

The second period was similar to the first. Again Sheffield took the penalties, again Tilburg wasted them, and again 'Rocket' Ron Shudra struck with a powerplay goal to make it 2–0. The Steelers' luck couldn't hold for ever, and Tilburg did finally manage to score on a powerplay of their own, the period ending with the Steelers 2–1 ahead. Whilst Tilburg had shown some nice touches, particularly in their own end and the neutral zone, they had looked ineffective up front and the Steelers must have been fairly confident by now that they could kill most of the penalties they were picking up. However, the effect of playing shorthanded for so long was that they were tiring. If this wasn't a factor in this game, it could be the next day when they were due to play Olimpija.

In the final period, Tilburg's spirit broke. Tony Hand cooly dropped the puck on to Nicky Chinn's stick for him to put Sheffield 3–1 up. With just 64 seconds remaining Hand then broke clear, effortlessly rounded the netminder, and put away Sheffield's fourth. This final goal, coming on a Tilburg powerplay, summed up the Dutch side's night. An excellent start for the Steelers. The question was, did they have anything in reserve for Olimpija, whom many of the Steelers players had watched on the first day and had been much impressed by? The next day, the early answer appeared to be no. The Slovenians were an impressive side. Individually, they were better skaters and passers than the Steelers, and their fluid style saw them lead 2–0 by the end of the first period and 4–0 by the end of the second. The Steelers were in danger of being outclassed. Then a strange thing happened. Sheffield scored and everything changed.

Perhaps feeling the game was won, Olimpija were careless enough to concede a penalty five minutes into the period, and when Kelland scored the first goal for Sheffield on the subsequent powerplay, you could sense some self-belief returning to the Steelers. Suddenly, it was a different match. Realising that they could not match the Slovenians for skill, the Steelers raised the physical part of their game, going hard into the corners whenever they could. Not so comfortable with this style of play, Olimpija looked vulnerable for the first time in the match. After Les Millie had come close on a breakaway, Nemeth picked up a rebound from a Chinn slapshot to pull a second back. Sheffield were revitalised. The challenges now came in thick and fast, but then an injury to one of the Herz players delayed the game, threatening to disrupt the momentum Sheffield had built up. Any thoughts that Olimpija harboured of this incident stemming the flow of pressure from Sheffield lasted all of two seconds, when immediately from the ensuing face-off, Justin George drilled home the third. Three goals in as many minutes. The Steelers fans were going bananas.

At this point, Herz were barely recognisable as the side that had coasted into a four-goal lead. Like a boxer grimly hanging on to the ropes, they clung on to their one-goal lead while Sheffield battered their goal. Yet the equaliser, now seemingly so close, would not come, both Hand and the impressive Ken Priestlay missing good opportunities.

Then, the turning point. Ron Shudra was called for a two-minute tripping penalty in the 58th minute, and against the run of play, Thomas Vnuk scored on the powerplay to seal the match for the Slovenians. For the Steelers it was a disappointment, but no disgrace. Herz were clearly the better side for the bulk of the match, yet the Steelers had undoubtedly rattled them and in the end were unlucky not to snatch a draw. Sheffield coach Clyde Tuyl was philosophical about the loss.

'I think we have to give our guys credit, going down four, and then to come back in the third and make a hell of a game of it. I feel that, as a club, over the last couple of games we've grown quite a bit.'

As regards qualification, however, things did not look quite so good for the Steelers. Assuming they would beat the Spaniards, they still needed Herz to lose against Tilburg, and on the evidence of the games so far, that was unlikely. Even in that event, the Steelers could qualify only on goal difference, unlikely given that Tilburg had also now managed a big win over Txuri, 14–1. The final game, against Txuri, was about as tense as a long relaxing soak in the bath. Sheffield knocked in four goals within the first seven minutes, and were six up by the end of the first, but from there they drifted along on autopilot, Txuri nipping a couple of consolation goals before the game ended 9–2. As it happened, the scoreline mattered little, as Olimpija completed their expected clean sweep of the group by beating Tilburg 8–2. Sheffield were out of Europe, any lingering hopes that they might have sneaked through as the best second-placed team extinguished when they learnt that Ust-Kamenogorsk (snappy name, guys) of Kazakhstan had qualified instead.

For the Steelers, the weekend had been an interesting diversion from the week-to-week routine of the domestic programme. It had been a lot of fun, not to mention hard work, and in the future it was possible that another Steelers assault on Europe would be more fruitful. There was talk that next season there might be some kind of European league run along similar lines to football's Champions League, which the Steelers found interesting, but that was too far ahead to worry about. In the meantime, they had business at home to contend with. There were titles to defend and new ones to win. Europe could wait.

# 6

# IT'S A KNOCKOUT

After sauntering through the group stages of the B&H Cup, the eight qualifying sides tend to find that when the knock-out stage commences in October, the intensity level goes up a notch. With the season in full swing – the coaches should all have been complaining about their team's injuries and bad luck for at least a month by now – the quarter-finals are usually entertaining affairs. Settled over the course of one weekend, the games are staged on a two-legged basis with the aggregate scores and, if needed, sudden-death overtime and shoot-outs, determining the winner. This year, three of the first-leg games were played on the Saturday night, and all proved to be extremely close affairs, with no more than one goal separating the teams in each of them, but the night before, in a game widely anticipated to be the 'tie of the round' and accordingly brought forward for the benefit of Sky television, the Steelers ran riot in Cardiff.

After a goalless first period, during which the Devils had laid siege to the Steelers goal, Sheffield stepped up a gear and established a three-goal lead by catching their hosts on the break. The Devils, playing in front of an enthusiastic capacity crowd at the Wales National Ice Rink, could have been forgiven for thinking that it wasn't going to be their night. However, this third goal seemed to sting Cardiff into finally making some of their possession count, and they rallied to pull a couple of goals back before the end of the second period. The momentum of the match seemed to have shifted, but Cardiff, aware that they needed to take some kind of lead to the return leg in Sheffield if they were to have a decent chance of making it through to the semi-finals, elected to throw caution to the wind in the final period. It was then that it all went horribly wrong for them. The Steelers simply said

'Cheers for playing with no defence, lads' and rattled in four more goals at the expense of just one to win the game 7–3. Superb though Sheffield's display had been, it was a wretched result for the Devils, and one that, to put it bluntly, gave them fart-all chance of progressing any further.

The three other ties, played the next night, were much closer affairs. Especially good was the match between the holders, Nottingham Panthers, and the home side, Basingstoke Bison. Basingstoke edged the first period with a solitary goal from Rick Strachan, and when Morrison and Sweeney made it 3–0 early in the second, it looked as though Basingstoke might take a commanding lead with them to Nottingham the next night. The Panthers, though, started to fight back, clawing their way back to trail 3–2 just after the start of the third period. When Richard Little put the Bison back in charge at 4–2 it looked like Nottingham's revival had been stopped, but Simon Hunt surprised everyone by pulling one back for the Panthers and then – just in case anyone hadn't been watching the first time – scoring again just eight seconds later. Just as Nottingham were about to congratulate themselves on getting out of gaol, however, Basingstoke snatched the game on a powerplay with just 21 seconds left to play; 5–4 to the Bison and an intriguing second leg in store in Nottingham.

The two remaining ties, Fife versus Newcastle and Humberside versus Durham, were equally close. Fife had already beaten Newcastle twice in the group stages and were presumably confident of repeating this feat again when, on the eve of the tie, they suffered a setback when defenceman Paul Hand walked out on the club. The dispute, apparently about money – Hand wanting more, Fife pointing to the sum he was contracted to play for, then Hand leaving for First Division Paisley anyway – could have been a shattering blow to the Flyers, especially as Hand had been their best defenceman and they had few others to take over. Instead, it seemed to pull the team together, and they produced their best form of the season so far. The quarter-final first leg in Fife was still no easy game, particularly when Newcastle took a 3–2 lead after being 2–0 down. However, Fife regained their composure, and the lead soon into the final period, and from then on the two sides traded goals, with Fife's Mark Morrison grabbing the last goal 67 seconds from time. It had been a thrilling game for the fans, who must have wondered if a 6–5 win would be enough to see Fife into the semi-finals.

Meanwhile, over in Humberside another close game was being fought, although with the Hawks jumping into a three-goal lead in the first six minutes it didn't look like a close game was going to be on the cards. However, the Wasps seemed to wake up once they had conceded the third goal and, after pulling a couple of goals back almost immediately, they made the Hawks pay for some needless penalties by going into the last period having scored five unanswered goals. The Wasps still contrived to let the momentum shift back to the home side, when Humberside rallied in this final period to level the score at five-all. Still, Durham felt, a draw away from home was no bad result, and one that they should be able to build on. So at the half-way stage of the quarter-finals, the Sheffield–Cardiff tie apart, everything seemed finely balanced.

The following Sunday was second-leg day. In Whitley, where Newcastle were still playing until their shiny new arena was completed, the Flyers and Warriors went at each other at a furious pace. Newcastle struck first, a pair of goals in the first five minutes putting them ahead overall, but when Stephen King pulled one back for Fife it triggered the start of a seesaw sequence of scoring in which first Newcastle, then Fife, then Newcastle again, took command. Fife got some breathing space when they grabbed a couple of goals early in the third, but almost immediately Newcastle came at them again and John Iredale grabbed the equaliser to make the score 5–5, and 11–10 to Fife on aggregate. Incredibly, thanks to some heroics in the Fife goal by netminder Ricky Grubb, that was how the score stayed, and that was enough to see Fife through.

It was equally dramatic in Nottingham where, if anything, there was an even better game in store for the fans. Defending their one-goal lead, the Bison gave Nottingham an early scare when they got a penalty stroke inside the first couple of minutes, which Scott O'Connor did well to block. The reprieve was short-lived, though. Basingstoke took a two-goal lead on the night, and a three-goal lead overall, when Scott Morrison and Richard Little both scored. With Basingstoke's GB netminder Bill Morrison in fine form, it looked grim for the Panthers, but a turning point came when their bump and grind tactics (a style of hockey, by the way, and not, as it sounds, the name of a Prince album) paid off and they pulled one back before the first interval. Soon after the break it was 2–2, Ashley Tait getting the equaliser for Nottingham, but just as Panthers felt they were getting somewhere, Basingstoke struck back to make it 3–2, and 8–6 overall, on practically their first attack of the period. It was at this point that Panthers' forward Simon Hunt once again stepped forward. At just over the midway point, he blasted the puck past Morrison from the blueline to make it three each. A few minutes later, he did it again. This time, however, the puck had been deflected in off Morrison's face mask, and so fierce was the shot that Morrison had been knocked unconscious. The referee halted play before the puck crossed the line. Morrison, thankfully, was all right after a few moments, but Hunt's effort was disallowed. Not to mind because Hunt let fly again and this time it counted; 4–3 to the Panthers, all square in the tie. Basingstoke snatched another, after a mistake by the Panthers defence, but this was balanced out by Randall Weber levelling the contest yet again with just over eight minutes to play. Simon Hunt still had some unfinished business, however, and his hat-trick marker in the 58th minute put Nottingham ahead for the very first time in the tie, and with Basingstoke forced to gamble on putting an extra skater on the ice, Paul Adey put away an empty-net goal to seal the tie for Nottingham. The crowd, you won't be surprised to learn, went crazy.

Whilst all this excitement was going on, further up the M1 Sheffield still had to finish the job at home to Cardiff. A four-goal cushion should have been comfortable enough for them, but on the day of the game they hit a snag. Netminder Martin McKay was suddenly struck down with appendicitis, and with the Steelers' new netminder, Wayne Cowley, not yet cleared to play, the Steelers' Alex Dampier had some fast thinking to do. An urgent phone call to Slough's experienced netminder Charlie Colon, followed by an even more urgent drive down from Sheffield and back to pick him up, resulted in the Slough player joining his temporary team-mates just moments before the game started. It was a good thing he was there, as Sheffield, drawn into defending their lead rather than playing their normal attacking style, found themselves largely outplayed by a Cardiff side determined to do themselves some justice after their poor home performance. In the event, whilst a 4–2 win for Cardiff restored some pride, it did nothing to affect the tie overall, and Cardiff were left to consider the irony of a sport that allowed a team's netminder who had had his appendix taken out to be replaced with a Colon . . .

With all these fun and games going on, it wouldn't have been unreasonable to expect the last quarter-final game, between the Durham Wasps and the Humberside Hawks, to be a slightly more mundane affair, but in the event that too was a remarkable game; not that you'd have thought so when Durham led 4–1 after the first two periods. At that point, the Wasps were cruising, 9–6 up on aggregate, and fully in command on their own ice. They had already beaten Humberside 9–3 earlier in the tournament, and must have been thinking that a repeat performance was imminent. They must also have been thinking, not unreasonably, that they were 20 minutes away from the semi-finals. Then a strange thing happened. Although the Durham team that returned to the ice for the final period was the same one that had started the match, strange hockey-playing alien beings must have kidnapped the Humberside players, and replaced them with superficially similar, yet superior players. The Hawks were a different team in this final period, astonishingly scoring six unanswered goals to take the game 4–7, and the tie 9–12. Amazing. The really spooky thing is that the previous season, also in a game against Durham, the Hawks had performed a similar saps-to-alien-hyperbeings stunt when they had come back from 6–2 down to score 11 times without reply to win 13–6. Whatever the mysterious explanation for these strange transformations – and we may never learn the real truth behind them, folks – one thing is certain: normal service was to be resumed in the Hawks' very next game, a league match at low-flying Milton Keynes, which the Hawks lost 8–1.

The draw for the semi-finals was made at the Sheffield arena the following morning, and was broadcast live on Radio 5, or at least a bit of it was. BIHA Chief Executive David Frame got as far as calling out 'Number 4 – Fife Flyers, will play . . .' and here he paused for dramatic effect, as the second ball was drawn. Unfortunately a technician at the BBC got the impression that this pause signalled the conclusion of the draw, and pulled the plug to move on to the next item. It was an hour later before Radio 5 was able to put us all out of our misery and tell us the draw, which shaped up like this:

## Benson & Hedges Cup Semi-final

| | | |
|---|---|---|
| Fife Flyers | v | Sheffield Steelers |
| Humberside Hawks | v | Nottingham Panthers |

It was a draw that kept alive the possibilities of a Sheffield v Nottingham final, the final everyone wanted to see (apart from Flyers and Hawks fans, of course, who somewhat selfishly wanted their own sides to win). Instead of both legs being played over the one weekend, this time they were staggered over two weekends, with Fife and Sheffield the first to get things under way. The Flyers, after suffering Paul Hand's walk-out just before the last tie, obviously felt that squad upheaval was a lucky omen for them before cup games, and so for the clash with the Steelers they decided the best preparation would be to sack coach Ronnie Plumb. With Plumb becoming marketing manager, the vacant coaching slot was awarded to player Mark Morrison, a Canadian forward who found that his very first job would be to stop a confident Steelers side. Against all the odds, the Flyers did just that. Overturning a 2–1 deficit in the first period, the Flyers crashed four goals past a Sheffield side that seemed half-asleep. Had it not been for Ken Priestlay grabbing a third goal for the Steelers near the end, the lapse in form would have proved more costly than it did. As it was, a two-goal deficit, surprising though it was, was well within Sheffield's capabilities and they remained favourites to win the tie. Of greater concern, perhaps, was the Steelers' poor performance and apparent lack of commitment. Later, Priestlay was blunt in his appraisal of the Steelers game: 'The worst in my time here. I think we thought we would just have to turn up. We were thinking of the final already, and Fife kicked us up the backside.'

There was more kicking of backsides the next night, too, as Nottingham travelled to Humberside. The Panthers got off to a solid start, leading 3–0 at the first break, and although the sides traded goals throughout the second period, by the time the third period was over the Panthers had pretty much sewn the tie up with a 9–3 victory, Paul Adey and Darren Durdle both helping themselves to hat-tricks. Player-coach Mike Blaisdell also grabbed a couple. It had been an impressive performance from the Panthers, particularly when compared to Sheffield's lacklustre performance the night before, and not even another alien abduction could save the Humberside Hawks now. In the return leg, a scrappy, bad-tempered affair, the Panthers duly confirmed their place in the final with a 7–5 win more notable for the amount of penalty minutes racked up by the Hawks (120) than anything else.

Meanwhile, over in Sheffield the Steelers and Flyers served up a corker. With the Steelers two goals behind, all expectations were that they would go right at the Flyers from the word go, and indeed they did, but what was less expected was that the Flyers were quite prepared to launch plenty of attacks of their own. The Steelers struck first, Tommy Plommer netting just before the end of the first period, but the Flyers stunned the home crowd with two goals in two minutes at the midway point to lead 2–1 on the night and 7–4 overall. Suddenly, Sheffield woke up to the fact that they had a game on their hands. Steve Nemeth grabbed an equaliser for Sheffield to set up an exciting final period but when Iain Robertson promptly scored Fife's third goal to restore the three-goal lead, it looked as though an upset was on the cards. Needing to score three goals in the remaining 16 minutes, the Steelers threw everything at the Flyers, whose lack of depth on the bench meant they were tiring fast. Tim Cranston started the fightback, with a goal at the 46-minute mark, then Nicky Chinn managed to get a touch on an André Malo slapshot to make it 4–3 on the night and 7–8 overall. The momentum was now with Sheffield, and an uncharacteristic slip by Fife netminder John McCrone let Ron

*Hilton Ruggles scores the first ever goal at the Nynex arena, and even the Cardiff fans seem happy about it.* MIKE SMITH, PLS LTD

*Two of the best – Sheffield's Tony Hand and Nottingham's Paul Adey.*
MIKE SMITH, PLS LTD

*Durham Wasps' talented netminder, Stephen Foster.*
MIKE SMITH, PLS LTD

*The Storm's Martin 'No Nickname' Smith.*
MIKE SMITH, PLS LTD

*Steelers' head honcho, Alex
Dampier.* MIKE SMITH, PLS LTD

*John Lawless (Shown actual size).*
MIKE SMITH, PLS LTD

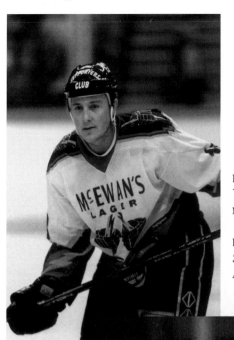

LEFT:
*Young bruiser, Nicky Chinn.*
MIKE SMITH, PLS LTD

BELOW:
*Shawn Byram looking happy.*
ANDY YATES, MANCHESTER EVENING NEWS

*Rick Fera, seen here playing for Telford. When this guy was with the Trafford Metros I swore he walked on water. (Which he did, if you included frozen water . . . )*
MIKE SMITH, PLS LTD

*Cardiff Devil and GB International, Shannon Hope.*
MIKE SMITH, PLS LTD

*Oleg Sinkov – a pleasure to watch, even at Blackburn.* MIKE SMITH, PLS LTD

*Hilton spreads the word . . .* KAREN WRIGHT PHOTOGRAPHY

Shudra tie the game up at 8–8 on aggregate.

With both sides now acutely aware that one slip could cost them the game, the final minutes of regulation time were tense. Sheffield nearly let it slip when they allowed Iain Robertson a last-minute breakaway, but their new netminder, Wayne Cowley, did well to smother the puck. The game went into sudden-death overtime, and after Fife came close on a couple of occasions they saw, to their horror, that Tony Hand had suddenly created a bit of space for himself. He calmly closed in on McCrone and, apparently unconcerned and unhurried by the pressure of the moment, let fly a smooth wrist shot that glided into the Fife net for the game-winner. Fife's Mark Morrison was mortified. Over the two games Fife had probably been the more deserving side, but in the end simple fatigue had caught up with them.

'All the guys gave 100 per cent and there's nothing I would have changed, or could have done, to make it different. We just didn't have the bodies,' he later said. You had to feel sorry for Fife; they didn't have the bodies so they just got bitter (sorry).

So, as had been widely anticipated, the final B&H showdown was to be between the favourites, the Sheffield Steelers, and their local rivals and cup holders, the Nottingham Panthers. The final was played at the supposedly neutral venue of Sheffield arena, with Sheffield as the 'home' team despite the fact that it was Nottingham who had won the toss of the coin beforehand, used so as to determine which side would use which dressing-room. Most people were surprised by Nottingham coach Mike Blaisdell's decision. With the Steelers on home ice, and enjoying the bulk of the support in the building, it was felt that making them play as the 'away' side, and so consigning them to the visitors dressing-room, and their away strip, might prove to be a psychological advantage for the Panthers. Instead, however, Blaisdell plumped for the away team dressing-room, perhaps feeling it would be a lucky omen for the Panthers as they had used the same room the previous year when they had won the trophy against Cardiff. Besides, the Panthers had already beaten the Steelers in the 'House of Steel' earlier in the tournament. They had also beaten them in the league just a couple of weeks previously, with a 5–2 scoreline that, if anything, had flattered the Steelers, so perhaps Blaisdell felt they had the psychological edge anyway.

The day of the final dawned with Sheffield Steelers' general manager Alex Dampier facing a difficult netminding problem. Martin McKay, the usual netminder, had been outstanding up to this point, but the Steelers' recent acquistion, Wayne Cowley, a netminder with NHL experience, was also pushing hard for a place. In what Dampier later referred to as 'probably the toughest decision I've ever had to make as coach of Sheffield' he gave Cowley the nod just before the start of the game. For Blaisdell, there were no such tough decisions, although his own appearance in the game was somewhat ironic given the fact that he had announced his intention to retire from the playing side the previous season, only to end up playing in the B&H final that year before 'retiring' once again. Here he was, one year on, still talking of hanging up his skates, yet due to appear again in the final.

By face-off time, thanks to some extra seating installed especially for the occasion, the largest crowd ever to assemble for an ice hockey match in Britain, 10,136, had squeezed into the Sheffield arena for the biggest game of the season. As well as being screened live by Sky Sports, the match was also broadcast live on Radio 5 – the first time ice hockey had been carried live on the radio in Britain for 58 years – another sign that the sport's profile was rising all the time. Hopes were that it would be a close game, and in the first period, so it proved. With both sides clearly apprehensive in the very early stages, the game took a while to settle, neither side wanting to lose an early goal. The first real chance of the game presented itself when both Darren Durdle and Paul Adey of the Panthers were sent to the penalty box. With Sheffield enjoying a two-man advantage, they sensed that the time had come to step up a gear, but when Adey returned, to leave the Panthers shorthanded by just one man, it seemed as though the Steelers were letting their chance slip. Then came the breakthrough. Chris Kelland drove the puck from the point to find Nicky Chinn, who was able to get off a quick wrist shot that sneaked past Scott O'Connor in the Nottingham net – 1–0 to the Steelers.

The goal sparked the game into life. With both sides tearing at each other, the remainder of the period was played at frantic pace, yet any feeling that this would lead to a bout of goalscoring proved unfounded as both netminders kept the forwards at bay for nearly 25 minutes. Although Ashley Tait and Simon Hunt had both come close to scoring, the Panthers, up to this point, had struggled to get their offensive game going, but because the defensive side of their game had been pretty solid they were still very much in the game. At the 35-minute mark, though, everything changed. As Sheffield pushed forward on another powerplay, the Panthers seemed to relax momentarily as, with just a couple of seconds of the penalty left to kill, the puck broke loose in the corner. Chuck Taylor moved over to clear, but Ken Priestlay checked him into the boards, allowing Tony Hand to pick it up. The Panthers stood off Hand, who appeared to be drifting ineffectually behind the net, but at the last moment he dropped back in front of O'Connor in the

Nottingham goal and, unchallenged, poked the puck into the net. Suddenly there was daylight between the teams.

With this lapse in Nottingham's concentration punished by Hand, the Panthers knew that they had a lot of work to do if they were to get back into the game, but, disastrously for them, Sheffield scored again on their very next shot. André Malo picked up a pass from Nicky Chinn, and skating to the point he let fly a shot that seemed to take a deflection, and the puck flew past O'Connor. The Panthers were shell-shocked – 3–0 down against a Sheffield side that looked like they were about to score with every shot. Nottingham had no alternative but to push forward. On their next attack, the Panthers' Chuck Taylor was robbed of the puck by Tony Hand, and the Sheffield player made a dash for the corner, but with no other Steelers players in support, and with three Nottingham players skating back to cover him, there seemed little danger. Hand, of course, was having none of that. He drifted almost to the point of the goal line, so that he had the most acute of angles from which to score. There was a pause as everyone seemed to wait to see what he would do, which was simply to pass the puck unerringly into the top corner of the net. Three goals in 90 seconds, 4–0 up, and suddenly the Steelers looked like they had the Panthers beaten.

As the third period started the Panthers fans must have been concerned about the possibility of the Steelers running riot, but Nottingham pushed forward, reaping some reward for their efforts in the 47th minute when Darren Durdle blasted the puck past Cowley from near the face-off circle. The flow of the Steelers' game stemmed, Nottingham now came back into the match, but when Paul Adey thought he had scored for the Panthers, only to see that somehow Cowley had managed to smother the puck, it seemed as though luck, and time, was running out for Nottingham. With Sheffield apparently content simply to hold on to their lead, Nottingham found their attempts to score met with increasing frustration. When they failed to score on a couple of late powerplays, allowing Sheffield off the hook, it looked all over. Just as the Nottingham fans were coming to terms with the fact that they had lost, Blaisdell teasingly gave them a tiny piece of hope when he back-handed a shot past Cowley to make it 4–2 with just over a minute remaining. With nothing to loose, Nottingham had pulled their netminder and seen Blaisdell cash in almost instantly. They stuck with the extra skater from the ensuing face-off, but the move didn't work a second time and, as the Steelers fans began to celebrate the impending victory, Tony Hand found himself with the puck in front of the empty net and duly sealed the match for the Steelers.

It had been an impressive performance from Sheffield, and Hand in particular. With both sides icing players with NHL experience, including Priestlay, Cowley and Blaisdell, Hand had stood out above all the others.

'I came here to win trophies, and I have won the first available,' he later said, ominously.

Still only 28 – though he has been prominent in the British game for so long now that it seems like he must be about 40 – it was clear that he was still hungry for success, and now that he was with the Steelers he had the chance to pig-out, big-style. It completed a great year for the Steelers. 1995 had been the year they won the British Premier Division and the British Championship, competed in Europe for the first time, and had now won the Benson & Hedges Cup. Just what would 1996 bring?

# 7

# FUN AND GAMES

After the initial bumper crowd for the opener against Telford, the Storm's early games were played in front of crowds around the 3,500 to 4,000 mark (in a league where the average was 764 the previous season). These supporters, the bulk of whom had never have seen any games of ice hockey before, started to make themselves feel at home at the Nynex. The atmosphere on game night seemed to develop a little more with every match. Partly, this was attributed to the music played over the public address system which, as at most rinks, was instrumental in firing up the crowd and getting cheers going. First-time visitors to the Nynex would be amused to see the audience respond to certain pieces of music in almost Pavlovian manner. For instance, a burst of Village People's 'YMCA' would have half the crowd leaping out of their seats to do the obligatory hand actions, likewise 'We Will Rock You' had the crowd clapping their hands in time-honoured tradition. Most worryingly, the between-period broadcasts of Stompin' Tom Connor's 'Hockey Night Tonight', which scientists believe may be the worst record ever made, went down a treat, many in the crowd joining in with disconcerting gusto. The announcer, Jon Hammond, also had an instrumental role in developing the game-night atmosphere. Although he was criticised in some quarters for a slightly shaky performance on his opening night – the first match he had ever seen, mind, not the best preparation you could have – he slowly managed to develop his own style with each game that passed. Not that he was, even then, without his critics.

Forget being a netminder, forget even being a referee, if you want a difficult job in ice hockey, go and be a rink announcer. It is a near impossible job. Beside the formal role of announcing the penalties, goalscorers and assists and so on, you also have to try to drum up the atmosphere, which is impossible to do without getting on at least half the crowd's nerves. Just ask David Simms, the Sheffield announcer, frequently criticised, perhaps 'widely despised' might be a more apt description, for his over-exuberant style. The problem is, how do you address the audience? Most rink announcers come across as failed local radio DJs, their vacuous repartee blended with a parochial amateurism that is both appalling and yet strangely endearing. Let's face it, if they were any good at this playing-records-and-announcing-things lark they'd be on the radio instead of working part-time at a suburban ice rink, wouldn't they? I don't mean to be unfair and have a go at any individuals here, but the mere fact that they even want such a terrible job means that they are undeserving of public sympathy. And I don't even mind them that much; I know plenty of people who hate rink announcers much more than I do.

So, how do you address an audience? Jon Hammond has the tricky job of addressing an audience with a large quotient of young children as well as adults. This means that anything witty, serious or well informed is right out of the window. Not his fault, I know, but the end result is that throughout the course of a game we get a constant stream of inane chirpy banter like 'Ladies and gentlemen, boys and girls, please keep your eyes on the puck, at all times,' said immediately after the puck has flown into the crowd and cleared some poor sod of their teeth; 'Let's have a Manchester wave starting in block 115!'; 'ladies and gentlemen, remember we don't boo the opposition at the Nynex arena, Manchester – we just cheer twice as loud for the Manchester Storm', and, to be repeated *ad nauseam*, 'Lets have a big hand for THE (Allsports sponsored) MAAANCHESTER . . . STORM!!' Taken individually, these remarks probably seem inoffensive enough, but I can assure you, the cumulative effect is devastating.

Cringeworthy though a lot of this is – being told what you could, or could not do throughout the course of a game – a lot of the crowd seemed to enjoy this kind of presentation. Fair enough, I suppose. Newcomers to the game, probably uncertain about how to act at a hockey game, welcomed the announcer's prompting. The rest of us, who don't say things like 'Good ball!' whenever a pass is made, or scream out 'Handball!' whenever a player catches the puck, probably enjoy ourselves just as much because it gives us something to moan about. It was only a matter of time, though, before the crowds took it upon themselves to provide their own entertainment. It was when this happened that ice hockey in Manchester really started to show signs of taking off.

Of particular infamy was a lady known at the start as 'the mad woman with the drum' – and later, when it transpired her name was Liz, as 'mad Lizzie with the drum'. She took it upon herself in the early games to spark some life into proceedings by occasionally banging out a short refrain – Dum, dumdum, dumdum – at the end of which she would implore people to shout out 'Storm!'. Amazingly, people did. Encouraged by this success, she subsequently decided to enliven games by materialising in different blocks and giving peaceful spectators the shock of their lives. Dum, dumdum, dumdum – Storm! Dum, dumdum, dumdum – Storm! The crowd, in the main, cheerfully adopted the chant as the regular Storm salute, and the lady responsible became a notorious regular on the giant screen as the cameras found her an ideal subject to home in on whenever there was a lull in play. Whether her frequent appearances on the scoreboard were in any way linked to the fact that, aside from obviously being of an extrovert nature and a good sport, she also had a prodigious cleavage and an unerring tendency to wear the kind of tops that would make Anna Nicole Smith blush, I wouldn't like to say, but it all helped to forge a 'unique family atmosphere', I suppose. She certainly managed to upstage Jon Hammond on a regular basis.

Another feature of the game-night atmosphere was the puck shooting contest held between periods. Anyone averse to Jon Hammond during normal play at least had the chance to slope off for a fag and a pint at this stage (including some of the adults) as Jon would come out on to the ice, wearing the kind of jacket that even Noel Edmonds would find distasteful. He would cheerfully conduct a little contest whereby members of the audience, mostly children no bigger than the sticks they were holding, got the chance to shoot a puck into an empty net from the neutral zone in order to win fantastic prizes (usually free tickets and the odd signed stick). Hammond would invariably try to coax shy youngsters into talking into the microphone, perhaps getting them to cheer out the name of Manchester's new ice hockey team. On one occasion, a toddler seemed somewhat overwhelmed by the whole experience when Hammond leant forward and gently pushed the microphone towards the child. 'And can you tell us who you support?' he prompted. The child looked at him and, now certain of what he was meant to say, bellowed 'United!' Okay, so there was probably more work to be done . . .

Another part of the public relations aspect of game night was the nicknames. The Storm had decided to follow Sheffield's lead and give the players nicknames, which Jon Hammond would shout out at practically every given opportunity. Some of the players had already got nicknames, of course. Hilton's renowned prowess for scoring goals had already seen him saddled with the nickname 'The Poacher' (and not, as it appeared in the Storm matchday programme, 'The Butcher') which suited him fine. Daryl Lipsey, who was known to one and all as 'The Lipper' at Swindon, tended to become the more prosaic 'Assistant Manager, Daryl Lipsey' at the 'Storm Shelter' – even the arena had its own nickname by this stage. Other nicknames included Dale 'Shotgun' Jago, Steve 'Barnstormer' Barnes and 'Smokin' David Smith'. Mark Stokes was 'The Engine' (although, sadly, I like that one)  and John Lawless was 'The Boomerang', as he continued the tradition he had begun at Cardiff of retiring, making a comeback, retiring, making a comeback, etc.

Not all the players were over-enamoured with their nicknames; James Manson could live the rest of his life without being called 'Baby-faced', I'm sure, whilst young Alan Hough coped well with the stigma of being referred to as Alan 'Hollywood' Hough all the time. Some of the players mysteriously managed to escape without a nickname. I asked Martin Smith why he didn't have one.

'Well, when I first came they wanted to call me "Citizen" Smith,' he said, visibly shuddering at the memory. 'I said, "no thanks", and so I don't have one – and I don't want one,' he explained.

I suggested Martin 'No nickname' Smith as an alternative, but he wasn't keen. Anyway, he had made his contribution to the game-night atmosphere already when, after scoring his first home goal for the club, the Storm goal celebration was born.

The scoreboard had increasingly been brought into play with new film clips and graphics being introduced all the time. After a good piece of play Bill and Ted would pop up to proclaim that things were 'excellent', and after miscreants had been sent to the bench for fighting, Oliver Hardy would point out what a fine mess they had both gotten into. The one that took off the most, though, was the one they used immediately after Smith scored in the home loss to the Humberside Hawks – Wayne and Garth dropping to their knees and wailing 'We're not worthy! We're not worthy!' In the context of a 9–3 home defeat, we certainly weren't, and the crowd humorously echoed the actions of mock adulation before returning to their seats. By the time the Storm had played their second home league match, a game against the hapless Billingham Bombers, the salute had clearly been adopted as the *de rigueur* celebration, although on this occasion, an 18–1 home victory, it started to loose a little of its charm around the 12th or 13th goal, if you ask me.

The crowd seemed to love it all, though, and for Ogden, that was what counted. One of the early successes of the whole venture was the appeal the Storm seemed to have for children and families. It is true that ice hockey in this country is very much a family sport, but in Manchester in particular, it seemed families were drawn to the games. The average age of spectators following the Storm seemed noticeably younger than, say, at Sheffield, where they attract a lot of over 40s as well as families. Whilst these differences in demographics were curious, they didn't prevent a good atmosphere which, by the time the Paisley Pirates played the Nynex, had really taken off. That game, the Storm's seventh in the League, was the first time that the crowd had really got behind the team and played a part in the result, and it gave a glimpse into the full potential of ice hockey in Manchester.

Prior to the game, the Storm had started a charge up the table. After the rigours of the B&H Cup maulings, the League programme seemed like a breeze for the Storm and the first six matches had all been won and, at home especially, won comfortably. However, because of some strange quirks in the fixture lists, the Storm found themselves still mid-table because their rivals had all played more matches. Paisley were third in the table at the time of their visit, and the general feeling was that they would give the Storm a decent match, something the crowd hadn't yet seen. Another thing the crowd hadn't really seen yet was a decent away following, which Paisley had brought down with them, complete with trumpets and drums, and when Mike Bettens scored the opener for Paisley after six minutes, the first visiting side ever to score first at the Nynex, they made sure their presence was felt in the 5,834 crowd. Some excellent play by Paisley, coupled with some pretty lax defending by the Storm, saw the Pirates 4–0 up inside the first 15 minutes. The home crowd, accustomed as they were to big home victories, could scarcely believe it, nor, for that matter, could the Pirates fans, who seemed somewhat bemused themselves. Finally, Daryl Lipsey scored for Manchester, and the home crowd hoped that that would be enough to shake the Storm from their torpor. It wasn't. Paul Hand (brother of you-know-who) promptly netted on a powerplay to restore the four-goal lead. Dale Jago brought some cheer back to the home support when he blasted one in from the blueline to make the first period score 2–5, but when the second period produced only two goals, one for each side, the Storms' 100 per cent record looked very much like it had just 20 minutes left to live.

Of course, the game wasn't over yet, we reasoned. Although 3–6 was a tricky position to overcome, it was not insurmountable. A couple of quick goals at the start of the third period and the Storm would be right back in it. Funny how these kind of thoughts always go through spectators' minds, isn't it? Naturally, all our constructive reasoning was blown away almost immediately, when Paisley took just 25 seconds to make it 3–7. John Lawless – unretired, at this point, due to the vacant import slot – took control of the puck and skated backwards towards his own goal with Pirates import Vas Vasilenko trailing him back in the half-hearted hope that it might be worth it. Lawless looked across the ice before making his mind up where to pass, and then calmly, and inexplicably, fanned the puck straight to Vasilenko who found that he was now about to score the easiest goal of the season. Aaargh! The silence from the home crowd was deafening. Lawless was abject; 3–7 down, the game thrown away. After a few moments, the crowd started up the drum chant. Dum, dumdum, dumdum – Storm! Not the most eloquent call to arms, I'll concede, but in the context of impending defeat, it was a stubborn rallying call – 'we may have lost, but let's still try Dum, dumdum, dumdum – Storm!'

The frustration in the crowd was evident. Paisley had clearly played very well, and deserved to lead the game at that point, but a four-goal lead seemed monstrously unfair, and the crowd were indignant that the fates had conspired to put them in this situation. For nearly ten minutes the Storm battled on without reward. The Pirates simply sat back, knowing that a four-goal lead should be more than enough at this stage. The Storm were forced to make use of that tactical ploy that teams trailing in games like this are invariably driven to use. They started mixing it. Fighting in situations like these often has the benefit of firing up the whole crowd, getting the team going, possibly putting the other side out of their rhythm. Not the most sophisticated of strategems, I grant you, but, hey, when it works, it's a lot of fun. As the game became more physical there were a couple of skirmishes that were greeted with loud cheers – evidence that if the players could give the fans something to cheer about, to get going, then they just might be able to turn things around. Finally Martin Smith's perseverance paid off, a goal with just over nine minutes remaining. The crowd cheerfully suggested that they weren't worthy, and suddenly Paisley wobbled. Within two minutes Jeff Lindsay had crashed one in from the point, and everyone sensed that the Storm had a real chance of pulling it out of the bag. Forty seconds later Ruggles had grabbed another and the crowd were going mental. The Storm were just one goal behind. Now every Storm attack was greeted with a massive roar. The Storm had got the adrenalin going and the Pirates were desperately clearing the puck whenever they got the chance in an effort to stem the tide they were now facing. It was marvellous stuff.

The game was now impossibly frantic, the Storm swarming all over the Pirates as the shots rained in. Martin Smith, playing out of his skin, spun round in front of the net and let fly a ferocious shot. It was blocked, came back to him. This time he hit it even harder. It ricocheted off the underside of the bar and crashed down a foot over the line. Bedlam. The crowd were so pumped up the noise was frightening. Jeeze. Imagine what the place would be like with another 10,000 fans inside. Martin Smith later told me it was the loudest roar that had ever greeted one of his goals. Four goals in four minutes. Seven-all with five minutes to play. Exhilarating. The Pirates were simply hanging on now, like a boxer clinging to the ropes. In an effort to halt the flow they called a timeout. It was possibly the only thing that could have saved them. Ruggles had a half-chance to score the winner, but couldn't get a shot away, and as the Storm piled on the pressure the clock raced down to zero and the Pirates scrambled over the line. The hooter sounded. Seven-all – a tie. The Storm had lost their 100 per cent record – but not their unbeaten one. As the crowd poured out of the building the excitement was evident. The Nynex had seen its first real match and loved it. There was a buzz about the place. As cars pulled away from the arena the horns sounded the clarion call – Beep, beepbeep, beepbeep – Storm! God knows what it would have been like if they had won.

After seven games the Storm stood seventh in the table with six wins and one tie – ruining a great joke I had planned, about how, if they had gone the entire league season without drawing, they would have been like Manchester *Untied* – oh well. Although the 100 per cent record had fallen, John Lawless was pleased with the result.

'The guys really showed some character, especially after hitting so many posts and having so many chances that we didn't convert. It would have been easy to say, 'Oh, I guess it's not our night,' but we just kept plugging away. Even when we were four goals down our fans were still behind us, but when we started the comeback the place went wild.'

In some ways, losing the 100 per cent record was a good thing – it had to go some time, and winning streaks tend to bring extra pressure. With a couple of tricky road trips coming up over the next weekend, away to Dumfries and again against Paisley, it is possible that the comeback gave the players a bigger lift than a normal win would have done. In what was the first really testing double-header the Storm had faced, they pulled out two big wins, beating Dumfries 6–3, and then Paisley 6–4. Both games were close affairs, with the Storm only pulling clear in the third period. Indeed, this had become something of a trend at this stage. The Storm players enjoying better conditioning than many of their part-time opponents, the third period was when other teams started to tire and the Storm were then cashing in. The wins allowed the Storm to leapfrog over both Dumfries and Paisley. They were now fourth in the table.

Above them, at the top of the table, stood the Blackburn Hawks. After the setback of a couple of early defeats the Hawks had put an amazing run together, and at the time of the Storms' back-to-back wins in Scotland, the Hawks led the table with 21 points from their first 13 games. The main reason for this success was the fact that the Hawks boasted the best first line in the League, and one of the best in the country, with French-Canadian Steve Chartrand, Scotsman John Haig and ex-Trafford Metro Oleg Sinkov forming an awesome combination. The three players stood first, second and third in the scoring charts, with the Hawks' inspirational player-coach Ryan Kummu not too far behind. It was a remarkable turnaround for the Blackburn club, who the previous season had been about as intimidating as a drowsy kitten. The bulk of the credit lay at the feet of Kummu, previously a favourite at the Fife Flyers. The Canadian defenceman, in his first job as a player-coach, had blended a handful of talented British players with his three imports to create a side that had managed the laudable feat of topping the First Division with fewer Canadian-Brits than anyone else. Of the import forwards, whilst Chartrand was the one clocking up the most points, Sinkov was the one the Hawks fans had fallen in love with, which is perfectly understandable to anyone who has seen Sinkov play.

The break-up of the Soviet Union has led to many of the Soviet hockey stars making their livings in the west; in the NHL, for instance, the Detroit Red Wings have Sergei Fedorov and the Vancouver Canucks Pavel Bure, both of whom have become major stars. Lower down the scale, Trafford somehow managed to get Oleg Sinkov, not as highly acclaimed as Fedorov or Bure, but, in his own way, just as great a player. At Trafford most people agreed that Sinkov was the most outrageously talented player they had ever seen. Here was a player who had broken into the top Soviet league while still a teenager, and whose first ever goal, for his side Sokol Kiev, was scored against the legendary Soviet netminder Vladislav Tretjak – a far cry from the Devonshire Road ice rink, Altrincham, it occurs to me.

'He was amazing in practice; you'd just look at some of the things he'd do and not know how he did them,' Tim Dempsey once told me. Part of the amazement at Sinkov's play was due to disbelief that a player of his quality was even here in Britain.

'I used to ask him how the standard of play in Britain compared to Russia,' said Tim, 'and he'd say, "Oh, in Russia . . . this (holds hand head high) . . . in England . . . this (holds hand waist high)," and I used to say, "Yes, Olly, but what does that actually mean?" His English wasn't great.'

'We used to give him a hard time when he was with the Mets,' a Blackburn fan said to me in the shop one day. 'You know, say he was rubbish and all that, but that was only because you'd got him. Now we've got him we can say how fantastic he is.'

Indeed they could. The Storm, due to having the rights to all the Metros players, had had first refusal on Sinkov, but Lawless had surprised some people by not going for him.

'I tend to go with the more North American style of play. I think Oleg Sinkov has proven the fact that he's got all the skills, and he can adapt to a North American style of play, but I still wasn't convinced he was right for us. Russians on a team together are, I think, better than North Americans, but as individuals on a team I'm not so sure. It was just my gut feeling.'

Manchester's loss was Blackburn's gain. Sinkov had responded to the move by playing some of the best hockey in all his time in England.

'He's been brilliant – the best I've seen him play,' said Paul Fleury, when I asked him how things had been going at Blackburn since his move there. 'I mean, he was good at Trafford, but he's been amazing this season.'

Was that why Blackburn had done so well?

'I don't know. I mean, we've got so few players, we've surprised ourselves, really. I don't know how we've done it, to be honest.'

In fact it was a surprise to most people. At the beginning of the season most people thought of Blackburn as play-off contenders, but no more. Now they stood between Manchester and the league title. The match between the two sides on 9 November looked like being a cracker.

# 8

# PREMIER DERISION

At the start of the 1995–96 season you could subdivide the Premier Division teams into probables versus possibles. Although most coaches started the season making noises about challenging for top honours, realistically only three teams looked like they could make a serious bid for the title. The Sheffield Steelers were the pre-season favourites, and it wasn't difficult to see why. Take a title-winning side, add Tony Hand and Nicky Chinn, and you should end up with another title-winning side. Having said that, Nottingham, after coming so close the previous season, were obviously going to be up there again, although having lost a few players mid-season, most notably Rick Brebant to Durham, it would be even harder for them to stay the pace this season. The Cardiff Devils were the other side most likely to challenge the Steelers for top honours. The loss of Lawless was a considerable blow, but he left the club in good shape, and the additions of Randy Smith and Steve Moria gave the Devils a depth of talent perhaps even more impressive than that of the Steelers.

Of the likely chasing pack, the Durham Wasps looked the best bet to sneak into a top-three place. Backed by Sir John Hall, the multi-millionaire property developer responsible for the Metro Centre, and, more recently, the man behind the resurgence of Newcastle United, the Wasps were the latest piece of the Hall 'Sporting Club Newcastle' jigsaw. He had acquired the club through one of his companies, after an acrimonious dispute between the owners of the Durham ice rink and the company that had run the Wasps. Now, although not directly owned by Newcastle United, the Wasps were under the umbrella of the club, and they even sported the club crest on their shirts. (The Billingham Bombers fanzine, *A funny thing happened when we got to the forum* claimed that Sir John Hall planned to change the Wasps strip so that it matched the famous black and white stripes of Newcastle United. The only trouble with this, they pointed out, was that it might cause some problems as that was what the officials wore.) The Wasps had a long-established tradition in British ice hockey, and until the recent trend towards arena-based teams, they had been one of the dominant forces in the game. Since 1983, and the advent of the modern era, the Wasps had won the British Championship four times, and collected the Premier Division title five times, both of them record totals. This tradition of winning was one that Hall intended to continue. They also played their home games in Durham, which was a tradition that Hall didn't seem so keen on.

Hall's plan was to build a new arena for the Wasps alongside Newcastle United's St James' Park. As well as staging ice hockey, this arena could be used to accommodate any overspill of football fans who couldn't get into the ground on matchday, who could then watch the game on giant screens. Sounds neat, huh? Unfortunately, there were a couple of snags with this plan. For one thing, Hall didn't have any planning permission, and the proximity of some listed buildings in the area suggested that it might not be easy to get. Sir John Hall decided it would be prudent to sort out such matters before sending the builders in, and with no new rink to move into, the Wasps were to play at the Crowtree leisure centre in Sunderland in the interim. As the season progressed and suspiciously little was heard about the proposed new arena, doubts began to fester about the likelihood of any of the plans coming to fruition. Besides, as Hall's plan stood, there was another blot on the landscape – the arrival of the Newcastle Warriors.

After another north-east consortium, led by the ex-manager of Jimi Hendrix, Chas Chandler, had made enquiries at Newcastle United about the possibility of building an arena adjacent to St James' Park, only to be told by the club that such a building would be unsuitable, they had decided to go ahead and build the Newcastle arena elsewhere in the city. The new building, situated just a mile from St James' Park and capable of holding about 7,000 people for ice hockey, would be home to a new team, the Newcastle Rockets; or so the initial plan went. After the Whitley Warriors expressed an interest, it was decided to let them move into the building instead, under the new title of the Newcastle Warriors. The new building wouldn't be completed until after the start of the season, but the BIHA agreed to let the Warriors continue playing at their old rink until it was ready. All parties seemed happy, except perhaps Sir John Hall, who now found that should he ever manage to get his Wasps into Newcastle, they would have the competition of another arena team right on the doorstep. Whilst Newcastle is undoubtedly a sporting hotbed, capable of supporting a team on a similar scale to Manchester or Sheffield, there were widespread doubts about whether it could support two such teams.

While Sir John Hall had all this to consider, the people of Durham had their own problem. One minute they had a successful team to follow, the next it was gone. Supporters were aghast. Without them there would have been no Wasps to acquire, but it seemed their feelings had been disregarded. A campaign to keep the Wasps in Durham was set up and received considerable local support, but beyond that there seemed to be little that they could do about it. There was some investigation into the machinations of the deal that had allowed the club to be sold against the wishes of the rink, and there appeared to be some doubt about whether or not the sale was legal. The BIHA, though, although sympathetic to the motives of the Durham supporters, were satisfied that the deal was legitimate, and so as things stood at the start of the season, we had the bizarre situation where the Durham Wasps, owned by Newcastle United, were playing all their home matches in Sunderland.

Unsurprisingly, not all the Wasps fans were prepared to transfer their allegiances to the new club. Apart from the sheer hassle of trekking down to Sunderland, there was the indignation felt at the club being uprooted in the first place. Many of the supporters shunned the Wasps in favour of a new club which was formed at the rink, the Durham City Wasps. This new club was entered into the English League, which is akin to football's non-league. (After the arrival of the Storm, the Altrincham ice rink went down a similar path and revived the Altrincham Aces.) This new club attracted a healthy level of support which, although not as good as that commanded by the old Wasps, was still far greater than most of the other clubs playing at that level. Although starting on the lowest rung, it was hoped that this new club would one day win the right to play at a similar level to the Wasps. Meanwhile, against the backdrop of all this uncertainty, the Wasps endeavoured to fashion a title-challenging outfit. With crowds considerably lower than they were used to, the Wasps would not find it easy, but with the financial backing of Sir John Hall they were on a sounder financial footing than previously.

Over in Whitley Bay, the newborn Newcastle Warriors had their own problems to contend with. Not least of these was that the team wasn't very good. Having narrowly escaped relegation the previous year, the main priority would be to consolidate their position. The upheaval of moving mid-season would do them no favours, but the addition of nine new players during the off-season would, it was hoped, give them some much-needed depth. Few people predicted anything other than a rough season for the Warriors, though.

A similar fate was predicted for the Slough Jets. After spending their entire history in Division One they had finally made it to the top flight. The trouble was, the recent history of promoted teams did not make happy reading, with many struggling to adapt in the tougher league and, all too often, surviving just one season in the top flight. Although Slough were conscious of this fact, and made a few signings with a view to bolstering their squad, they were mindful that with limited resources, and playing out of a rink that can hold only 1,500, they would never be able to compete for the best players, and would just try to hang on to their new-found status as best they could.

Other likely strugglers included the Milton Keynes Kings, who the previous season had done what many predicted Slough would now do – they were relegated in their first year at the top. Of course, the withdrawal of Murrayfield had provided a reprieve for the Kings, and now a year older and a year wiser, they felt they had enough experience to keep themselves up. Time would tell. Of the middle pack of clubs, Basingstoke looked best equipped to have a decent season. They had an experienced roster, and with GB coach Peter Woods at the helm, they were unlikely to be an easy side for anyone to beat. The play-offs seemed an odds-on bet for the Bison. It also seemed to be within the grasp of the Fife Flyers, Scotland's sole Premier Division outfit. Without much in the way of financial clout, the Flyers had put their faith in a lot of British talent and, indeed, had probably more talented Brits than any other club. Their youth system was one of the best established in Britain. The question was, with the new import ruling, how easy would it be to survive without the help of dual-nationals? Fife would find out soon enough.

The final Premiership outfit, the Humberside Hawks, were generally earmarked for a mid-table finish. Although a good home side – most sides would not relish the trip to Hull – the summer departures of the three Johnson brothers and Malcolm Bell, who had moved *en masse* to Durham, was a blow. On the other hand, they did manage to acquire netminder John Wolfe from Telford, which would bolster a previously suspect defence. Alas, it seemed as though on-ice considerations might prove to be the least of the Humberside outfit's problems. The county of Humberside itself ('England's newest county' gush the road signs in the area) was set to be England's newest ex-county. The people in the region have never taken to it being called 'Humberside', some stubbornly insisting that all correspondance be sent to them marked 'East Riding'. As a result, it was decided to scrap the moniker 'Humberside' and to disband the council at the same time.

Whilst the disbanding of the Humberside council may have caused no tears, it does cause some alarm to the ice hockey fans in the area. The team, and the rink, are funded by the Humberside council, and while it seems that the future of the rink is safe, the future of the club is decidedly less so. Against this, the summer strengthening of the team reportedly left the club in debt – paid for by the tax payer. This is not ideal for endearing a club to its community. The local paper, quoted in *The Ice Hockey News Review*, was, shall we say, stinting in its support for the Hawks:

'[Ice hockey] has little or no value as a promotional aid for the city, because success or failure in the sport leaves non-fans unmoved. Yet we see attempts being made to grab monies from libraries . . . in order to cover a £100,000 overspend on a failing ice hockey team. The inevitable conclusion is that someone, somewhere, has a cock-eyed sense of priorities.'

Against this kind of local feeling, which is understandable given the circumstances, things do not bode well for the Hawks. Success this season for the Humberside Hawks would inevitably be measured in terms of off-ice developments.

The early leaders of the Premier Division were Basingstoke, who led after three games, but they were to be soon overtaken by the Cardiff Devils who had played a couple of games more than the other sides at the top. Sheffield, surprisingly, drew their opener at Milton Keynes, in what was later described as one of the best games ever played at the Bladerunner. It all looked like it would run to plan earlier in the game, when Sheffield held a commanding 6–1 lead with less than half of the game played, but then they went to sleep as the Kings underwent one of those Humberside 'players-to-hyperbeings' transformations and reeled off seven goals to lead 8–6 with ten minutes to go. The Steelers, shocked at such *X Files*-type goings-on, stirred themselves sufficiently to draw level before the end, but, even so, it was a warning to the Steelers that there would be few nights where they could just turn up and win.

No such delusions for Slough. They started off with four straight defeats, including demoralising home losses to Sheffield (5–13) and Cardiff (2–10), before regaining their composure and snatching valuable wins at Milton Keynes and at home to Newcastle. Indeed, these victories seemed doubly valuable, coming as they did against fellow strugglers. Milton Keynes, finding the going just as tough, managed just one win from their first nine games, but because they had managed to secure three ties they stood above Newcastle who, not to be outdone, managed just one win from their first 12 games, just a solitary 8–6 vicory over Slough spoiling their 100 per cent record. Of defeats, that is. Fife were another side who struggled early on. A surreal 8–17 home defeat by Cardiff was the start of a poor run of games that sent Fife to third from bottom of the league after ten games with just two victories to boast of.

It was an alarming scenario for the Scots, who at the start of the season had been worried that Murrayfield's withdrawal would have negative knock-on effects on them, loss of gate revenue, increased travel costs etc. Realising that they could now get embroiled in a relegation dog-fight if they weren't careful, they moved quickly, installing Mark Morrison as player-coach after moving Ronnie Plumb upstairs. The early benefits were felt most in the B&H Cup run which, although it ended in defeat at Sheffield, did enough to suggest that the Flyers had the spirit to prise themselves away from the bottom of the table. Another side to start badly were Humberside, who lost four of their opening five games, including a terrible drubbing in Milton Keynes where they lost 8–1. By October, though, the Hawks had managed to pull clear of the relegation zone, leaving the bottom four to scrap out the last two play-off positions throughout the remainder of the season.

After their early, dizzying, lead, Basingstoke seemed determined to spend the entire season in mid-table obscurity, the occasional worthy victory, e.g. 6–3 over Cardiff, neatly counterbalanced by a poor showing at a lesser side, 9–3 at Fife, for instance. Come play-off time, the Bison would be there. Capable of upsetting anyone on their day, they were unlikely to attract too much attention to themselves. Nottingham were much more likely to be found hogging the limelight. They got off to a brisk start, winning their first four, and after eight games they stood third in the table with seven wins. Tucked in behind them were Sheffield, whose tie at Milton Keynes and defeat at the hands of the Devils consigned them to fourth place at this stage, although they held games in hand.

Above these two stood Durham and Cardiff. The Wasps had got off to a useful start, just two defeats in 13 games in all competitions – although a November 8–2 defeat in Milton Keynes posed serious questions about their ability to win the title, and the stunning loss to the Hawks in the B&H Cup suggested a frailty in the side on the big occasion. One note of cheer, though, came when player-coach Rick

Brebant passed the 2,000-point mark in his British career, only the second player to do so. (Would you be surprised if I tell you Tony Hand is the other player to have reached the milestone?) This achievement was to be overshadowed, however, when Brebant retaliated to a check from Gary Stefan in a game with Slough, which left Stefan needing 21 stitches in his chin. Brebant seemed to have a thing about hurting Slough players – the previous season he had broken the Jets' captain Warren Rost's nose. This time the BIHA had come down heavily on him. He was suspended for 12 games. The ban hit the Wasps hard, although perhaps not as hard as Brebant hit Stefan, but without him as either player or coach, the Wasps would struggle.

No such drama for the Devils, who simply got their heads down and got on with the business of winning. After a setback loss to Durham, Cardiff put together a winning streak, only to lose in their first league encounter with the Steelers, the Devils going down 6–3 in front of a crowd of 9,000 in Sheffield. The favour was returned when the Steelers visited Cardiff a few weeks later, and left after being beaten 5–4, despite holding a 4-1 lead at one stage. The defeat, Sheffield's first of the season, left the Steelers five points behind the Cardiff team, but with three games in hand. This was to slip to four games in hand when, a fortnight later, Cardiff slipped up at Basingstoke whilst Sheffield had no game.

By now, the middle of November, the league had taken definite shape, the strugglers struggling and the contenders contending. Cardiff led second-placed Durham by three points, but tucked in just behind them were Nottingham and Sheffield with enough games in hand to overhaul the leaders should they win them all. With Basingstoke and Humberside in a comfortable mid-table position, much of the interest was at the bottom of the table, where Milton Keynes narrowly led Fife and Slough. Four points adrift at the bottom of the table were a worried Newcastle. After bidding an emotional farewell to their Hillheads rink, which they celebrated in typical fashion by being blown out 2–9 by Durham, they faced some big changes. Not only were they to take up residency at the new Newcastle arena, but they also needed a new coach.

After five successive games ending in defeat, including a nasty 14–1 home loss to Sheffield and a 12–1 drubbing from Durham, the Newcastle management felt that they weren't exactly going into their new building on a roll. The Storm had shown that a winning team in a new arena could draw big crowds, but just how many would turn up to watch a team beaten every week was less clear. Long-serving coach Terry Matthews agreed that it was in the best interests of the club to hand over the reins to player Chris Norton. It was a sad end for Matthews, who had a long association with the Whitley club stretching back nearly forty years in various capacities, and who had also led the GB team at one point. It was indicative of the fact that teams playing out of new arenas were playing for much higher stakes. The pressure is greater the bigger you get, and Chris Norton was under no illusions about the task now facing him.

'Basically, they presented the chance to me because they were making the change and needed someone to take over . . . now,' he said simply.

He set about turning the club around and, aided by an injection of cash by Ogden, the Newcastle arena operators, he put on his recruitment hat and went looking for players. Telford pair Simon Leach and Dean Edminston were quickly added to the roster, with the promise of more to come. Before that, though, the Warriors had to open their new building, and the historic first clash was set to be against fellow strugglers Fife. An encouraging crowd of 4,089, three times the normal Warriors gate, turned out hoping to see the Warriors score the first goal in their new home. Alas, for Newcastle fans at least, it was Fife player-coach Mark Morrison who netted the game's first goal after 10 minutes.

The Warriors, without the injured duo of David Longstaff and Jason Smart, responded quickly, equalising 37 seconds later; but then Fife started to get hold of the game, two goals from ex-Murrayfield man Chris Palmer setting the Flyers up with a 3–1 lead at the end of the first period. The two sides shared a goal apiece in the second period, and hopes of a Warriors comeback were fanned when Steve Brown made it 3–4 with 18 minutes to go. Suddenly there was talk of a fairytale début for the Warriors, as the crowd urged the home side on. Unfortunately, the Flyers don't believe in fairies, and Mark Morrison and Doug Marsden both scored to put the game out of Newcastle's reach. Although Dean Edmiston scored a late consolation goal for the Warriors, there was no denying that they didn't yet have a fine team to play in their fine new home, and time was running out.

# *9*

# RUDE AWAKENINGS

Less than four months after their first game, there was no doubt that the Manchester Storm were starting to eke their way into Manchester's public consciousness. Crowds were up to around 5,000 and growing, and visiting the arena on game night you were confronted with a plethora of fans attired in their new Storm shirts. In Sportspages you were almost as likely to see customers coming in with Storm gear on as you were with United stuff. There were other telltale signs, like people who had previously expressed no interest in the place suddenly announcing that they intended to go on holiday to Canada. All in all, it seemed very much like the people of Manchester were taking to ice hockey.

It was becoming clear, also, that people had started to have favourite players. After missing the initial part of the season, Dale Jago had established himself as one of the most influential players in the squad. Those spectators used to watching the Trafford Metros, that is to say, those supporters who felt innately superior to other Storm fans by dint of having watched the game for years – like myself, for instance – all agreed that he was our best player. Not that it took a genius to work out that he was a fine player. Banners started to appear at the arena with Jago's name on, and early chants of 'J.A. – J.A.G. – J.A.G.O. – JAGO!' were, I felt, touching and affectionate tributes. Colin Downie, who had started the season strongly in goal, also enjoyed some popularity, and Martin Smith was pleased by the fact that a couple of fans had gone to the trouble of having 'Smith 19' put on the back of their shirts, though only, I assured him, because his was a cheap name to do it with.

The clearest barometer of any player's popularity, however, is when the rink announcer reads out the team roster at the start of the game, and at Manchester the winner of the 'biggest cheer when his name is called out' competition was always Hilton Ruggles, although, for the life of them, a lot of the old Metros brigade couldn't work out why. He was of course, our first big-name signing, he had been the Premier Division's leading goalscorer the previous season, and in 1993, during Cardiff's amazing European run, he had been the tournament's top scorer, winning, as a prize, a radio cassette recorder for his efforts (Oooh!) So big things were expected of him. In goalscoring terms, he didn't disappoint; as well as notching the historic opener in the game against Telford, he was the Storm's top goalscorer, reaching the 50-goal target before Christmas. Although he never looked like troubling the top of the overall First Division scoring charts, in a team that spread the scoring around far more than any other side, it was still an impressive haul. He was also black. Nothing remarkable in this other than the fact that because few blacks play ice hockey in this country, it made him instantly recognisable to an audience who were so new to the sport that Wayne Gretzky could sell popcorn in the stands unnoticed. From a marketing point of view, the Storm had wanted a star player they could use to sell the sport to the public and Hilton fitted the profile better than any other player. The *Manchester Evening News* described him as 'Hockey's answer to Andy Cole', which wasn't a bad analogy except that Ruggles could actually score goals and hadn't cost £7 million.

But there was something about him that some fans didn't like, something they couldn't put their finger on, although some tried.

'He's crap. He can't skate, he can't pass, he can't shoot. Waste of money. He's rubbish,' was the forthright view of one old Metros fan when I mentioned Hilton to him.

I knew what he meant. After all, when you watch Hilton, it is noticeable how often he loses control of the puck, he isn't all that fast, his shot isn't all that fierce, and quite often, when presented with a good chance, he'll spoon the puck hopelessly over the bar from practically any angle. But there he was – the top scorer. I mentioned the fact that the long-time hockey fans in Manchester were more critical of Ruggles than the newcomers were to Anthony Beer, a hockey writer and long-time follower of the Cardiff Devils. He wasn't surprised.

'You'd get that all the time in Cardiff, when he was with us,' he explained. 'People were saying he was no good, that he was lazy and what have you; but he was top goalscorer here with us the last two years.'

'People expected things from him that weren't in his game. He's called "The Poacher" and that says it all. I did a preview piece on a game with Sheffield last season and asked their coach who the danger man was. He said Ruggles. I bet whenever you ask the opposing coach they'll tell you he is the one to watch. He takes all this stick in front of the net, players hitting him and holding him, and he just comes back for more.'

Martin Smith understood the criticism but thought it unfair. 'When you hear about a guy who scores 92 goals in the Premier you think about a slick, smooth skating, finesse player who flies with grace across the ice – that's what you think. All of a sudden, you see this guy. . .' he smiles, 'and I dunno if anyone else plays like that. He's choppy, he shoots off the wrong leg all the time, and around the net he slaps at the puck. But his hand-eye co-ordination is unbelieveable, the bouncing pucks he slaps and controls – I'd like to see him play baseball. You have to give him a lot of credit. His ability to find the goal . . . He goes to the net. He takes the whack, and he stands there. He gets more fired up the more he's hit and bounced around. If you leave him alone, sometimes he goes to sleep . . . but get him fired up and he shows up, especially in the big games.'

He was right. I could see Ruggles's faults, and nearing the end of his career I suppose he may have lost some of his speed, but he was still there, banging in the goals. In front of the net, in traffic, he was still the biz. Besides, how can you not love a guy who chooses 'The Biggest Moaner' when asked to choose three words to describe himself in the matchday programme?

He was also the main source of entertainment for the rest of the team. Martin Smith told me about his unusual dress routine. Most players, in most sports, have superstitions about the way they dress, perhaps always putting on the left skate, before the right etc.

'Hilton does what no other guy does. He puts his shoulder pads on first – you know everyone else kind of starts with the skates and works their way up, but not Hilton. He puts his pads and shirt on first. And he's got these really skinny legs, right, so there's this guy with all this gear on top, he looks massive, but there's just these skinny little legs sticking out. I said to him, "Hey Hilton, are those your legs or did you ride here on a chicken?" He wasn't too pleased.' Poor old Hilton. Yet when a pregnant woman took part in the puck-shooting contest one game after writing to the arena saying it would be a good way to settle a dispute over the baby's name, and promptly won the shoot-out, guess who she said the baby would be named after? Little baby Hilton. The mind boggles.

Some of the pressure was taken off Ruggles's shoulders when Lawless finally made his move and signed up the third import. Forward Shawn Byram was joining the Storm. Not that many of us had heard of him. He had played in the NHL, but only five games over two seasons, for the New York Islanders and the Chicago Blackhawks, (no goals, no assists, but a healthy 14 minutes in penalties) but that still meant that he would probably be better than most of the other guys in this league. He had played in Europe a bit, in the Italian First Division, and in the early part of the previous season with the Bracknell Bees, averaging one goal, one assist and one penalty per game. He hadn't exactly set British ice hockey alight, it was true. In fact he hadn't even managed to singe it a bit, but hey, he might be good. He was big, though, 6 foot 3 inches, which was what was needed, and playing alongside Martin Smith and Hilton, it looked like he might complete a useful first line.

Due to his work permit arriving earlier than expected, he made his début for the Storm in an away game at low-flying Billingham. It was a low-key début – he only scored six goals, and made four assists. We were impressed. It was only Billingham, sure, but even so, ten points. The next night he made his home début against Solihull and scored a hat-trick, along with another four assists. Seventeen points in your first two games is no bad start, even against bad teams. Now that we had had a look at him, we felt happier about our new acquisition. He was a good passer of the puck, and quite quick too, although his size made that deceptive because he looked as though he was barely moving as he skated. I was especially pleased by the way that he seemed impervious to checks. At one point a Solihull player hurtled towards him by the boards, and flung himself unflinchingly at him. He just bounced off, and Byram, apparently oblivious to the whole incident, skated off without even a glance back. Nice one. The question was, now that we knew he could carve apart weaker teams, how good was he against decent opposition? We would soon find out. The next game was against Blackburn.

I don't think I have ever looked forward to a game so much. In the days building up to the game it was evident that my anticipation was shared by other supporters. Storm fans coming into the shop could talk about nothing else, and the Hawks fans who came in (Blackburn being so close to Manchester, there are quite a few Hawks fans who work in Manchester) were equally excited about the prospect, although they faced the game with a certain degree of trepidation.

'I think our first line can beat yours,' one fan said to me. 'It's the rest of the team I'm worried about.' Indeed, that was the general feeling shared by most people. In his programme notes for the preceding game against Solihull, John Lawless had written:

Blackburn have an awesome first line with Steve Chartrand, John Haig and Aleg (*sic*) Sinkov topping the scoring charts. Those three players alone account for 70% of Blackburn's goals. Contain their first line and you should contain the Hawks.

Rumour from the Blackburn camp had it that the Blackburn team shared this concern.

'They're really scared!', a Storm fan with a 'reliable source' told me. 'They're worried that we'll slaughter them.'

Oh, this was going to be good. Just before the game Paul Fleury popped into the shop, and laughed when I asked him if the Hawks had any nasty injuries they were hiding.

'No, 'fraid not. Sorry,' he smiled. I contemplated tripping him up as he left the shop to try and break his leg, but thought better of it. After all, he is a nice bloke for one thing, but, more importantly, he doesn't play on that first line so I might be wasting my time.

The Blackburn Hawks were not the only visitors to the Nynex arena that night. Sky television's *Ice Warriors* programme was also coming to town, and the game was going out live. This, in fact, was why the game was being played now; originally it had been scheduled for late December, but it had been brought forward a few weeks, to fit in with Sky's schedule. A small price to pay, we thought, when it allowed us the opportunity to tape the game off the telly as well as watch it; a great souvenir of the first season, eh? A win over Blackburn, on tape. The only thing that could spoil it would be if I got home after the game to find that, instead of recording a hockey match, I had done my usual trick of taping the shopping channel for four hours instead.

Although it was still relatively early in the season, the general feeling was that the League title was going to be won by one of these two teams. Manchester were still unbeaten, only the draw with Paisley blemishing their 100 per cent record, and since losing to Medway back in October the Blackburn Hawks had won their following six games to lead the table with 25 points from a possible 30. A win here, though, would put Manchester top of the table with three games in hand, a position they would surely maintain for the rest of the season. Although early predictions of the British attendance record being broken were a little too optimistic, a bumper crowd of 8,974 turned up for the first ever local derby meeting between the two sides. The prospect was mouthwatering.

The teams came out on to the ice to a tumultuous reception. The Hawks fans, clearly fired up for the occasion, were there in their hundreds, with flags, banners and drums, making as much noise as they could. It was by far the largest contingent of away fans the building had seen, and it made for a great atmosphere. There was a brief hush as the anthems played, but then a roar as the puck was dropped and the sides went into battle. After just 34 seconds Ruggles broke free and made it 1–0. The crowd went wild; just the start they wanted. Blackburn, however, were not rattled by this, and Paul Fleury scored the equaliser after three minutes. Not to worry, though, Ruggles did his trick again to make it 2–1. It was around this point that the game got more physical. The Storm obviously felt that one of the ways to stop the first line was to rough up Chartrand, Haig and Sinkov. To this end, the game became very scrappy, as Manchester made sure their presence was felt. Trouble was, the Hawks seemed prepared to take it.

Oleg Sinkov pulled the Hawks level after ten minutes, and Chartrand put them ahead for the first time on a powerplay as the Storm increasingly found their key players in the penalty box rather than on the ice. Although Martin Smith got Manchester's third, it was clear that by the time Ryan Kummu had put the visitors 4–3 up on another powerplay, the Storm's tactics were not paying off. In an effort to stop Sinkov, Lawless, hardly the first person you'd expect to goon it up, tried to get him to fight. The Storm fans could not believe it. Those of us who had watched Sinkov play for years knew that, although he didn't play well in physical games, he never retaliated, and the attempt to get him to do so was sheer folly. Sinkov was awarded two minutes for roughing; Lawless, on the other hand, faced 14 minutes in the penalty box for his troubles. The Hawks led 4–3 at the first interval. Things were not exactly going to plan.

If we thought the Storm's lack of discipline had cost them dearly in the first period, we were stunned by what happened in the second one. As the Storm racked up the penalty minutes, the Hawks racked up the goals. Chartrand, on a powerplay, Fleury (what had Lawless said about him coming back to haunt us?) and then Cotton all scored to make the score 7–3 to the Hawks. The Storm were in disarray. Colin Downie, superb all season, chose this match of all games to have an off-night, at times looking like he couldn't stop a beachball, but he wasn't solely to blame by any means. There were plenty of others who simply weren't showing. Byram's high-scoring games now looked like they took place a long time ago. We were briefly reminded of the spirited comeback against Paisley when Steve Barnes drilled one in to make it 7–4, but the Hawks slammed the door shut with two more powerplay goals from Kummu, and another from Cotton. The Hawks were irresistible. It was now a slaughter. Their passing was superb as Sinkov and Chartrand tore through the Storm defence time after time. Every time they got the powerplay they seemed to score, and the Storm seemed hell-bent on allowing them this opportunity whenever possible. The Hawks fans were having the time of their lives, each goal greeted with a euphoric cheer as the Storm were run ragged.

It got worse at the start of the third. After five powerplay goals, the Hawks decided that even strength goals were just as much fun, Haig making it 11–4. They had a goal disallowed, not that we thought it would make the slightest difference, but it did seem to bring a halt to the onslaught. The Hawks took their foot off the pedal, allowing Mark Stokes and David Smith to pull a couple of goals back, and after Kummu had sealed his hat-trick, the Storm got the consolation of a further three goals as Jago popped in a couple and Ruggles got his third: 12–9 to the Hawks the final score. The late Storm goals added a veneer of respectability to what had been, in truth, a hugely disappointing performance by the home side. The hooter sounded, and the subdued crowd filed out of the arena towards the nearest pubs to drown their sorrows. It had not been a good night to be a Storm supporter. When I got home that night I found that my luck was out again with the attempt to tape the match off the television. It had worked perfectly. Typical.

The next day the post-mortems began. What had gone wrong? The Storm had been well beaten, no argument. Perhaps the only consolation was that they had played poorly and lost – not as bad as playing well and still losing, which would mean that the Hawks were a much better side. How had Blackburn won so comfortably, though? The Hawks had been brilliant, their passing exemplary, their discipline good, and netminder Ian Young had played a good game, but surely it was their teamwork and will to win that had won the match. When I was finally able to stomach watching the game on video, one of the most interesting things to notice came not during the game itself, but during the interval, when the Sky cameras were allowed to film around the Storm dressing-room. The home players, despite trailing 4–3 at that stage, were lounging around, apparently unconcerned about the state of the game. Perhaps they were conscious of the cameras, wanting to appear nonchalant, but perhaps they were also overconfident as a team, not giving Blackburn the respect they deserved. Before the game all the talk had been about the Hawks' first line, but in the end it was about the bottom line – they had come to the Nynex determined to win, whilst the Storm had showed up expecting to win. Big difference. Perhaps the Storm were simply not as good as they thought they were. It had been a sobering experience.

# 10

# PASSPORT TO BRITAIN

Here's a little quiz for you. Of the top ten scoring leaders in the 1994–95 British Premier Division season, how many players were both born and trained in Britain? The answer is one – Tony Hand, who in fact was the top scorer that year with 292 points, more than 50 points ahead of second-placed Rick Brebant. In fact, when you consider that Mr Hand is a freak in the first place – I mean, he's far too good to be British – you are looking at one of the hard facts about British ice hockey. The game is, and always has been, dominated by imports. In theory, this can work out fine. By allowing clubs to import some players, you can have a pool of British players at a club and ship in a couple of stars from Canada. The Brits then learn how to be better players from following the example of the Canadians, who in turn enjoy a higher profile playing the game in Britain than they would have at home and the fans are happy because the hockey is better. Sounds all right, doesn't it?

Needless to say, it doesn't often work out like that. In an ideal world your import would come over, play his heart out, coach all your junior players and generally be an excellent ambassador for the sport, but in the real world, some of them just prefer to play golf instead. People, therefore, are often critical of imports. They are just mercenaries, it is claimed, with no commitment to the development of the sport in this country. Certainly you could point the nasty stick at many imports for this very reason, but while you were at it you'd probably have to wave it in the direction of a few Brits, too – they don't all play the game with the Corinthian ideals of sport uppermost, either. The problem is that whilst replacing a British player isn't easy, it is still easier than summoning up a new import player, and because your best players are always likely to be imports, if your import doesn't cut the mustard you are in trouble.

It was felt, therefore, that some effort should be made to ensure that players arriving here from abroad should be of sufficiently high standard so as to be of benefit to the British game. Before any import is allowed to play in Britain, he has to be granted a work permit by the Department of Employment, and the criteria were changed so that only players who had been playing in the élite league of a Pool A European nation, or in the higher pro-hockey leagues in North America, would be granted one. In theory this was a good idea as these players would presumably be of a higher standard than the British players they were likely to be replacing, but it was still far from perfect. Rather than protecting clubs, it was argued, this new ruling might actually damage them, since inevitably, the higher the league a player plays in, the more it is going to cost to lure him to Britain. Even then, once you had wedged out on your new player, who was to say he'd be of any benefit to the British game?

Critics were quick to point out that many of the best players who have come to Britain had previously played in leagues that are now deemed not good enough for British hockey. These included players such as Darren Durdle of Nottingham, Chris Kelland of Sheffield and Steve Moria of Cardiff, not to mention any imports who had come from the old Soviet Union. Some of these players had been so good as to be revered as demi-gods by their fans. When the Trafford Metros somehow managed to lure Oleg Sinkov from Sokol Kiev to Altrincham, some of the fans, hypnotised by his prowess on the ice, took to driving Ladas in tribute. To think that in the future players like these would be barred from our game, effectively told they weren't good enough, was not on – it would be an opportunity lost. Besides, you can't tell how useful a player is going to be just by the league he plays in. For example, if you take the National Hockey League (NHL) which nowadays is without question the élite league for the world's best players, you would expect any player good enough to play in that to be good enough for the British league which, by comparison, is absolutely cack. Right? Well, no.

The trouble with playing as an import in Britain is that so much is expected of you. Some teams rely so heavily on their imports that they play them for anything up to 50 minutes a game. In the NHL some players may only get a few minutes of ice time each game, and even then, they will be assigned specific roles – like going up to the opposition's star player and jabbing their stick repeatedly into his face. A forward in the NHL wouldn't dare deviate from the strict game plan laid down by his coach, and would surrender his natural style of play so as to conform to the team ideal. Here, we want imports to play as many shifts as they can without busting blood vessels, and to cover the ice more thoroughly than the Zamboni. If we could make the sods play in goal at the same time, we would. Needless to say, this isn't going to suit every NHLer. However, the player who, in Canada, was always being vilified by his coach for trying to play in three positions at once, and has never made it past the junior leagues as a result, could be just the man for the British game.

Whilst it is understandable that we don't want every goon that has ever picked up a stick to qualify for a work permit, it is a shame that some great players will now be denied the chance of coming here. For instance, John Lawless, who has had an enormous impact on British hockey, not just in Cardiff and Manchester but in Peterborough also, would nowadays not even qualify for a work permit. Mind you, if you think it gets confusing when you look at who is going to be selected to play as an import in Britain, you should look at how messy everything gets once they arrive here. Take that 1994–95 season, for instance. Each team could sign as many imports as they wanted, but a maximum of five were permitted to play in any one game. Of these five, at least two had to possess a British passport (dual-nationals, in other words) and only three such players could be on the ice at any given time. The whole business of who counted as a dual-national player and who was an import was further confused by the issue of reclassified players. These were guys who had originally started as imports, but who had been playing long enough in this country to be eligible to play for Great Britain. You with me so far? Well, it doesn't really matter whether you are or not, because at the start of the 1995–96 season everything changed. On 29 May 1995, the BIHA announced that, as far as the clubs were concerned, anyone eligible to play for Great Britain under International Ice Hockey Federation (IIHF) rules counted as British, regardless of where they had been born and trained. The announcement, made shortly before the work permit issue was addressed, completely overshadowed the debates concerning the quality of imports and had two immediate effects. Firstly, it led to clubs racing to stack their teams with Canadian-trained British passport holders, and secondly, it brought more cries of 'We're doomed!' than a season of *Dad's Army* repeats.

In retrospect, the new ruling had been on the cards for some time. Legally, it was becoming more and more suspect that the BIHA could treat anyone holding a British passport any differently from anyone else in the country. The continuing threat of legal action from some clubs, challenging some of the rulings concerning imports, was too much for the BIHA to face. Sooner or later they would have to give in and, with regret, they had finally done so. The implications were potentially massive. In the past, restrictions on import players had been made primarily to protect home-grown talent. It was a balancing act, in many respects. The BIHA felt that one of its main obligations was to ensure that the game had as healthy a future as possible. This meant doing as much to help the development of our own players as possible. On the other hand, clubs would naturally want the best players they could get. Inevitably, this meant players from overseas, usually Canadians. Not all the best players are from Canada, of course, there are plenty of Russians, Swedes and Finns who could skate rings round our British lads, but bearing in mind the fact that so many of our coaches are Canadians, it doesn't take Carol Vordermann to work out why so many Canadians seem to top their shopping lists. This new ruling suddenly presented coaches with a golden opportunity to grab as many of these players as they could afford. If the amount of imports in the domestic game had been of questionable benefit to the British players before, now they seemed an out-and-out threat.

The new ruling meant that any player who held a British passport, either through their parents' nationality or through long-term residency, could now play as British provided they hadn't played for, nor held citizenship of, any other country. As there were a large number of players in that position, once the announcement was made, there was a massive scramble among the clubs to sign as many of these new Brits as possible. Teams that had previously been allowed to ice only three imports could now start the new season with 10 or 12 players who had learnt the game overseas. There were two obvious losers in this: firstly the poorer clubs who couldn't afford the wages these players were now commanding, and secondly, the British players now out of a job.

It had been one of the ironies of the old imports system that, ultimately, success at the higher levels depended more on the quality of your domestic players than on your overseas talent. Everyone was allowed the same number of imports, it was reasoned, therefore teams would be more or less equal in this respect providing that their imports didn't get injured, walk out on them, or retire suddenly and inexplicably at the age of 26. The British guys would therefore be the deciding factor in where the silverware went at the end of each season. The best illustration of this can be found when you look at the careers of Brits Ian and Stephen Cooper. The Coopers, both GB internationals and both among the top ten British scorers of all time, have always been seen as a pair. Sign one, and you have to sign the other – not a bad deal, by any means, when you consider how good they both are. They started off at Durham, when the Wasps enjoyed a spell as the dominant side in Britain, winning the British Championship in 1987 and 1988. They then, sensationally at the time, signed for the First Division Cardiff Devils, winning promotion in their first season there, and winning the championship again the very next year, 1990. They went back to Durham, and lo and behold, won another couple of championships. Then they re-signed for Cardiff and, guess what, won the championship again in 1993 and 1994. (Getting a little too close to the Twilight Zone here, if you ask me. . . ) This meant that they had won the championship six times out of seven, only denied a clean sweep because of that one season in Division One. It seems to me that the secret of how to win the British Championship at this point was simply to buy the Cooper brothers, which goes to show that having the best Brits did give you a slight edge.

As a result of the impact that premium British players could have on the domestic game, they became very much prized assets. Coaches complained that these Brits were asking for more money than they were worth, although they still seemed prepared to stump up the cash. With the new ruling in place, suddenly these Brits didn't look quite so indispensable. Why pay through the nose for top Brits when the sudden glut of new Brits meant better players could be snapped up cheaper? Finding a job as a top British player wasn't as easy as it had been. Of course, not every one of these new players was as good as Randy Smith or Paul Adey, but it's not difficult to see why they appealed to the clubs so much. By the time the 1995–96 season was in full swing, there were 154 players in the British League who had learnt their trade overseas, yet, of these, only 70 were registered as imports. Closer examination of just which clubs had all these guys on their rosters revealed something about as surprising as drinking 12 pints of lager in one go, only to find that you need the toilet. Which clubs had all these players? Why, the ones with money, of course. Immediately, there were concerns that such an unequal distribution of talent would be detrimental to the game. How could Billingham possibly compete with Manchester in the First Division when Manchester could afford ten players trained in Canada and Billingham could only afford three, if that? Well, the answer was quite straightforward. They couldn't.

If some of the clubs were worried about the sudden influx of so many Canadians, it's fair to say many of the players shared their concerns. Tony Hand was particularly vocal in his condemnation of the new ruling. He argued that the only reason that he had become the player he was was because of being thrown in at the deep end and playing first-team hockey as a teenager. The experience, although difficult at the time, had paid dividends in later years, and other top British players like the Cooper brothers had had similar experiences. The quality of young British players is probably higher now than it has ever been, but with so many Canadians grabbing all the ice time this talent will be lost if youngsters aren't given their chance.

'They've got to . . . compete with Canadian players who have had Canadian training . . . some of them were playing NHL three years ago, and how can you expect an 18-year-old kid to compete with that?' asks Hand.

'Players who are not given their chance at this stage, who look at the Canadian players in front of them, are going to think, "Will I ever get a chance?" They could be lost to the game altogether.

'It's going to take an exceptional British player to come through, actually to get the ice time they're going to need to develop. I worry for the outcome of this, whether in four or five years time there is going to be hockey around . . . '

Alarmist though this may sound, Hand had a point (although, do bear in mind that he has always been a card-carrying pessimist). The influx of Canadians into the game was of questionable benefit, and some of these Canadians now playing in the British game weren't that great; in many cases, British players could have been just as effective. Having said that, the old argument that 'British = Good, Canadian = Bad' was far too simplistic to stand up to close scrutiny and, as far as some of the older Brits were concerned, they had been demanding such high wages previously that you couldn't blame club owners plumping for the cheaper Canadian product. Besides, it could be argued that, as hockey stands on the threshold of a new level of popularity, anything that improves the quality of the game in the short term is worth the risk. Although it would be a shame if any British players decided to give up the game, that might be outweighed if some dazzling new Canadian talent helped to sell the sport to the public.

It was true, admittedly, that it was possibly damaging to the sport's credibility if all the players were seen as foreigners; also that it would be harder to gain media recognition as a consequence, but media coverage hadn't exactly been at saturation point beforehand, so what was there to lose? Anyway, if the explosion of foreign talent in the football Premier League was anything to go by, it seemed the British public welcomed the colour and skill that overseas players could bring to the game. Everyone gives lip service to the notion that it is vital for British players to develop, but, where the fans are concerned, as long their team wins, do they really care that much where the players come from? Sure, it is nice for the top players to be Brits, but how many Steelers fans felt their Championship triumphs were negated by the fact that they had so many Canadians playing? (Answer: None.)

However, just a few weeks into the 1995-96 season, before you could say 'thank goodness this import palaver has finally settled down', it all flared up again. The BIHA announced that some of the players they had cleared as being 'British' should not have been cleared after all, and recommended that any clubs with such players should suspend playing them until the matter was sorted. The clubs were furious at this latest development. Most had signed these players in good faith, and those who had realised that the players weren't really British were indignant that the other clubs had gone and signed them anyway, leaving them up the creek without a kayak. It was, to put it mildly, an unfortunate state of affairs. The confusion had stemmed from the earlier statement that any player qualified to play for Britain was no longer an import. They had to hold a British passport, and, crucially, not have held citizenship of another country. Some of these new Brits held British passports because they had been born here and moved away at an early age. This was fine. The problem arose with players who were born elsewhere and held passports because their parents were British. In these circumstances, they could not qualify to play as British because being born in Canada automatically meant that they held Canadian citizenship. They would only become eligible to play for Britain after they had played here for three seasons. The whole situation was becoming messier than a pig's bottom.

The clubs claimed that the BIHA had moved the goalposts. First they had said that some players were British, then they had said that they weren't. In truth, this was unfair. To say the BIHA had changed the rules mid-season was incorrect; to say the BIHA were a bunch of hapless dundering incompetents was probably nearer the mark. Originally, the BIHA had requested certain documentation regarding the new players' citizenship, and had cleared several of them. Once the Canadian High Commission looked at the papers, however, they deemed them to be worthless and the BIHA realised that they had screwed up. Clearly, some clubs were now icing players as British who should have been classed as imports. Oops!

Although this wasn't the clubs' fault – in fact, they had been told that they could sign these players by the BIHA themselves – they were now being told that any points gained in matches in which the players concerned took part could be forfeited. Some of the clubs, including the Manchester Storm who had three such players, took legal advice. They felt that if the BIHA were to insist that these players be reclassified, they had reason to pursue a legal case against the BIHA. The BIHA, realising that they had no chance of surviving such action, did a U-turn faster than you can say 'crippling damages and legal costs', and everything went back to the way it was before, albeit with the BIHA somewhat red-faced.

While all this had been going on, the machinations of the Bosman case rumbled on in the European courts. It soon became clear that ice hockey would be just as affected as soccer. If a player from another EEC country wanted to play in Britain, the BIHA would be compelled to treat that player as if he was British. If the British players had been worried about competition from Canada, now they had Europe to worry about also. Within days of the announcement that there would be no restriction on EEC players, some of the clubs had already made a move, most notably Durham who wasted no time in beefing up their squad with the addition of four Finns. In a relatively short space of time, the role of the British player in the game had been turned on its head. Of course, there was nothing stopping British players from going abroad themselves, but, strangely, this didn't seem much consolation to many. Although everything would probably take a season or two to settle down, it seemed likely that the British game would never be so 'British' again. And that is probably as much as you can read about imports in one chapter without your brain hurting, so I'll talk about something else now.

# 11

# BACK TO BASICS

It is often noted that the way a team responds to defeat is a good indication of the character of that side, and after losing to Blackburn at the Nynex, the Storm resumed their league campaign determined to bounce back and prove themselves. Any hope that they might be able to get back into the swing of things with an easy match against one of the struggling sides was soon put to rest, however, when they consulted the fixture list to see that it had provided little in the way of respite. Their next game was at home to third-placed Telford, another stern test for Manchester. Indeed, a win for Telford would see them leapfrog over the Storm, not to mention posing some serious questions about the Storm's championship aspirations. A crowd of 5,819 were at the Nynex to see how the Storm would respond, and within a few minutes of the start of the match it was clear that the Storm were in no mood to endure another home defeat.

Manchester took control from the start. Ruggles scored after three minutes, and just 38 seconds later Mark Stokes made it 2–0. Suddenly, it was like Blackburn had never happened, as the Storm passed the puck fluently and confidently. Ruggles scored his second, followed by Martin Smith pouncing on the puck to make it 4–0 at the end of the first period, a Ruggles assist on this goal giving Hilton his 1,000th British point. The Storm were in complete control now, and Telford, clearly bewildered, had no answers. In fact, they didn't even look like they knew what the questions were. Ruggles made it 5–0 after 26 minutes, and although Claude Dumas scored a powerplay goal just after the half-hour mark, Martin Smith put them back in their place with a goal to make it 6–1 at the end of the second. Within three minutes of the start of the third it was 8–1, Jago and Ruggles both scoring. The game now over as a contest, Lawless elected to give more ice time to the third line, and as a result, Telford were able to claw some goals back as Manchester took their foot off the pedal. The final score of 9–5 did not reflect what had been a commanding display by the Storm. After the Blackburn nightmare, it signalled a return to form.

Peterborough were next to visit the Nynex, and a first-period score of 5–1 was pretty much what everyone had expected. To liven things up, Colin Downie was rested in the second period as the third line went to battle with Nathan McKenzie between the pipes. Unfortunately, McKenzie struggled to find his form, allowing four goals in to give Peterborough a glimmer of hope, although in fairness to McKenzie, he was not much helped by a defence who seemed to doze off for the period. Manchester still led 9–5, though, when the third period, and normality, resumed. With Downie restored, Manchester got their act back together, and scored a further six goals past a beleaguered Ian Young – ironically, the same Blackburn netminder who had frustrated the Storm attack just a few days previously. He was guesting in the Peterborough goal after the Pirates regular netminder, Simon Wren, had been slightly injured in a car crash. 15–6 was the final score; the ship back on course.

Manchester now travelled down the road to Telford, who were in danger of slipping out of the title hunt altogether, and eager for revenge after their recent defeat at the Nynex. Unfortunately for them, the Storm were in a determined mood. By the end of the first period, after a devastating display of hockey, the Storm amazingly led 8–2 – probably their finest display of the season up to that point. Telford were shell-shocked, and probably greatly relieved that the Storm eased up for the remainder of the game. The final scoreline of 6–11 clearly illustrated a gulf of ability between the teams. Manchester were on a roll now. Swindon were the next side to visit the Nynex and although they played a tight, defensive game, there was little they could do to keep the Storm in check as Mark Stokes chose this game to remind fans that it wasn't just Byram, Smith and Ruggles who scored the goals. Stokes had a superb match, scoring four times, including one outrageous goal where he decked the Swindon netminder about four times before electing to sweep the puck into the net. The final scoreline of 8–2 to the Storm was harsh on the Wildcats, who had played better than just about any other side to visit the arena, but in the end the Storm, and in particular Mark Stokes, were irresistible.

Swindon did not have to wait long for the chance to exact revenge. After a thrilling midweek home win over a useful Bracknell side, Swindon entertained the Storm on the following Saturday and were confident that they could get some kind of result at the Link Centre. Considering that during the close season Swindon had suffered the double blows of the influential Daryl Lipsey moving to the Storm and, somewhat controversially, Steve Moria defecting to Cardiff despite being under contract, it had not been a bad season for the Wildcats. The loss of those two had many predicting that the Wildcats would struggle to make the play-offs, but in the event Swindon had gelled together, winning six of their first seven starts, and during the course of the season they had racked up some impressive results. Earlier in the season they had even managed to win at Blackburn, 12–9, twice overcoming four-goal deficits. They were prone to the odd infuriating defeat, a home loss to Peterborough for instance, but generally they seemed well on course for that play-off spot.

The main reason for their success had been the impressive form of two of their imports, Gary Dickie and Brad Rubachuk, the latter a feisty but talented forward playing his first season in Britain. The two had formed a useful partnership and were as potent as any two-man combination in the league. They were also determined. 'We aren't a team to back down,' Rubachuk was reported as saying at one point. Indeed he wasn't, as he proved when he set a new record for penalties in one game, racking up an impressive 45 minutes against Bracknell in a game Swindon lost 11–2. With that loss now avenged, it was Manchester's turn to face the fury. In front of a sell-out crowd of 1,400 Swindon were quick out of the blocks, Davison, Dickie and then Nell putting the home side 3–0 up in less than 15 minutes. Eventually, Hilton Ruggles pulled one back for the Storm, but two quick goals from Swindon at the start of the second from Rubachuk and Crawford put Swindon back in command at 5–1. Byram managed to pull one back before the end of the second, and former home favourite Lipsey got Manchester's second soon after the start of the third – but not before Rubachuk had struck again to score Swindon's sixth.

On a tight, confined rink such as Swindon's it was always going to be difficult for Manchester to get back into the game; by now Swindon were buzzing, Rubachuk and Dickie in devastating form as they pulled Manchester apart at the back and threatened to score on every breakaway. In fact, for 76 seconds soon after Lipsey's goal, they did, scoring three more to make the score 9–3 to the 'Cats. There was no way back for Manchester, although Jago banged in a couple and finally, after Rubachuk scored again, his fifth of the night, David Smith closed the scoring with a goal that was, strangely, credited instead to Daryl Lipsey. (Perhaps it was because they still loved him so much. He got a great reception at the start and was even invited to write in the Swindon programme. 'Number 14 in your programme, Number 1 in your hearts,' he wrote. How sweet.) 10–6 to Swindon the final score and really the Storm had no complaints – apart from the fact that they had played poorly, obviously. Swindon had been much the better side, Rubachuk and Dickie combining for 13 points between them, and they had exposed a weakness in the Manchester defence that, unless it was strengthened, would surely be further exposed by better sides in the future.

Overall, though, the defeat was not as worrying as the Blackburn defeat had been. Swindon were a good side, as they had suggested earlier at the Nynex, and besides, up to that point, Manchester had won every other road game in the league – one loss out of seven wasn't too bad. (Guess which was the one away game I went to out of all of those, go on . . . ) A road trip the next night to Murrayfield proved successful, the Storm winning 2–8, so the away record now stood at seven wins out of eight. Blackburn's lead at the top of the table stood at four points, although the Storm held two games in hand. Besides topping the table, the Hawks were also pulling in some big crowds – 3,332 that weekend in a home game against Bracknell, which they won 11–4. Back in 1990, the arrival of the Blackburn Hawks had vitalised the Trafford Metros, the local rivalry spicing things up and providing some cracking local derbies. Now, five years later, the arrival of the Storm seemed to be having a similar effect on the Hawks; aside from the two Premier Division arena sides, these two were, at that point, pulling in the biggest crowds in the country.

Manchester's good away form continued. After winning in Edinburgh, they drove down to Gillingham to face the Medway Bears, and won 16–7, Downie and McKenzie again sharing the netminding. They then travelled to Peterborough, where finally Downie got the shut-out he had been looking for, the Storm winning 7–0 against a Pirates side depleted by injuries and suspension. Ironically, considering that Downie had just claimed his first ever shut-out, there was now speculation that he would be replaced as the Storm's number one netminder by Sheffield's former GB netminder Martin McKay. McKay was reportedly unhappy at being usurped in the Steelers goal by Wayne Cowley who, since his arrival in Sheffield, had been given more starts in goal despite McKay's continued form, including, of course, the B&H Cup final. In the end, the speculation came to nothing when the Storm decided it would cost too much to bring McKay to Manchester and he decided to stay in Sheffield. The episode did signify that Lawless was keen to strengthen the squad, and with McKenzie looking unlikely to make the jump to first-choice status, it was clear he was looking for another netminder.

However, the next addition to the Storm club, introduced to the fans before a home game with Billingham, was not a netminder or any other kind of player. In a move redolent of the *It's a Knockout!* tradition of dressing up geezers in funny, oversized costumes, the Storm had decided to introduce their new mascot. After Sheffield's 'Steeler Dan' and Humberside's snappily-named 'Harry the Humberside Kid' came 'Lightning Jack'. Best described as a bright yellow Jack Nicholson look-a-like wearing dark glasses, a cape and a Storm shirt, Lightning Jack was to make a spectacular entrance. Before the game, with the arena shrouded in darkness, the crowd were astonished to see a mysterious figure, high up in the rafters. To the accompaniment of pounding rock music, and picked out by spotlights, the crowd held their breaths as Lightning Jack prepared to abseil his way 80 feet down on to a waiting platform below. Taking a firm grip on the rope, Lightning Jack confidently strode off the walkway and, as he fumbled with the ropes for a second, there was a pause as the crowd waited for his dramatic drop to the ground. But, as he continued to fumble with the ropes, the pause grew longer and longer.

As Lightning Jack, still picked out by spotlights, hung there helplessly up in the roof, slowly spinning round, it crossed people's minds that he was stuck. His cape was entangled in the ropes and he seemed unable to move either down or back on to the platform. After about three minutes of this top-drawer entertainment which, judging by the amount of gleeful laughter in the crowd, the audience seemed to be enjoying, Lightning appeared to move. Just as most people, bored with watching the hapless rubber-headed mascot dangling from the roof, had turned their attentions to the game, he seemed, at last, to be making some progress. Gingerly feeling his way down the ropes, Lightning slowly descended, in a way that suggested that he was trying not to draw too much attention to himself, which was, of course, impossible by this stage. To the good-humoured applause of the crowd, Lightning finally touched base, by which time the music had long since ended and the match gotten under way. With our attention now drawn firmly to the ice, Lightning slunk away unnoticed, presumably to wash his underpants.

After such a beginning, the game itself was an inevitable anti-climax. Downie and McKenzie were both in action as the Storm ran up a routine 15–1 home drubbing of the Bombers, notable more for a worrying injury to Dale Jago than anything else. McKenzie got the nod to start in the next game, away to Billingham. He was beaten five times, but as the Storm racked up 18 goals it had little or no bearing on who was going to win the points. The next night promised to be much tougher, though. Another road trip, this time to the third-placed Bracknell Bees, who had put together a run of 11 games unbeaten at home. Relegated from the Premier Division the previous season, Bracknell had been one of the favourites to go back up, and had consistently maintained a play-off berth without really catching fire all season. The Storm would be without Jago, who had been advised not to play for a few weeks after injuring his shoulder against Billingham, which, coupled with the Bees' unbeaten home record, made Bracknell slight favourites. It also marked Shawn Byram's return to his previous club, where he felt he had a point to prove after failing to make the kind of impression there that he was now making in Manchester.

The Storm were out of the blocks first, Ruggles scoring in 31 seconds, but the Bees didn't take long to respond, Chris Brant firing in the equaliser after two minutes. From then on the game was a corker. With both sides going at each other full pelt, and the challenges flying, the penalties started to accumulate as fast as the goals. The Bees, who had earlier led 4–2, were trailing 9–7 with just 37 seconds left, when they called a timeout and elected to pull the netminder in favour of the extra skater. This gambit paid off when Rob Stewart scored with 15 seconds left, but then there were some fun and games as the fight that had been threatening all night finally broke out, with Byram provoked after a punch to the face. To cap what had been a marvellous performance in which he had notched seven points, Byram responded to his assailant's pawings with a single blow which ended the contest. Fifteen seconds later the match was over too, a thrilling 9–8 win for the Storm in which Byram had made his point. 'He was amazing,' Alan Hough later told me.

Whilst all this had been going on in Bracknell, a strange thing was happening in Blackburn – the Hawks were losing. Since their victory in Manchester, Blackburn had just carried on, winning every match. Apart from the prodigious output of the first line, the Hawks had a new addition to thank for their string of victories. Canadian netminder Horatio Schlinger who, in addition to challenging Ruggles for the title of 'Most Absurdly Named Ice Hockey Player 1996', had also proved to be a mean performer between the pipes and had quickly eclipsed Colin Downie at the top of the First Division netminding charts. This night, however, there wasn't much he could do to stop the Telford Tigers, who now counted Rick Fera among their numbers. The Tigers, aided by some solid checking from Mark Pallister, were able to contain the Sinkov-Haig-Chartrand line, and there were few complaints from Blackburn manager Mike Cockayne when the Hawk's 15-game winning streak was ended as the Tigers won 10-6. 'Unbeaten runs are there to be ended,' he said, philosophically. The Storm were now level on points with Blackburn, with one game in hand.

If the weekend proved to be a turning point in the title race, the more significant day was probably the Saturday, even though the Storm were not playing that night. Following up a tip, John Lawless put his scouting head on and went to watch Chelmsford take on the Paisley Pirates. Chelmsford were a struggling mid-table side, not so bad as to be fighting it out with the stragglers at the bottom, but generally the last of the mid-table teams. They had recently produced a couple of good results, including an eye-catching 2–2 draw at Bracknell, the first points the Bees had dropped at home up to that point. Such a low-scoring game was a surprise given Chelmsford's defensive record, but they had just aquired a new netminder called John Finnie, and he was gaining some rave reviews, saving 49 of the 51 shots he faced in that début against Bracknell, a statistic that had immediately caught Lawless's eye. Who was this man?

Although from Detroit, Finnie had been playing in Florida, enjoying the sunshine and working at Disneyland in his summer vacations. It had never occurred to him to play in Europe until a friend got a job playing hockey in Austria. Suddenly deciding that playing in Europe might be fun, Finnie asked his friend if there were any openings for him. The friend said that there wasn't a slot open for a goalie, but why not try Britain? With Scottish parents (his dad had played in goal for St Mirren) Finnie held a British passport, and so thought it might be worth a try. Originally, he was put in contact with the Slough Jets, but they already had a couple of good goalies and so put him on to Steve James at Chelmsford. James, who has an impressive record in bringing over talent from North America, took the gamble and signed him not even knowing how good he was. When they saw him play, Chelmsford were delighted with what they'd got. So, too, was Lawless. He took one look and was convinced. 'I could see straight away that the trip was worth it.' After quickly negotiating a deal with Chelmsford, Lawless spoke to Finnie and asked him if he wanted to join Manchester. Finnie, slightly bemused that he was being signed after just nine games for Chelmsford, happily said yes, and Manchester had a new netminder. They'd also saved themselves a lot of money after coming so close to splashing out on McKay.

Storm fans got their first look at Finnie in the home game against Peterborough, although not before Colin Downie had shut out the Pirates in the first period. When Finnie came on, the Storm were already ahead 7–0, and it was 17–0 before the Pirates scored, Stuart Parker denying Finnie a début shut-out. The final score of 18–1 was emphatic enough, every player getting on to the scoresheet, and Finnie's début was solid, although he had little to do. But the most encouraging thing about the night was the crowd. Lured by the promise of a chance to meet the players after the game, 8,367 people turned out, and about 2,000 queued up for a couple of hours after the finish in order to get their favourites' autographs. For the players, it was the clearest indication yet that Manchester was falling in love with hockey.

'We came up the stairs not knowing what to expect,' said Martin Smith to me later. 'I thought there'd just be a table and a bunch of guys stood around – that's what I thought. I didn't think there'd be a queue down the concourse. As we walked up, they started cheering us, clapping; they were roped off, but, just . . . it was amazing. I've never ever experienced anything like that.'

A further indication that the city was taking to the sport was the nomination of Shawn Byram for Sports Personality of the Year, awarded by the *Manchester Evening News*, an award for the whole team as much as an individual accolade for Byram.

'I've never won anything like this before, it's great,' he said, genuinely pleased to have been nominated.

The *Evening News* had also chosen ice hockey to promote their sports coverage. A picture of Hilton adorned many of the billboards dotted around the city bearing the legend 'Manchester Evenmore Sporting News'. Considering that the city of Manchester boasts more than its fair share of sporting heroes, it was satisfying to see an ice hockey player chosen. For the Manchester Storm, in their own city at least, stardom was beckoning.

# 12

# TAKE-OFF

Manchester saw out 1995 in a celebratory manner, slapping 16 goals past Murrayfield for their first ever home shut-out in front of another 8,000+ crowd. With the attendances growing larger for each game, it seemed likely that Sheffield's record for average attendance in a début season would be broken. In their first season, the Steelers had averaged 5,760. Manchester's average crowd at this juncture was 5,815, and with three months of the season yet to come, there was every possibility that that figure would be pushed even higher. Sooner or later, these teams would start meeting each other on a regular basis, and heaven knows what kind of crowds they would generate then. It was a mouthwatering prospect. In the meantime, the Storm had league business to attend to.

The first visitors of the new year were the Telford Tigers, now without Rick Fera, who had been lured to Newcastle along with Simon Leach and Dean Edmiston. Rumours of financial instability had surrounded the Telford outfit all season, as they seemed to every year, and at one point it was even suggested that the Tigers would do well to survive the season. Now, with large cheques being waved in front of some of the players' faces, Telford could do little apart from step aside and let the players go. Ironically, this exodus coincided with a good run of results that had seen the Tigers climb from sixth in the table back up to third, although with many of these games coming against the weaker opposition, it was perhaps a false position. They arrived at the 'Storm Shelter' on 2 January more in hope than expectation then, but Manchester had managed to come up with some problems of their own.

Still without Dale Jago, whose shoulder injury looked as though it might drag on for a few weeks yet, they now also had Mark Stokes on the casualty list after Stokes was struck down with a nasty dose of glandular fever. At one point he was even hospitalised with the condition but, thankfully, the fever receded. It would be several weeks before Stokes was well enough to resume playing, and probably longer still until he had recovered his full fitness. At around the same time, youngster James Manson was also sidelined through injury, leaving the Storm with just three recognised defencemen. They still had Shawn Byram, though, and it was he who opened the scoring after just 20 seconds to set them on their way. The final scoreline of 8–4 to the Storm possibly flattered the Tigers, but Lawless had given the third line a fair run-out and Claude Dumas had pounced against the more inexperienced Storm players to grab a couple of consolation goals.

Still, Lawless's ploy had allowed young Alan Hough to grab a rare goal to the obvious delight of the small, yet devoted, Alan Hough fan club, who tirelessly sing his name whenever he gets anywhere near the ice. He waited until there was just one second left to play before prodding the Storm's eighth goal over the line. Although hat-trick hero Martin Smith had also played well, the man who had got most of the crowd's attention was Telford defenceman Mark Pallister, cousin of Manchester United's Gary Pallister. A couple of solid early checks on the Storm forwards had not gone unnoticed by the crowd, and Pallister's United connection seemed to carry no favours as he was paid the ultimate compliment by the Nynex crowd and soundly booed every time he got near the puck. In the light of the Storm's lack of defensive cover, it was easy to understand the rumour that he had been coveted by the Storm management for some time now.

Three days later, the Guildford Flames made their first visit to the Nynex arena, and a healthy crowd of 6,334 turned up knowing that, should Manchester win, they would go top of the table for the first time – albeit briefly, in all likelihood, as Blackburn were due to play the next night. The Flames were the underachievers of the First Division. Sitting just outside the play-off zone, although with games in hand, they had not done justice to themselves considering the amount of talent they had, with several dual-nationals including Darren Zinger, Fred Perlini, Terry Kurtenbach  and Troy Kennedy. On paper, at least, it was a formidable line-up. Trouble was, it didn't look so good on ice. Guildford struggled to find the right blend, an unsettled import line-up doing them few favours, and they were struggling to pick up points against the better sides, particularly on the road. They were an ambitious club, though, playing out of the Guildford Spectrum, which was a modern £30 million complex opened in 1992. They were also one of the best-supported sides in the country, although I did hear a rumour that their attendance figures tended to include everyone in the complex at the time of any game – swimmers, squash players etc. Not a bad way to do things, I suppose. The same trick at the Nynex would probably bump up the Storm crowds by a couple of thousand; after all, the arena abuts Victoria station, and with all those train passengers . . .

It was John Lawless (un-retired for the 56th occasion) who opened the scoring, but within three minute the Flames had pulled ahead on a brace from Ferster and Kurtenbach. Tempers flared when Ruggles and Dave Gregory were both ejected from the game after 10 minutes for roughing, but this only seemed to focus the Storm who scored four straight, to lead 5–2. Ferster got his second, only to see an old friend of his, Martin Smith, go one better and score his third to make it 6–3. The Flames dug their heels in, clawing their way back to 6–5 down with 15 minutes to go, setting up a pulsating finish. Then controversy. The Flames were enraged that Byram escaped without penalty after elbowing one of their guys right in front of their bench (although in my unbiased opinion thier guy should have been thrown out of the game for bruising the great one's elbow . . . ) and then, almost immediately, the referee called a hooking penalty on the Flames that did not look any worse than several that had just preceded it. With the Flames shorthanded at such a critical point in the match, they were distraught to see Jeff Lindsay step up to the blueline and crash in a shot that gave David Graham in the Flames goal no chance.

Guildford threw everything forward but could not get past Finnie, who had been superb all night, and when they pulled their netminder in a last desperate gamble – the first side ever to do so at the Nynex – they saw Linsday again in a shooting mood as he converted the empty net opportunity with a confident shot from deep in his own zone. 7–5 to the Storm. Easily the best game seen at the Nynex since the Paisley thriller. The Storm were worth the win, although only just. After the game Guildford coach Ivan Brown was full of praise for the officials: 'That's the worst referee I've ever seen,' he claimed. Life's like that, Ivan.

The Storm's stay at the top of the table, enthusiastically greeted by much tooting of car horns as the crowd left the building, was short-lived. The next night, Blackburn regained the advantage when they exacted revenge for their earlier defeat and beat Telford 6–4. Blackburn and Manchester were level on points now, and although the Storm enjoyed the better goal difference and held a game in hand, Blackburn stood at the top because their win at the Nynex gave them a better record in the head-to-head clashes between the two, which was what counted when teams were level on points. The only other side to have gained anything from visiting the Nynex had been the Paisley Pirates, and they were Manchester's next opponents, as the Storm battled to keep the pressure on Blackburn.

Any Storm fans turning up hoping to see a game as good as the first between these two sides were going to be disappointed; although considering the Storm won 9–1, they were presumably able to cope with the let-down. Despite having to play their third game in just six days, the Storm were in a different class. Passing the puck fluidly and smoothly, they controlled the game, seemingly able to step up a gear whenever a goal was needed. The Pirates simply weren't in it, not that this came as any great surprise to their supporters, mind. After leading the table early on, the Pirates got worse as the season progressed. The early blistering performances of their Russian imports Vasily Vasilenko and Dainus Bauba were a distant memory as the two seemed to lose understanding and their partnership lost its venom. Paisley seemed also to have developed the knack of tossing away leads. Apart from letting a four-goal lead at the Nynex slip, they later did the same trick and lost at home to Medway 7–6 after being ahead by four goals. The exasperated coach, Martin Shields, felt that his side lacked 'will-to-win', and in an effort to fire things up, he released several players during the course of the season, including Bobby Haig and Dean Smith. Although new players were brought in the gambit failed, and the Pirates were destined to lose out to Guildford in the chase for the final play-off spot.

Manchester now had the pleasure of a midweek jaunt down to Telford, who were enjoying a four-game losing streak. With the brash Storm in town, however, they buckled down, determined to give Manchester a run for their money. At the half-way point, after the sides had taken turns to hold the lead, it was four apiece and Telford were in with a shout of victory. Lawless made the decision to swap Downie for Finnie, who, once installed, looked unbeatable. Soon after, Ruggles scored to make it 5–4 with 25 minutes to go. Amazingly, this proved to be the winning goal, as Finnie, playing with total authority, resolutely snuffed out every Telford advance. The Storm couldn't add to their tally in the final period either, but as they were already winning they didn't care so much. Telford were crestfallen. Had it not been for Finnie, they felt, they would have won the game. This defeat, their fifth on the bounce, effectively ended their play-off hopes.

In the nether regions of the table, things looked pretty settled. The honour of a last-place finish was now down to a straight dogfight between Billingham and Murrayfield, two former Premier Division clubs fallen on hard times. The other ex-Premier outfit, Peterborough, were looking like they would finish 11th, a long way off the pace but 11 points clear of bottom. Their season, however, would ultimately be most memorable for just one game, and indeed, just one goal, but as goals go it was a real collectors' item. The game was a home match against Bracknell (which the Pirates ended up losing 7–5, incidently) and the goal that made all the headlines came right at the start. Pirates netminder Tony Melia had cleared the puck up the ice, where it was collected by a Bracknell defenceman who, under no pressure at all, passed the puck across to Chris Brant only to see it take a bizarre deflection past Dave Langford in the Bees goal.

As Melia had been the last Pirates player to touch the puck he was the one credited with what was in reality an own goal. After the game, it dawned on everyone that no one could remember a goalie ever having scored in a game whilst the other netminder was on the ice. (Goalies had scored empty-netters before, but even then, it was a rare event.) News filtered through to Canada, where the *Hockey News* picked up on the story. It seemed that no one, anywhere in the world, had ever managed it before in a professional game. It was suggested that Melia's jersey be hung in the Hockey Hall of Fame in Toronto, although as no video evidence of the goal exists, sadly that honour may be denied. Either way, it was something that Melia could boast about in future years.

Up at the top of the table, Manchester led once again, but this time Blackburn, playing at Swindon two days later, were unable to peg them back. Swindon, in a bid to strengthen their side, had taken advantage of the Bosman rulings to bolster their squad, adding three Finns to the side. They all made their débuts against a Blackburn side that seemed to be running out of steam. Swindon took full advantage, and as the Hawks crashed to a 6–3 defeat, it looked as if Manchester's visit to Blackburn a couple of weeks later might be the Hawks' last chance of ever catching up with the runaway Storm. And still Manchester pressed on. Away at Paisley, they won 6–3, and the next night in Edinburgh, the Royals were taken apart 10–1. Blackburn hung in there, beating Dumfries at home, only to see Manchester whip Chelmsford 9–1 in a midweek game. By Sunday 21 January, Blackburn faced Manchester four points adrift of the Storm, having played one game more. They knew that, in order to keep the title race alive, they somehow had to beat the Storm. They had managed it before, of course, but there was a nagging suspicion that this would in fact make it harder to repeat the feat. The Storm had a score to settle.

As face-off approached, the atmosphere in the sell-out Blackburn crowd of 3,500 was electric. The Storm had been awarded a large allocation of tickets, which they had easily sold, and peppered among the ranks of the home support there were further Storm supporters, bringing the level of away support to something like 1,000 fans. And what a noise they made. Before the start, the announcer invited the away fans to show their support for the Storm, and was rewarded with a massive roar as the Storm fans flexed their vocal muscles. Impressive stuff, I thought to myself. But there was an even bigger roar for the Blackburn Hawks. I was even more impressed. (Although I later twigged that whenever the Hawks fans were asked to cheer they fed the noise through the PA system to boost it up. Cheats!) The combined noise level was terrifying, the kind of atmosphere you only ever get in local derbies, games with a bit of needle. We could hardly wait. Our anticipation was further heightened when we learnt that, aside from what we hoped would be a cracking match, there was also some bizarre between-period entertainment in store; the Blackburn arena management had arranged for some figure-skating nuns to take to the ice and put on a show for us. If the Hawks were going to be as inventive in their play as they were in their match presentation, we were in for a hell of a night.

The game took off at a frantic pace. With every attack from either side greeted with howls of encouragement, the atmosphere was enough to curdle porridge. Inevitably, there was an edge to the play, Manchester drawing several early penalties as both sides fought for every inch of the ice. Blackburn were awarded three separate powerplay opportunities in the first period, but facing a resolute defence backed by the dependable Finnie, they saw every chance come to nothing. Manchester, still without the trio of Jago, Stokes and Manson, defended stubbornly, but could do nothing when John Haig swept in to put the Hawks 1–0 up. According to the script, tormented by the memories of the earlier home defeat, the Storm should have wobbled at this stage. Instead it was Blackburn who looked the more uncertain. Within a couple of minutes, Lipsey had broken clear to get on to a pass and fired Manchester back into contention, and on their first powerplay opportunity of the night, Ruggles put the Storm 2–1 up. The balance of the game had swung Manchester's way, the Storm fans could tell, but even so, they were little prepared for what happened in the second period. Forget the figure-skating nuns, something really surreal was about to happen. Manchester scored seven, yes, count 'em, seven goals without reply.

Martin Smith scored first, to the delight of the away support, and from then on it was a procession. David Smith, Steve Barnes, Hilton Ruggles, John Lawless, Shawn Byram (am I missing anyone out here?)

and then Martin Smith again as the Hawks were routed by a rampant Manchester. The pick of these had been Byram's. Collecting the puck on the half-way line, he took a step or two forward, apparently limbering up, ready to sprint towards the Blackburn goal. Instead, with barely a glance upwards, he suddenly hit a slapshot that took everyone by surprise and tore into the goal just an inch or two above the ice. Young, flat-footed by the shot, could do nothing apart from throw his head back in disappointment as the shot took a second or two to register with the crowd. There was a roar from the Storm fans, and scattered applause from the Hawks fans who knew a good shot when they saw it The Storm had clearly wanted to erase the 6–1 second period defeat in Manchester, and they had done so, big style.

It was probably the most imperious, spellbinding period of hockey I had ever seen them play; and against Blackburn too. With Dale Jago running the bench, and mixing up the lines so as to unsettle the Hawks' powerful first line, the Hawks were simply torn apart. Byram, playing as an attacking defenceman in place of Jago, was in one of his 'you'll never get the puck off me' moods, elegantly striding across the ice and picking off team-mates with languid ease. Steve Barnes, who throughout Dale Jago's absence had raised his game, was, yet again, outstanding. Daryl Lipsey, who had started the season looking somewhat out of sorts in his new surroundings, had got better as the season progressed, and was now playing like the Lipper of old, or more literally, the Lipper of young. And John Finnie was playing like, well, John Finnie. The period ended with the Storm 9–1 up. Tangible disbelief was evident in both sets of supporters. Manchester were going to win the league. No doubt about that now. And they still had 16 games left to play. 'We are number one. Say, we are number one!' sang the gleeful away fans, mirroring the song the Hawks fans had themselves sung at the Nynex. At the back of the arena, behind the Blackburn fans, was a banner bearing the legend '12–9', in reference to that game back in November. Well, I thought to myself, peel off the '2' and you've got it spot on again tonight, fellows.

The final period began in slightly muted fashion, both sides fully aware of who had won this particular battle. 'We want ten!' clamoured the Storm fans, stupidly. Needless to say, they scored no further goals. John Haig did nick a couple, both cheered ironically by the Storm supporters, but the final score of 9–3 to the Storm was, in the end, as flattering to the Hawks as the 9–12 had been to the Storm. Blackburn coach Mike Cockayne was stunned.

'I honestly don't believe we could play that badly again. It was a total disaster,' he moaned. 'In the second period we lost our discipline and it cost as heavily as is possible. You can't play like we did against a side of their calibre and expect to get away with it.'

The Storm were jubilant. They had gone to even up a score, and done so in devastating fashion. It was all too easy.

In fact, the ease was of some concern to Lawless. With the Storm's winning streak now standing at 17 games and counting there was, he felt, a danger that complacency might set in. It could prove costly come play-off time. To this end, he arranged a home and away challenge match against the Cardiff Devils. A defeat by the Devils might just keep the Storm's feet on the ground. A trip to Cardiff, greeted with less than total enthusiasm by some of the players, did indeed result in a loss; 12–6 to the Devils, but no disgrace, considering the opposition, and a useful pointer to the kind of improvement needed to be competitive at the higher level.

'It was no friendly, though,' said Martin Smith. 'They were checking pretty hard,' he added ruefully. Hmm, a score to settle in the return, perhaps . . .

It was back to league business, with a trip down to Chelmsford, which was won 12–3, followed by another game against Solihull. There was only ever going to be one winner in this one, although it did provide some entertainment for the watching crowd of 8,356. The game was drifting along in predictable fashion, the Storm leading 11–1 nearing the end of the second period, when suddenly it all got a bit silly. Evidently, there had been some needle between the Barons' netminder, Stephen Doyle, and several of the Storm players, and it came to an abrupt head when a massive brawl broke out, several players getting involved. The crowd went wild, loving every second of it, and when Doyle was thrown out of the game he seized his opportunity for stardom by wiggling his bottom discourteously at the crowd and skating off in exaggerated Robin Cousins style. I thought he was brilliant. Suddenly, Solihull's slapdash performance had turned into a slapshot one. The crowd bayed for blood. Of course this meant war . . .

The Storm, annoyed that Solihull had forgotten to behave like gentlemen, turned venomously on the Barons. Egged on by a delighted crowd who greeted every goal as if it were the first of the night, the Storm, somewhat farcically, scored another 15 times. It was the Barons' worst ever defeat, and the Storm's biggest ever win. Watching in one of the executive seats with his son was a certain Monsieur Cantona. What must he have thought about the game as yet another fight erupted in the third period, Dale Jago, now back from injury, getting a standing ovation for punching one of the Baron's players squarely in the face and only getting a two-minute penalty. 'I'm in the wrong sport . . . ' possibly. It was Solihull's own fault, anyway. If they hadn't roughed it up, they would have only lost about 16–1.

What was it like to play in a game like that? 'It was boring,' said Martin Smith. 'I guess the crowd didn't help, they just kept on wanting more goals, and you don't want to let them down – but I didn't enjoy it. I've played in matches where we've lost like that, though not as bad, and it's not much fun.'

Deadline day approached and we wondered if John Lawless would take the chance to beef up his squad with some Europeans now they could play as Brits. At the inaugural supporters club meeting, held before the Solihull game, he was asked during a questions and answers session if he had any in mind.

'No, I don't think so. It's not that there aren't good players there, because many of the European players are good players, but to be honest I wouldn't know who they were. So we won't be looking to Europe just yet. In the close season, perhaps, we'll take a look, but not just now.'

Fair enough, we thought. There was no doubt that some other clubs had taken a chance and got some new players in from Europe, some of whom would prove to be good players, others perhaps less so. It was a gamble Lawless was not prepared to take. If a player was brought in and didn't come up to scratch there was a danger that, apart from the waste of time and money this would involve, it would disrupt the balance of the team. Lawless would rather know exactly what he was getting. Besides, as it turned out, he already had his eye on someone.

Daryl Lipsey and Steve Barnes dropped into the shop on deadline day and Lipper, obviously feeling pretty satisfied with the way things had developed that morning, asked me if I had heard the news about the big signing.

'David Longstaff to Sheffield?' I suggested, stupidly, thinking this must be what he meant.

'Well, yeah, but Manchester's got someone too,' he teased.

'Who?'

'Mark Pallister.'

Oh yes, I thought, nice one. Lipper was obviously well pleased about it. Pallister was exactly what the Storm needed – a big defensive presence. He had originally played in Billingham before leaving to join Telford when the Bombers' financial state worsened. Now that Telford had given up all hope of reaching the play-offs they had released him because they could not afford to pay his wages. This time, though, surely, he had found a team that wasn't going to go and run out of money just yet.

The Storm faced a run of games against stern opposition, not least that return game with Cardiff. The Storm were keen to prove a point, and with Finnie yet again outstanding, they shocked the Devils by beating them 3–2. For Lawless, the win, although only a friendly, was one of the most satisfying of the season.

'Personally, it was very big. I didn't have signs posted around the dressing-room saying "Guys, this is a really big game!". The guys just respected everything that the game meant. It was like "You're with me now, so, are we the future, and that was the past?". It was a level the guys believed they could play at and it was just tremendous.' It was also another game in which Finnie had shown what a difference he had made to the club.

'You know, I don't think people realise how good Finnie is,' I said to Alan Hough the next day.

'Don't worry. They soon will. You don't keep Cardiff to two goals without people hearing about it.'

He was right, they'd better watch out next season, he was a hell of a netminder. Strange thing was, he never planned to be one.

'No, I never wanted to be a goalie,' he admitted to me in the shop one day. 'I wanted to play as a forward. I keep pestering John to let me play up front against Billingham or someone but he won't let me. He says "No! You'll get injured!"' He shrugged. His arrival had also had benefits for Colin Downie. Rather than sulk about losing his place, Downie had buckled down and tried to improve his game. Finnie had been happy to help him.

'John's arrival has forced me to concentrate on my game much more. While he's here to take my job, he has actually helped me along the way,' Downie told the *IHNR*. It also helped that Finnie was a nice bloke, very affable and likeable – mad as cheese, it must be said, but likeable.

He was next in action the following Sunday, after Downie had played in an 8–4 win over the Medway Bears on the Saturday. The Sky cameras were once again in attendance as Manchester entertained the Bracknell Bees, who now lay third in the table, pretty much secure of a play-off spot. The Storm announcer, Jon Hammond, had implored everyone at the previous game to bring along a friend so that there would be a big crowd for the Sky cameras. He was not let down. As everyone took their seats it was quite clear that a remarkably large crowd was in attendance. For the first time, the upper tier of the Nynex was packed over half the way round, with the bottom tier sold out completely. The players skated out at the start of the game to be greeted by the awesome sight of a massive wall of people. 'Between periods, that was all we kept talking about – the attendance. Did we get the record, did we get the record?' said Hilton Ruggles after the game. Yup, they had. There was a delay before the attendance figure came through, by which time the match was well under way, but when it did it was an astonishing one – 12,386. We had known all along that one day Manchester would break Sheffield's attendance record, but when it finally happened it came as a bit of a surprise. I mean, the old record had been smashed by more than two thousand, which was incredible enough, but where had all these fans come from? Overnight, Manchester seemed to have found another 4,000 fans. Not that anyone was complaining, but two games ago (for a rearranged midweek game) the crowd had been just 3,687, so the attendance had increased by 335 per cent – boom time.

It seemed that the large crowd was having an unsettling effect on the players, as the game was somewhat scrappy, the puck frequently given away by both sides. Manchester did get an early goal, though, Hilton Ruggles emerging from behind the net to tee up Martin Smith who pounced to score his 65th goal of the season. Within a few minutes Bracknell were level, when an innocuous-looking pass from Matt Cote was smartly deflected past Finnie by Mike Ellis. From then on the game was very much a defensive one. Manchester, mindful of the 21-goal scoreline the last time they had been on Sky, were determined to play a much tighter game this time around and, for their part, Bracknell came to the Nynex intending to snuff out the Storm forwards and build from solid defence. Not that they could do anything about Manchester's second goal, a peach from Byram. Picking up on a pass from Steve Barnes, he skated behind the net, holding off a Bees defenceman, and with exemplary control guided the puck in a smooth arc around the net to pop it past Langford, as sweet a wraparound as you could ever wish to see.

There were no more goals in the first period and just two in the second, both from Ruggles. The first came when he finished off some good work from Byram to steer the puck in from the crease and the second when Jago intercepted a loose pass and fed Byram, who in turn laid it off for Hilton to grab his second. In between these goals the Bees were unlucky not to score when Rob Stewart's shot appeared to have been smothered by Finnie at which point referee Ken Taggart called the puck dead, only for it to slither out from under Finnie's pads and creep across the line. But Manchester rode their luck, and at 4–1 going into the third appeared to have the game won. There was a scare when Brian Wilkie made it 4–2 with ten minutes to go but it proved to be the final goal of the evening, although for the watching Sky viewers the best moment was still to come.

With just a few minutes of the game remaining, the Bees only two behind and the game staged for a tense finish, Sky's Gia Milonovich seized her moment for a live interview with John Lawless. Watching from the other side of the rink, we could see her home in on Lawless as he tried to edge away from her; not that he could do anything about it. Gia, a graduate of the Gary Newbon School of Intrusive Sports Reporting (once, at a boxing match, Newbon strode into the ring and grabbed a victorious Chris Eubank for a memorable interview. 'I'm in excruciating pain . . . I need to go to hospital,' said Eubank, trying to get away. 'So, Chris – you must be feeling on top of the world') collared Lawless just as the Storm gave away a penalty. At this stage, Lawless was obviously more concerned about the game than he was about giving a good interview, but not wishing to appear rude, did his best to answer the questions as quickly as possible.

'John, can you tell me, what are the correct tactics for you guys to stay ahead in the game?' asked Gia.

'Well,' started Lawless, glancing at the scoreboard, distracted by the game, 'we just got to stay five on five . . . but we just got a penalty there . . . ' glances up again, obviously agitated, 'we gotta kill this one off and, uh, hopefully, you know, that'll be enough . . . ' Play resumes, Lawless hops about trying to see what's happening, 'but, it's one of those games, erm . . . look, SHIT! It's just hit the crossbar!' Nice one, John. Grace under pressure.

This minor PR slip aside, it was a good evening for the Storm – new attendance record, a win over the third-placed side, and a winning streak that now stood at 22 games. And the best was yet to come.

# 13

# UNCERTAIN TIMES

Back in October, a story had broken that threatened to be the biggest of the season. It seemed that plans were afoot for a drastic restructure of the British game and rather than being organised on the basis of playing ability, it would be facility led. After a meeting held in London between the BIHA and representatives of some of the clubs, a statement was issued entitled 'Ice Hockey – The Way Forward'. It caused quite a stir. In a nutshell, the statement outlined plans for a new élite British league, starting in the 1996–97 season, consisting of 'financially sound and well-managed clubs' and run by the clubs themselves with the full co-operation of the BIHA. 'A working party has been set up to develop the proposal, liaising with other clubs and interested parties,' the statement claimed. The league would be a closed one, that is to say, there would be neither promotion to nor relegation from this league, simply that a team would have to apply for membership and, once accepted, uphold certain off-ice criteria.

Although specific details were infuriatingly hard to get hold of at this early stage, it quicky became apparent that certain teams had been involved in these preliminary talks and that, more interestingly, some others hadn't even been invited to the meeting. Among the Premier Division clubs represented at that inaugural meeting were the Sheffield Steelers, the Durham Wasps, the Cardiff Devils and the Fife Flyers. Also represented were Ogden Entertainment Services, who ran the arenas in Manchester and Newcastle, and the First Division clubs Guildford and Bracknell. The understandable, albeit hasty, conclusion many observers drew was that these teams were going to break away from the rest and everyone else was going to be left behind. There was immediate uproar.

'If there is going to be a Super League, the best teams have to be involved,' said John Flavill, chairman of the seemingly excluded Panthers, in *Powerplay*. 'We are always at the top, or thereabouts. It seems strange. I would like to know what references are being required, what does a team have to put up to qualify for membership? I would like to say we want to be part of a Super League but the way we're being treated at the moment, I have to say we're not very happy. We weren't even told "We're having a meeting."' The Panthers fans were aghast. How could there be a Super League without Nottingham, consistently one of the best-supported clubs in the country? What would happen to the likes of current Premier League teams like Slough and Milton Keynes? No matter how good their sides were on the ice, it seemed like they would be left behind for ever because other teams had bigger arenas. What about ambitious clubs in the First Division? What was the point of Swindon, for example, ever trying to assemble a decent side when they knew that they would never be allowed into the top flight because their building was too small?

From the moment the Super League story broke, the season was dogged by uncertainty. There was talk of other arenas coming on line, perhaps a team at the London Docklands arena, or Wembley, and possibly the Birmingham NEC getting a team. There seemed to be a gang of seven teams pushing for the new league – Sheffield, Manchester, Cardiff, Durham Wasps, Guildford, Basingstoke and Bracknell. Meanwhile, those clubs apparently excluded from the Super League talked about forming their own league, which would cover the gap between the likes of Sheffield and Manchester and the English League sides like the Bradford Bulldogs and the Altrincham Aces. The idea would be not to compete with the Super League, but to complement it, to provide a structure in which the medium-sized clubs could still operate. However, no one knew for certain what was going to happen and speculation was rife. The only official announcement to be made about the Super League was that there would be another announcement in March (which never happened, by the way). Until then, everyone had to soldier on, not knowing which league they would be in the next season, and try to get their minds back on to the business of playing out the current season.

Going into Christmas, the Cardiff Devils led the Premier Division by six points, although behind them the Steelers had four games in hand. The Nottingham Panthers had also enjoyed a brief sojourn at the top of the table, but a narrow defeat away to Durham knocked them off the top, although with games in hand over the Devils, they were still in contention. Down at the foot of the table, the Newcastle Warriors, after moving into their new arena, were doing all they could to clamber off the bottom. They appointed a new coach, Gary Douville, formerly of Telford, and after the arrival of several new players they slowly started to turn things around. Their 11–4 win over Humberside on 9 December snapped an 11-game losing streak and also marked their first win in their new building. They were still adrift at the bottom of the table, however, trailing Slough by four points, but with four games in hand and renewed confidence slowly starting to seep back into the club, they were hopeful they could turn things around.

After their Benson & Hedges Cup triumph, the Sheffield Steelers had set about retaining their Premier Division title. They had won seven of their next eight matches, dropping just one point, which was the result of a thrilling 6–6 tie with Durham. Unfortunately, that game was overshadowed by a nasty injury to Ross Lambert, who came close to losing an eye after a reckless challenge by the Steelers' Nicky Chinn. The incident led to a massive brawl, as players from both sides became involved, and by the time things had settled down the referee had awarded 236 minutes of penalties and several players had been thrown out of the game. After the match, Chinn was arrested, though later released on bail, and the game made for some sordid headlines in the press.

The incident diverted attention from what was shaping up to be an interesting title race. Over the festive period the Steelers had a busy programme and by 7 January they had caught up with Cardiff in terms of the number of games played, cutting the deficit from six points to just one in the process. Had they not had the misfortune to run into Humberside on one of their hyperbeings days on 2 January – they were well beaten, 8–3 in Hull – they would have taken over as leaders. With the Steelers breathing down their necks, Cardiff decided to strengthen their roster. Steve Moria's reclassification as British meant that they had room for another import, and so they signed veteran star Doug Smail, an ex-NHLer with 13 years experience of the big league. As well as adding considerable depth to the side, the versatile Smail could also double as Cardiff's answer to Steeler Dan, should they ever need him to.

This new acquisition, coupled with the fact that Paul Heavey seemed at last to have settled on the best line formations for his team, saw the Devils play their best hockey of the season and from December to February they put together an unbeaten streak that extended to 18 games – championship winning form. But the Steelers were doing much the same thing. After losing in Hull, Sheffield embarked on an unbeaten streak of their own. Although they were denied a win in

Nottingham when Garth Premak had tied the scores at three apiece with just 39 seconds to go, they bounced back the next day and beat Fife 9–1 in Sheffield, and from then on looked unstoppable. Their next port of call was a return to the Crowtree rink in Sunderland to face the Wasps. Any worries that Nicky Chinn might do something really silly after his last visit there proved unfounded when he did something only slightly silly, and was thrown out of the game after just 29 seconds for roughing. With no Chinn, there was no chance of a repeat of the earlier fracas and Sheffield's 4–2 victory was not only Durham's first home loss of the season, but also the game that saw Sheffield lead the table for the first time in the season. Three days later, it was Durham's turn to visit Sheffield. This time they were beaten even more convincingly, 9–3, and although Cardiff were swift to respond, beating the hapless Jets 12–0 the next night, the Steelers still led the table and were clearly in no mood to give it up.

Elsewhere in the Premier Division, Nottingham were starting to fall off the pace. Before that loss to Durham, the Panthers had put together an impressive run; they beat both the Steelers and the Devils and were in a position to move clear at the top. The Durham game, it seemed, was a turning point. Their next game was the B&H Cup final, which of course they lost, and one point from their next two league matches did not augur well. Although they still occupied a reasonable position in the league, they seemed unlikely to put together the kind of runs that Sheffield and Cardiff were enjoying and a good showing in the play-offs now seemed the best hope. Below them, the Durham Wasps were having an unsettled season. Playing out of a rink with less than half the capacity of their old one must have been disheartening enough, then to see that on some nights it wasn't even half full must have been even more demoralising. With all the uncertainty surrounding the club the one consolation must have been that with rich uncle Sir John Hall looking after them they could, at least, afford decent players.

Kim Issel, Kip Noble and the Lambert brothers, Ross and Dale, all started the season with the Wasps and made their presence felt. The signing of ex-NHL defenceman Randy Velischek appeared to be a good one, but Velischek was lured away from the Wasps by a lucrative media job, and as a replacement the Wasps signed another player with NHL experience, Bruce Bell. As well as raiding North America for additions to their squad, the Wasps were also prepared to go to Hull and back to get the right players, Todd Bidner and the three Johnson brothers, Stephen, Shaun and Anthony, all making the trek north from the Hawks. The sudden availability of European players after the Bosman case also opened doors for the Hawks. They quickly signed a quartet of

Finns – Janne Seva, Mikko Niemi, Kimmo Maki-Kokkila and Kristian Fagerstrom. On top of all this, the Wasps also had an abundance of British talent including netminder Stephen Foster and Paul Dixon, both GB internationals. With such a burgeoning roster it soon felt like there were more people on the team bench than in the stands at Durham home games. The Wasps, though, ran into injury trouble in December and January, and were seriously depleted when they had the misfortune to run into Sheffield four times in little over a month. A final haul of just one point from the possible eight all but put paid to the Wasps' title aspirations. On their night they could give anyone a tough match, but an unsettled line-up playing under difficult circumstances was never going to be the best preparation for a serious stab at the title and they were too vulnerable on the road to put together the type of consistent run needed.

After winning seven of their first 12 matches, the Basingstoke Bison started a slow slide down the league. At the start of the season, with several dual-nationals on their roster, they were one of the stronger sides, but as other teams scrambled to pack their squads with Canadians and Europeans they were overtaken. The loss of form was most noticeable in December, when they won just once in six games, but results often failed to reflect the effort the side put in. On Boxing Day, for instance, they threw everything at the Steelers, outshooting the champions 50–15, but still contrived to lose the game 3–4. Their cause wasn't helped much by an injury crisis that, at one point, saw them missing eight players and were it not for the fine form of netminder Bill Morrison they could have flirted with relegation. They were another side, though, who on their day could beat anyone; over the course of the season they managed to beat every other side at least once except for Humberside, but having said that, they also managed to lose at least once to everyone else. They were nothing if not fair.

Humberside managed to occupy a mid-table position throughout the season. Amidst the uncertainty surrounding the club's future with the abolition of the local council, the players did the best they could to get their heads down and get on with the job. At home they were a force to be reckoned with. Away from home they stank. Whilst the memorable 8–3 victory over the Steelers was probably the highlight of the season, you had a choice if you had to plump for the worst moment. Take your pick from losing 14–1 in Nottingham, 14–3 in Sheffield, 17–6 and 15–5 in Cardiff, or even an 8–1 drubbing in Milton Keynes. The Hawks were consistently inconsistent, and their physical style saw them top the Premier Division penalty count. They weren't helped by the sheer number of players that came and left during the season, not to mention swapping their coach before the season had even started – coach Peter Johnson's departure preceding that of his three sons to the Wasps – but in the end a mid-table finish would mark their highest league placing since they first entered the Premier Division in the 1991–92 season. If it was to be the final season of top-class hockey in Hull, at least they had achieved their ambition of making the play-offs.

The Fife Flyers had a tough season, but this was a reflection on the new import rulings which had allowed other teams to get stronger whilst the Flyers stayed loyal to British talent. The Flyers had fewer imports than any other side in the Division, and it was ironic that, to compound their problems, the status of these players meant they could only ice three out of four of their imports in any one game. Considering that most of the sides the Flyers faced had eight or nine imports or Europeans compared to Fife's six (including the one who would have to sit out the game) they did well to finish sixth. In a way, it worked in their favour as they were able to get the best out of their Brits who felt they had a point to prove every time they stepped out on to the ice. With the return of Sheffield's Les Millie to the team, alongside another ex-Flyer Scott Plews, the Flyers were gradually able to strengthen their squad, and backed by a vociferous and passionate home crowd, rookie-coach Mark Morrison wrung some gutsy performances out of his players. It had been a learning curve for players and coach alike, but in the end the Flyers had shown more than enough heart to hold their own.

The Slough Jets, by comparison, struggled all season. The previous two seasons had seen the Jets unbeaten at home in the league, the Slough 'Shed' being a place where no team wanted to play, but sadly this season the Jets may just as well have put up a sign outside their building saying 'Collect your two points here' as every team managed at least one win there. From very early on it became clear that the Jets were out of their depth in the Premier Division and by the season's end they had managed just five wins out of 36. Although they never gave up, their penchant for tenacious, but ultimately fruitless performances – they lost 2–3 at home to the Wasps, and 5–3 in Cardiff, for example – meant they got little reward for their efforts. They did manage a couple of away wins, though, and to the horror of the Kings, they were both in Milton Keynes.

From the turn of the year it became clear that the relegation spots would be filled by two from Slough, Milton Keynes and Newcastle. For a long time, the Warriors were bottom of the league, only lifting themselves off it with four weeks of the season to go, but as they had several games in hand over the Jets it had always looked a misleading position. With Slough almost certain to finish bottom, the race was on

*Tony Hand. The best British trained player, ever. Fact.* MIKE SMITH, PLS LTD

*Behind the bench. Storm versus Billingham.* ANDY YATES, MANCHESTER EVENING NEWS

LEFT:
*'Let's go Devils.'*
*Unfortunately, they*
*didn't. The Steelers win*
*this one 7–2 in Cardiff on*
*their way to winning the*
*B&H Cup.*
MIKE SMITH, PLS LTD

BELOW:
*Fun and Games at*
*Basingstoke.*
MIKE SMITH, PLS LTD

*The Panthers making life hard for Tim Cranston, Wembley 1996.* MIKE SMITH, PLS LTD

*Wayne Cowley denies Paul Adey in the exciting final shoot-out – the only thing yawning here is the goal . . .* MIKE SMITH, PLS LTD

*Sheffield Steelers, 1996 Grand Slam winners.* MIKE SMITH, PLS LTD

*Manchester Storm 1995–6 (Left to right, back row) John Finnie, James Manson, David Smith, Daryl Lipsey, Simon Ferry, Hilton Ruggles, Shawn Byram, Martin Smith, Steve Barnes, Stefan Barton, Dale Jago, John Lawless. (Front row) Colin Downie, Alan Hough, Nick Crawley, Jeff Lyndsay, Mark Stokes (Mark Pallister was injured).*
ANDY YATES, MANCHESTER EVENING NEWS

PREVIOUS PAGE:
*Manchester Storm versus Dumfries Vikings, 24 March '96. 16,344 fans pack the Nynex to see the Storm clinch promotion. (That's me in the top right, block 106. Unfortunately, I blinked just as the picture was taken . . . )* ANDY YATES, MANCHESTER EVENING NEWS

between Newcastle and Milton Keynes to grab the last play-off spot. After a horrendous first half of the season – the Warriors managed to garner just six points from a possible 36 – they knew they had to improve a hell of a lot if they weren't going to end up in the relegation play-offs. After their December win over Humberside, only their second of the season, the situation had still looked hopeless. Subsequent defeats by Cardiff and Nottingham, although not unexpected, did little to suggest that they could turn it round, but gradually they did.

A thrilling 5–4 home win over Basingstoke on Christmas Eve brought renewed hope, but in their next contest they lost at home 7–13 to the Kings, and with such a crucial win under their belts, Milton Keynes looked odds-on to make the last play-off spot. Newcastle trailed the Kings by seven points, albeit with a couple of games in hand, and needed to improve fast. They had beefed up the squad considerably since Gary Douville's arrival, adding Richard Laplante, Scott Morrison, Scott Campbell and Swede Lars Blomberg. They had also taken advantage of Telford's precarious financial state to snap up Rick Fera from the Tigers barely three weeks after he had joined them. The rumour mill also suggested they had attempted to lure Hilton Ruggles up north, but Hilton was happy where he was. The results started to improve. They beat Humberside at home, then tied at Basingstoke. Although they were beaten away at Humberside they bounced back to get a terrific draw with title-chasing Cardiff in front of over 5,000 in Newcastle. They were beaten 8–4 in Sheffield, but considering the Kings had just fallen 10–1 there, there was still hope.

The Warriors team now bore little resemblance to the one that had started the campaign. Just six players remained from their opener, and there was no doubt that the additions to the squad had improved the team considerably, but there was a shock in store when they announced that one of their players, David Longstaff, was on the way out. Longstaff, one of the best young British players in the league and a current GB international, was being released on loan to Sheffield. It seemed that there was some kind of disagreement between player and coaching staff, but even so, it was a surprise that Newcastle thought they could do without him, and the move was widely criticised.

The showdown between the Kings and the Warriors at the Bladerunner rink on 27 January looked like being a key game, but a heavy snowfall prevented the Warriors from travelling down – perhaps a blessing in disguise, because further additions to the Newcastle team had yet to be given clearance to play, but would be ready when the teams finally met.

Luck appeared to be with Newcastle now. While Milton Keynes were losing, Newcastle grabbed a point at home to Nottingham and then took both points in a trip to Basingstoke. February would be the real test, however, with successive games against Cardiff, Nottingham and Sheffield surely too much even for the revitalised Warriors. It certainly appeared so when the Devils beat Newcastle 8–4, but then Newcastle pulled off one of the biggest shocks of the season. They travelled down to Nottingham, who hadn't lost at home all season, and came back with a 7–5 win. The result had two effects. It was a massive boost for the Warriors, who now really believed they could escape, and it completely traumatised the Panthers who suddenly lost all form and spiralled to a run of six successive defeats which, coupled with their traditional injury crisis, completely wrecked their distant title hopes.

After that result, the Steelers were careful not to take the Warriors too lightly and were relieved to win 5–3 in front of another 5,000 in Newcastle. Milton Keynes still couldn't pick up any points, and as Newcastle won in Slough the gap between the two sides had now closed. Milton Keynes were not about to be overhauled yet, though. After both sides went down at home on 18 February, the Kings bounced back and got a vital win in Humberside. They followed this up with a home triumph over Basingstoke to put the pressure back on Newcastle. The Warriors, who presumably would have chosen an easier fixture than Sheffield away at this point, responded superbly, though, and after falling 3–0 behind early on rallied to take a point in a nerve-jangling 5–5 tie. The Kings and Warriors were due to meet at each other's rinks in successive games, with the destiny of both teams surely hanging on the outcomes.

The first game was at the Bladerunner in Milton Keynes. In a tense, low–scoring first period, Newcastle struck first through Laplante. The Kings came back into the game when, in the middle period, they took the lead with goals from Patrick Scott and Doug McCarthy. Before the end of the second period, however, the game turned. Doug McCarthy was controversially called for elbows and Scott Morrison scored for the Warriors to tie it at 2–2, and with the momentum now flowing their way, Newcastle scored two more in the third and, despite a late Kings marker, hung on for a 4–3 win. They still trailed the Kings by a point, but knew that if they won again in Newcastle on the following Wednesday they would be lifted into a play-off spot for the first time all season with just the final weekend to go. They had come too far to let it slip now, and easily beat a dispirited Kings side 13–4 to take over the driving seat. It was their biggest win of the season – and the most important. With Milton Keynes apparently now beaten, Newcastle could afford to lose in Fife on the Saturday and still clinch their play-off spot with a 7–3 home win over Slough on the final day. For the Kings, the final losses at home to Nottingham and away to Fife typified their collapse. Newcastle had come back from the dead, and Milton Keynes had blown it.

In comparison to the enthralling relegation dog-fight between the Warriors and the Kings, the title race proved to be somewhat anti-climactic although, for the victors, none the less gratifying. By the time the Devils and Steelers were due to meet in Sheffield on 27 January, both had put together impressive unbeaten runs. Clearly, something had to break. Unfortunately, it turned out to be the weather, and the same blizzards that had halted the Warriors–Kings match forced the game to be postponed. The sides eventually met on 21 February, by which time it was clear that one of these two would take the title. The Steelers were unbeaten in 12 games, the Devils in 18. A crowd of 9,743 packed into the Sheffield Arena to see the biggest game of the season. (At the same time, there were 16,280 in Manchester – it was a great night for British hockey.)

It was a classic game. Sheffield got off to the better start; Tim Cranston and Ken Priestlay both netted inside the first six minutes to set the Steelers on their way. After no further scoring in the opening period Priestlay swiftly made it 3–0 early in the second, only for Cardiff to wake up and grab two goals through a powerplay Doug McEwen effort and Mike Ware's close-range shot to make it 3–2. Priestlay showed his class by first converting a Steelers powerplay and then grabbing his fourth of the night from a seemingly impossible angle just eight seconds before the break. With the Steelers in command, and roared on by their fans, the final period was goalless and the Steelers had taken a giant stride towards the title. The two sides had four games each remaining, including the Steelers' visit to Cardiff on the final day, but with the Steelers having three more games at home they hoped to have the title in the bag before then. They didn't start too well, dropping that point at home to the improved Warriors. Anxiously, they waited to hear how the Devils had fared in Fife.

The Devils had not had a good time. They were trailing 4–1 to an inspired Flyers side when they finally managed to get themselves going, eventually tying the game at 5–5 with six minutes to play. The Devils had done well to come back, but Fife had been superb throughout and would not be denied. Kevin St Jacques, taking a pass from the classy Chris Palmer, fired in a winner which was as appreciated in Sheffield as it was in Fife. The Devils now desperately needed to get something from their game in Durham the next night, and were in with a chance of doing so with the game tied at three apiece with two minutes to go. Then controversy. The Devils were penalised twice, giving the Wasps a five-on-three advantage, and when Ross Lambert duly blasted the game-winner through a pack of bodies the title was all but Sheffield's. The Steelers now needed just one point from their last three games to win the league. They took just one. The fixture list kindly pitted them against Nottingham, much to the Steelers' fans glee, and the subsequent 7–2 win sealed the title for the second year running. The partying began.

For the record, the Steelers won their next game too, 14–3 against the Hawks, and the Devils were left to reflect on what might have been as they gained some consolation with an enjoyable, but ultimately inconsequential, 6–1 hammering of the champions in Cardiff. Whatever the reasons for the Welsh club's failure – and it certainly wasn't home form, as they managed to win all their league games at the Wales National Ice Rink – they couldn't deny that they had lost out to the better side. They'd better pick themselves up in time for the play-offs, though; Sheffield were looking at the Grand Slam, and it was going to take a very good side to stop them.

# *14*

# TOP OF THE WORLD

After the record-breaking crowd against Bracknell, the Manchester Storm could start counting the days until they were crowned First Division Champions. After a routine 13–3 beating of Solihull at the Nynex they led Blackburn by eight points. Glancing down the table, you could see that Bracknell, Swindon and Dumfries all looked odds-on for a play-off spot. Behind this lot were Guildford, and it was they who now played host to the Storm. Their season had ambled along without ever really taking off, although it looked as if they would be the ones to bag the final play-off spot now that Telford had dropped off the pace. The mood in the Guildford camp was that it was about time life was made more difficult for the Storm. What they didn't know was that Manchester seemed to have come up with a way to make the games tougher all by themselves. This was when the Storm invented a new game to keep their fans amused called 'Give the other team a two-goal head start'.

Obviously, after winning 23 successive games, a certain degree of nonchalance was starting to creep into their play. To make things more interesting, they started a trend of dithering around for the first quarter of an hour, apparently not bothered about winning, letting their opponents think that they might just snatch a win, only to shake themselves from their somnolence and come screaming past their bewildered rivals to take the points with a late flurry. So when Guildford found themselves 2–0 up against the Storm, it was to the delight of their fans. However, these same fans were considerably less delighted to see the game finally end up 2–6 to the Storm. Ha, fooled you! Obviously impressed with this new method of tormenting their opponents, the Storm tried it out again the next night against Swindon at the Nynex. This time, because they were at home, they didn't stop until they had won 8–2. Although more exciting for the spectators, this business of giving away a two-goal head start was a bit rough on John Finnie, who would have to battle away furiously at the start until his team-mates stirred themselves sufficiently to start scoring. Still, it was what he was paid for, I suppose; and it didn't go unnoticed by John Lawless.

'When we made a mistake – he came up big for us. He was also very consistent. When we had Colin Downie, Colin was making a lot of good saves but would occasionally let a weak one in. That would have a double effect – it would drop our confidence and raise the confidence of the opposition. They'd think, "Hey, we can get some goals here." But with Finnie, when teams were outplaying us he would come up big. He doesn't show any emotion – which is really good. Goalies, he knows, are going to let goals in, so if one goes in he just thinks "So what? I'll save the next one." To have a good goalie is so important.'

Bracknell were next to fall for the 2–0 gag, which by now was so popular that the Storm even let the Bees lead 3–1 before getting serious and eventually winning 8–5. They then went to Swindon and did it all over again, trailing 2–0 before running out 7–3 winners in the end. Quite a gas this 2–0 lark, eh? One team not laughing were the Blackburn Hawks. While the Storm kept on winning, they had started to run into a bit of trouble, and as the losses started so the attendances tumbled. They lost 5–3 in an excellent game in Guildford, and then fell at Telford, who responded to a five-game losing streak by springing a surprise 7–5 over the Hawks. These losses meant that if Blackburn and Manchester both won their next home games, against Paisley and Chelmsford respectively, which they were both expected to do, the match-up between the Hawks and the Storm on 21 February at the Nynex could see Manchester clinch the title against their local rivals. It was a galling prospect for the Hawks. Blackburn coach Mike Cockayne was determined that the Hawks should spoil the party, and they did. On 18 February, Blackburn, somewhat lamely, lost at home to mid-table Paisley whilst Manchester were beating Chelmsford and, without anyone at the arena realising it until the Storm game was over, the Manchester Storm were the 1995–96 First Division champions.

In truth, it had turned out to be a bit of an anti-climax. The Storm couldn't even be bothered to let Chelmsford hold the traditional 2–0 lead, and Martin Smith scored the Storm's first when the Chieftains were only 1–0 up, the Storm eventually prevailing 14–5. And so the return of the Hawks to the Nynex was not to be the title-decider we hoped it would be; not that it was a damp squib either, mind. At least it meant certain celebration. The Storm were champions, after all. The BIHA had arranged for the First Division trophy to be sent to the Nynex, ready for the presentation on the Wednesday. When they saw it, John Lawless and Daryl Lipsey were underwhelmed. It was tiny. Forget about drinking champagne from it, it was so small you wouldn't use it to eat your boiled egg out of. If they presented that after the game it would be a joke. No one would be able to see it. Instead, Lawless and Lipsey took an executive decision and strode into Manchester to buy the biggest trophy they could find. They had it engraved 'Manchester Storm First Division Champions 1995–96', and had the names of all the previous winners engraved on it too. At least people in the upper tier would be able to see the damn thing.

Enticed by the prospect of seeing the Storm's first ever piece of silverware, another massive crowd turned up on the Wednesday night to see the Storm take on the Hawks. The British attendance record was smashed again. This time an astonishing 16,280 people packed in to the arena to see the party, and what was more, they were in the mood to celebrate. They wanted goals. They wanted blood. They got 'em both. Dale Jago, who had been injured when the Storm avenged their earlier loss in the win at Blackburn, obviously still felt that he had a personal point to prove. After three minutes he crashed in Manchester's first with a trademark slapshot that went in at about 180 miles an hour. In case that had been too fast for some to see, he popped up on the blueline again for the encore and repeated the trick to make it 2–0. Ryan Kummu went in determined to wrestle Hilton Ruggles for a loose puck, only for Ruggles to smack him in the face with the end of the stick, which would surely have had Kummu's dentist twitching nervously, had he been there to see it. Ruggles, quite rightly, was ejected from the game, as the Zamboni fans in the audience got an extra treat as the ice-clearing machine had to come back on to the ice to clear up the blood. Kummu, visibly shaken by the incident, was subdued throughout the remainder of the game, although by a small token of justice, John Haig cashed in on the resultant powerplay to make the score 2–1. Not that it mattered much.

George Powell, an ex-Trafford Metro player who had joined the Hawks when they were originally formed, ran into Mark Pallister. Pallister, half-man, half-wall, had been threatening to show the Nynex crowd what a good hitter he could be for some time now – he had warmed up by checking an opponent clean through the Plexi-glass at Bracknell just a few games beforehand. Powell was just about to turn and clear the puck out of his zone when Pallister came from nowhere to hit him full on with a ferocious check, an absolute beauty. Pallister seemed just absently to step back from Powell, as if he hadn't even noticed he was there, and skated away, apparently impervious to the damage he had just inflicted. Powell, for his part, didn't move at all. There was no question of any foul, it was a perfectly clean hit, you could almost say text-book – although I doubt such controlled violence often makes it on to school reading lists – but Powell was in a bad way. After a couple of minutes, he stirred and, looking rather groggy, got to his feet. Such had been the force of the impact, it transpired, Powell had actually vomited on to the ice. The Hawks players now looked as concerned for their own safety as they had been for his, as the ice was cleaned up again. The crowd, needless to say, were absolutely loving it.

After that, Blackburn didn't want to know. Byram put the Storm 3–1 up before the end of the first, and in the second and third periods the Storm scored at will. With the score standing at 11–2 with just a few minutes to play, and the crowd preparing to celebrate the impending victory, John Finnie set up the softest goal ever conceded by any team, ever. Intercepting the puck near the boards, Finnie drifted back towards the goal looking for the pass to a team-mate. He saw Oleg Sinkov in open space, and with an endearing disregard for the normal protocol in these circumstances, passed it straight to him right in front of the unguarded net. Sinkov, looking slightly embarrassed at the ease of it all, duly scored. Finnie's team-mates looked at him, and failed to keep straight faces themselves. Still, it proved even the mad one could make mistakes, and as Blackburn were unlikely to sniff the scent of victory, still being eight goals behind, the misdemeanour was quickly forgotten. It was time to celebrate.

The whistle blew, and the Storm received a standing ovation. David Frame and David Pickles of the BIHA were in attendance to hand over the suspiciously large and new-looking First Division trophy as the crowd cheered. As the festivities began – players dancing on ice, throwing yo-yos into the crowd, dunking buckets of water over the heads of their coaches, that sort of thing – it began to sink in what they had achieved. Winning the league was great, obviously, although expectations at the Nynex were such that it would ultimately count for nought if promotion after the play-offs didn't follow, but the greater achievement was simply the number of people there to see it. In hockey terms, 16,280 people is a massive crowd – that same night in the NHL there were seven games played yet only one of them could boast a bigger crowd. In British ice hockey terms it is stupefying. Add to this equation the little matter of Manchester United playing at home down the road on the same night, just about the biggest competition you could get in sporting terms, and it becomes all the more staggering. All things considered – the crowd, the trophy, thumping Blackburn – it was hard to imagine how the evening could possibly have been bettered. Unless you happened to be my girlfriend, Tracy, whose winning number in the 50/50 draw won her £321 on top of it all. As memorable nights went, it had been a good one.

The festivities carried on well into the small hours of the morning. For that matter, they started to creep into the big hours of the morning, too. For Alan Hough in particular, the celebrations were something that he wouldn't forget, that is if he could remember them clearly in the first place. Dancing down Deansgate clutching the First Division trophy, giddy from the euphoria of victory and imbued with about a gallon of celebratory champagne ('blind drunk' in other words, according to one insider) he spectacularly failed to negotiate a tricky puddle and fell crashing to the ground. He recalls being somewhat alarmed to see the First Division trophy in a worse state than he was, not so much dented as disintegrated. Scooping up the various fractured pieces, with the nagging suspicion in the back of his mind that John Lawless might be compelled to kill him when he found out, he left the trophy in a safe place overnight before returning the next morning and taking it to be repaired in Altrincham. When the trophy came out of hospital, although no longer in pristine condition, it looked better than he had feared. When he found out about the incident, to Hough's immense relief, Lawless didn't mind that much, and spared his life. Besides, it kind of looked more how it should do now, he felt. 'It's got that worn look, now,' admitted Daryl Lipsey.

When the hangovers receded, the Storm faced another five games before the play-offs. With the winning streak now standing at 29 games and counting, it was just a matter of keeping things ticking over and avoiding injury. Along the way, there were a few records to be picked up. In beating the Medway Bears 9–3 in their next game, Hilton Ruggles scored the goal that took the season's tally to 486, beating the old record for the most goals in a season held by Milton Keynes (whose average of over 11 goals per game would still stand at the season's end, however). The game was unusual for the exceptional intensity with which it was played, as not a single penalty was recorded. Oh, and it was also watched by the fourth biggest crowd ever for a British hockey match, 10,487. This was probably the least noteworthy thing of the night, especially as by the next night it had dropped to only the fifth biggest crowd, 11,580 turning up to see Manchester play Dumfries.

Dumfries came to the Nynex determined to put on a good show, and in fact played very well, taking an early lead and even out-shooting the Storm in the opening period, but the Storm were in superb form and proceeded to take Dumfries apart, winning 10–1. The final goal, scored by Stefan Barton, was the Storm's 500th of the season, another record. In the space of just five days the Storm had pulled in over 38,000 fans, which was probably yet another. The home league campaign was wrapped up with the visit of Guildford, who paid the price of bringing just 12 players to the Nynex, as they were eventually overrun 11–2 in another impressive display from the Storm, and in particular, Finnie. Just two games left, now – away at Chelmsford, but firstly, the return to Blackburn.

Relationships between the two sides were not good. Ryan Kummu and Mike Cockayne were both critical of the new champions in the press, and, for his part, John Lawless didn't wait long to get his oar in, too. The Storm were just a brutish dump-and-chase side, said the Hawks. They had only won the last game between the sides by being dirty, and they were only top of the table because they had a big arena and loads of money. The Hawks were just a one-line wonder, said the Storm, lucky to be as high in the league as they were. If the coaches didn't get on, neither did the fans. Although the Hawks fans were traditionally a friendly and accommodating lot, and capable of providing terrific support for their team in the big games, a few of them had taken a distinct dislike to the upstart Storm. Entering the Blackburn arena, the Storm fans were greeted with a banner suggesting that the Hawks fans were the true hockey fans for supporting a side that wasn't a big-money team (as a whopping crowd of 400 for the previous game against Solihull showed, eh?) and, furthermore, accusing the Storm of having bought their success, which was a bit rich coming from the town that brought you Jack Walker and Blackburn Rovers. It was also, I'd like to add, rubbish. Of course, the Storm had an enormous advantage with the facility they had, but they had not simply 'bought' success.

If you buy success you go to the Premier League and buy the top players. Granted, Ruggles was a big-name signing, but nearing the end of his career, and while Jago and Lyndsay had made an enormous contribution to the team you could hardly call the signing of a defensive pair from a relegated side 'buying success'. Shawn Byram didn't, according to local sources, 'make much impression' at Bracknell, another relegated side, and half a season with the Trafford Metros had failed to make Martin Smith a household name. Other players, such as Stokes, Lipsey, Downie, Ferry and David Smith, had all come from within the First Division and no one had even heard of Steve Barnes or John Finnie before the season started. Had the Storm managed to lure Paul Adey, Shannon Hope and Martin McKay along, perhaps the accusation would have stood up better. It was true that the Storm had a lot of dual-nationals, but so too did Guildford and Bracknell, neither of whom had enjoyed anything like the same level of success, and the change in the foreigner ruling had allowed Swindon to dive in and grab three Europeans, which the Storm could easily have done. Given the money, anyone can assemble good players. Turning them into a good team is another thing entirely, and it is ironic that it was Blackburn that had done so much to help the Storm make it happen.

The 9–12 home loss to Blackburn was, according to Martin Smith, 'the best thing that happened to the Storm all season.' Being humiliated at home, live on telly, had done more to bring the team together than anything that had gone on before. 'When we lost that game, you could see the mood change. We really learnt a lot about ourselves. That was what pulled us together.' Before that game the Storm were really just a collection of players, 'everyone, I guess, had a bit of an ego . . . ', they were all used to being the main players with their previous teams and the Blackburn loss brought them down to earth. They had become arrogant, thinking that all they had to do was turn up. Even when trailing, they hadn't been worried, because they had been so confident of bouncing back. They had been unprepared. 'We didn't know Kummu was going to jump into the play and go toward the net like that, but we knew the second time.' The second time it had been a different story, and the third time, too; and now this meeting. 'I guess we wanted to rub it in,' Martin said to me later, although, to be honest, I had figured that much out for myself.

The Hawks came out flying, scoring first through Chartrand, but then it went all pear-shaped . . . First Jago scored, then Byram, then Stefan Barton striking a blow for the third line, then Byram again putting Manchester 4–1 up at the end of the first. Sinkov briefly raised Blackburn spirits with a goal to make it 4–2, but that only irritated the Storm. They fired in another six goals before the end of the period. It was a slaughter. The Hawks were badly missing Kummu, who had had to return briefly to Canada for business reasons, not that he would have prevented the onslaught. Blackburn scored their fourth goal with seven minutes to go but by then Mike Cockayne's earlier comment that Blackburn could not possibly play any worse than they did in the 9–3 defeat was looking horribly misguided. The goals kept on flying in, 11, 12, 13 – The Storm fans were dancing the Conga around the rink – 14, 15, 16 . . . just a couple of seconds left to play now . . . time for one more . . . 17! Thank you and goodnight. The Storm had, I think it was fair to say, murdered them.

To go to the second-placed team in the league and score 17 times probably says more about that second-placed team than it does about the victors. John Lawless was reported as saying that on current form the Hawks would have finished eighth in the league rather than second – an opinion Ryan Kummu hotly refuted, although just one win in their last nine games did not do his argument any favours. The Hawks had been sussed, Lawless said, not just by the Storm but by everyone else. The game preceding the visit of the Storm had even seen lowly Solihull leave Blackburn with both points. It was a shame for the Blackburn season to end like this; after all, to finish second, given the resources and the depth of talent in the squad, was a remarkable achievement, but in the end the Hawks finished the season with a sour taste in their mouths – grapes, probably.

If the final weekend had been traumatic for the Hawks, spare a thought for poor old Billingham. Although the Murrayfield Royals were to finish the season with just nine points, two behind Billingham's 11 at this stage, even they didn't hit the kind of depths that the Bombers reached on that final weekend. On the Saturday they travelled to Solihull, who hadn't exactly set the league alight themselves, and lost 20–6. Unbelievably, they got worse the next night, losing 35–6 in Swindon. At first it looked as though Swindon had gone mad, sending a message to the other play-off teams, but on reflection the scoreline owed more to various players chasing club scoring records and Billingham playing a shambolic game. Arriving with just ten skaters (and allegedly having to prise one of their netminders out of the pub immediately before the game) the Bombers probably didn't do much to help their cause when they elected to change netminders – while the puck was still in play. It was a wretched final weekend for the Bombers, although absurdly they managed to spring one final surprise when they beat Peterborough 10–9 in their final match a week later. It could only happen in British ice hockey.

The Storm, by comparison, ended the season on a high. They had just one more game to go, away at Chelmsford, which, for the record, they won 11–7. The game itself was, according to all accounts, a poor one, with a lacklustre Storm performance just about enough to win both points. Still, as it counted for nothing in itself, and with John Lawless away (spying on the Slough Jets in Newcastle) and the play-offs looming you could, I suppose, forgive the Storm for being a little half-hearted about this one. Besides, there was much else to celebrate. The Storm had, over the course of the season, smashed all attendance records, becoming the best-supported club in Britain, and within just a few weeks of formation their supporters club had purportedly become the largest in Europe. They had won 33 games on the trot, becoming the first side ever to win the First Division in their début season, and what's more, winning it by 23 points, a record margin. They had scored 539 goals in the process, another record, won 99 points, another record and finished the season with a winning percentage of 95.19 per cent and a goals against average of 3.55. Both, surprise surprise, were records. There was no doubt that the Manchester Storm were the rightful owners of the 1995–96 First Division trophy. They even had the receipt to prove it. Now for the play-offs . . .

# 15

# PLAY-OFF TIME

After clinching the title, the Storm began to think about the relegation/ promotion play-offs. They would share their group with whichever side finished bottom of the Premier, which increasingly looked like being the Slough Jets, and two other First Division sides. Blackburn, by dint of finishing second to the Storm, would be in the other group alongside Milton Keynes. The rest of it was up to the draw, and this is how it all turned out:

| Group A | Group B |
|---|---|
| Milton Keynes Kings | Manchester Storm |
| Blackburn Hawks | Swindon Wildcats |
| Bracknell Bees | Slough Jets |
| Guildford Flames | Dumfries Border Vikings |

As far as Manchester were concerned, it wasn't too bad a draw. They would probably have preferred to have avoided Swindon, after the Wildcats had managed to inflict the Storm's only away league defeat, but Dumfries, whom they had swept away 4–0 in the normal season, didn't pose too many problems. Slough would be tricky, they felt. Suffering an anxious attack of pre-play-off jitters, I asked *Powerplay's* editor, Simon Potter, how he thought the Storm would fare. 'No problem,' he said, reassuringly. I needn't worry about Slough. 'Losing is a habit,' he said, simply. I wasn't wholly convinced. In the other group, it was probably going to be very close, but I felt that Milton Keynes might just shade it, as Bracknell and Guildford would probably take points off each other and Blackburn, I thought, would not win a game. Overall, the play-offs looked like being tense, exciting affairs, the

143

only cloud on the horizon being the nagging thought that they were utterly meaningless.

Plans for the Super League looked well advanced by this stage, although no official announcement had yet been made, possibly because the clubs involved wanted to keep up the pretence that the play-offs would have a genuine bearing on who played where next season. After all, if everyone knew they didn't matter one jot, who would bother paying to go and see them? Although it didn't do much for the sport's credibility to go through with such a charade, the basic truth was that some of the clubs were counting on the money. However, there still remained a tiny doubt about whether these Super League plans might not yet slip back a year. With the Solihull Barons announcing that they would move into the Birmingham NEC, but only in time for the 1997–98 season, there seemed reasonable grounds for putting the whole thing back until then, assuming Manchester won the play-offs, of course. The thought that the Storm might fail in the play-offs and thus be consigned to another year of pointless hammerings was not a particularly alluring one. Besides, British hockey needed the Storm's crowds in the top flight. It seemed to me that if the Storm won in the play-offs there would be no need for the Super League just yet, but if they failed, they'd probably bring in the new set-up pretty sharpish; which, when you think about it, was a pretty good safety net for Manchester. In fact, so good, that it might work against them.

With this Super League business looming, I asked Martin Smith if it mattered to the players how the play-offs went. After all, one way or the other, the Storm looked certain of going up.

'Yeah,' he conceded, 'the team might, but we might not.'

Although some of the players were on two-year contracts, a lot of them, like Smith himself, and Shawn Byram, weren't. If they wanted to come back the next season, they still had things to prove. Besides, a contract sometimes doesn't mean a whole lot. If you play badly you can be out at any time, so perhaps none of them could be sure of retaining their place. But one thing was certain, they all wanted to. Martin Smith felt that he'd just had the most enjoyable season of his career, and he wasn't the only one who felt that way.

'This is the greatest place to play, maybe in the world, because the number of people who come to watch the games and the facility you play in – it's got to be up there. Obviously, it's got to be great to play in the NHL, but as far as minor league goes, this has got to be the best place to play. I've never had so much fun going to the rink. 'Besides,' he added, 'we didn't work this hard, all year, not to win.'

The play-offs would tell Lawless a lot about his players. Great though the normal season had been, these were the games that counted the most.

'He's going to be able to see who shows up – it's just like showing up on the road. Anyone can play in their own rink, but when they go on the road that's a tough environment, and that's where you have to pick up your game. You look at a lot of NHL players, guys that might have 50, 60 points in a year – but 45 of them are at home and 15 are on the road. You don't want a guy like that in the play-offs because is he going to go to the wall for you? Is he going to take that check? Is he going to take that slash to score? And those are the things he [Lawless] is going to find out now, for next year – because that's what you're going to have to do in the Premier,' Smith explained.

In some ways, it was a shrewd move for Lawless to have key players in a position where they were playing for their contracts at this stage. He would find out who wanted it the most.

'Hilton – he's disappointed that we didn't get Guildford and Bracknell in the play-offs, because he thinks they will be the better teams. He loves a challenge, and wants the toughest opposition – that's what he's like. Me, I think Swindon and Slough are going to be tough enough,' concluded Smith. We would see.

It was generally felt that the way a team started in the play-offs set the tone for the whole stage. 'We have to come out flying,' said Martin. The same thought was obviously on Slough's minds. Their opener was at home to Dumfries, which they won 8–1. A terrific start; the Jets, boosted by the timely return of Joe Stefan from injury, were back on the winning trail. It was a warning to the Storm that the Jets were determined to put up a good display in the play-offs. Not that this would have been uppermost on Storm minds, I suppose, for that same night they were facing Swindon away, a stern opener. In front of a near capacity crowd, boosted by a considerable contingent from Manchester, the Wildcats and the Storm tore at each other from the off. It was a surprise to everyone in the building when, after a frenetic opening, the game was still goalless after 11 minutes of play. It couldn't possibly last, we reasoned. Indeed not. Mark Stokes popped up to score, unassisted, and make it 1–0.

The lead lasted all of 37 seconds, the time it took for Robin Davison to break away, steady himself, and then drill a belter past Finnie in the Storm goal; 1–1. Suddenly, it was goal time – Stokes again, in a scramble, within 16 seconds, and then a Ruggles shot somehow crept in a minute later; 3–1 to the Storm. After this flurry, things settled down, and there was no further first–period scoring. We didn't have to wait too long after the break, though, for the next goal to arrive. Byram pounced on a loose Swindon pass to steal away and make it 4–1 and when Ruggles danced clear after a super Jago pass and made it 5–1 less than a minute later, I turned to Tracy, watching the game with me, and proclaimed: 'Game over.' What a stupid thing to say. Swindon came roaring back into the game. For the next 15 minutes they dominated. Although Finnie was not having one of his best games, he kept the Storm in it with a couple of kicked saves, but he was unable to stop first Dickie, and then Crawford from scoring. It was now 5–3, and the Wildcats were getting closer all the time.

I suddenly realised that after all his talk about showing up in the big games, Martin Smith had not got into the game himself. It was nearing the end of the second period and he'd been held scoreless. So, right on cue, with the Storm battling to stem the Swindon tide, he grabbed the goal that changed the game. Picking up the puck in traffic, with seemingly every player crowded on to about six feet of ice, he dwelt on the puck for about, oh, a quarter of a second before unleashing his shot. It tore in; 6–3 and relief again for the Storm. The goal seemed to take the wind out of Swindon's sails, and although they continued to battle away in the third period, the Storm were now more resolute in defence, and of the two sides, looked the more menacing on the breakaway.

After 14 minutes of scoreless play in the third, however, Swindon scored on the powerplay to make it 6–4 and set up a close finish. Lawless now called a timeout in order to steady the nerves. It was simply a matter of holding out for the last few minutes. With less than two minutes remaining, and the game drifting away from the Wildcats, the Storm got a breakaway and Ruggles bore down on the goal. He feinted one way, then went the other. Dowd left just the merest of gaps at his near post and in an instant Ruggles was past him with the puck, but the angle seemed impossible, the chance missed, surely. Somehow he pulled the puck backwards whilst still moving forwards himself, and, incredibly, squeezed the puck through a gap that, standing just six feet away, I could have sworn wasn't big enough. He must have flipped it on its side to get that one through. But there it was, a goal: 7–4 and no way back for Swindon now.

There was even time for another goal from Martin Smith, which restored the Storm's four-goal lead. In truth, the 8–4 win flattered them, although it was well deserved. For their part, Swindon had played with considerable passion, but in the end a lack of depth on the bench told. The result may have been ground out somewhat, but that was what play-off hockey was like. The players left the ice to a standing ovation from the Storm fans – although, as the bulk of them had had nowhere to sit during the game, that wasn't a surprise. As Ruggles made his way through the crowd to the changing room he walked past a young Storm fan. Without breaking his stride or looking back, he thrust his stick into the boy's grasp and before the boy knew what had happened he was gone. The look on the kid's face was a picture, utter astonishment, then as it registered that he was actually meant to keep the stick, delight. It was a nice gesture. Hilton hadn't made a big thing about it, but it was good to see. Ruggles may not have finesse, I thought, but he has class.

After mugging the kid in the toilets later, and getting the stick for myself, my thoughts now turned to the Sunday game. If the Storm could beat Slough, and beat them convincingly, then they would be in a very strong position for the rest of the play-offs. We filed into the Nynex that Sunday not knowing what to expect from Slough, but what we did expect was another bumper crowd. Not so. Although it might be churlish to describe a crowd of 9,940 as 'disappointing', I couldn't help feeling that the Storm fans weren't really taking this play-off thing seriously. Considering that the meaningless double-header with Medway and Dumfries had attracted more on both nights just a fortnight before, I expected a bigger attendance. Mind you, the prices had gone up a quid, so perhaps that had something to do with it. Those fans who missed it, missed a good one. Slough came determined to show the Storm that they still had much to learn, and in a tense, defensive game, they played the best hockey any visiting side had ever done at the Nynex.

At first, the Storm couldn't break Slough down, although with Finnie playing a solid game, Slough couldn't make any impression either. It was 15 minutes before Martin Smith popped up to bang in a Jago rebound to make it 1–0, but any thought that the goals would now flow proved unfounded. It was to be the only goal of the period. The second period was even closer. Jamie Organ was playing a blinder in the Jets' goal, and when the Storm spurned a five-on-three chance – Jago unlucky to glance one off the post – it looked as if they would never score again. Ruggles, denied any service up to that point, changed to the second line, and it was he who got behind the net neatly to set up Stokes who made it 2–0. Going into the third, Martin Smith came up big again, and now it was 3–0 and everyone was happy. Not for long. Almost immediately, Rob Coutts fired one up into the roof of the net, and when Slough got a powerplay opportunity they produced the best move of the night, carving the Storm defence apart for Kyle Dolman to make it 3–2. The final 15 minutes were compelling, but ultimately uneventful. The final hooter sounded and the Storm had just about done enough to scramble home.

Entertaining though the match was, it raised a few points. Firstly, how good a victory was it? Assuming Slough won all their other games, which, judging by that performance, they were certainly capable of, then the return game in Slough took on enormous significance. If Slough could beat the Storm by more than one goal, they would become favourites to win the group and those two late goals would have proved invaluable. On the other hand, Manchester still controlled their own destiny – a draw in Slough, and then winning the remaining games would be enough. Another thing to consider concerned the question of how much the current squad would have to improve in order to compete next season. Although the win over Cardiff had been much enjoyed at the time there was no disguising the fact that it had only been a challenge match. By contrast, this had been for real, and although the Storm had prevailed, it had been by the narrowest of margins, and this against a side that had finished bottom of the league. Clearly, further improvements would be needed, and not just to the squad. I felt you could say much the same about the crowd.

The Nynex crowd, reared on a diet of 15–2 victories, had taken a while to get into the Slough game. It had been tense stuff, and far more engrossing than all the other games which the bulk of the crowd seemed to realise, but it was at this point that I was reminded how much the fans, as well as the team, had to learn. Imagine your team is winning 3–2 in the most important game they've ever played, a goal for either side having devastating implications. There's five minutes to go. The netminders are both playing superbly. One mistake from either side could change the whole season. Around you, other fans are so tense they daren't breathe. What do you do? That's right. You start a Mexican wave. 'Wahay!' the fans gleefully roared. Suddenly, as Slough bore down on the goal, the Storm's fate hanging by a thread, everyone in front of me threw their hands in the air and laughed. What fun! 'It was better last time,' – when they had won 11–2 – I heard a fan complain to her boyfriend as we left the arena. Real edge-of-the-seater, that one.

I'm probably being a little harsh here, but there was no doubt that a lot of the Storm crowd paid more attention to the Village People dance routines than the game. In time, the Storm crowd would become more appreciative and sophisticated, as they had done at Sheffield over the years, but for the time being they were similar to the 15-year-old brother who gets hideously and embarrassingly drunk on punch at parties. In a way, it was hard to knock; after all, I'd rather have 16,000 fans like that who have a good time and enjoy themselves than the 400 diehards who know all about the game but moan about the music being too loud. The players certainly enjoyed playing in front of the Manchester crowd, in fact, a few of the Canadians in the team preferred them to their own crowds back home.

'The thing about supporters here is, they are supporters, they are hockey fans, and at home, a lot of them are just critics,' said Martin Smith. 'But it's nice to see people catching on to something that we take for granted.' In Canada, the crowd would have behaved very differently. For one thing, they wouldn't hang around to watch a game if it was turning into a rout, they'd go home. In Britain they stayed. And so the Storm had often carried on scoring goals just to give the fans what they wanted. This time they just had to make do with the points which, hopefully, they'd appreciate counted for a lot more.

Meanwhile, whilst Manchester were beating Slough, the best game ever played at the Dumfries Ice Bowl was taking place. After crashing to that big defeat in Slough the night before, which Dumfries had felt flattered the Jets considerably, they had been further hit by news which added injury to insult when they learnt that forward Martin Grubb had broken a bone in his wrist during the game and would miss the rest of the season. It was hardly the best start to their first ever home play-off game; nor was the way they handed the Wildcats a 4–1 lead after just 15 minutes. It was all going wrong for the Vikings. However, Craig Lyons gave them some hope with a strike that made it 4–2, and Moray Hanson then did his bit by pulling off an heroic double save to deny Swindon. The second period saw the tempo rise, along with the tempers, as Dumfries pulled another back and Brad Rubachuk collected a 2 + 10 minutes penalty for Swindon. The same player then managed to convert this to a game misconduct early in the third period, when, still sat in the bin, he vehemently disputed a penalty called on team-mate Joni Virtanen, resulting in both of them being thrown out of the game. Any thought that this might swing things Dumfries's way proved horribly misguided when Robin Davison scored a shorthanded goal on the subsequent five-on-three to make it 5–3, which should have killed off Dumfries – should have.

With ten minutes to go, Craig Lyons got his second to make it 5–4, and suddenly Swindon were on the ropes. Although Jamie Thompson made a great save to deny the Vikings' Gordon Whyte, he could do nothing about Paul Pentland's screamer from the blueline which tied the scores at 5–5 with six minutes to go. The Vikings crowd went wild as they scented victory, only for despondency to come crashing back around them as Jari Virtanen atoned for his brother's misdemeanour and made it 6–5. In a classic finish, Rob Hartnell equalised with a thunderous shot two and a half minutes from time and, by way of an encore, grabbed the winner with 87 seconds to go. It brought the house down.

It didn't do much for Swindon, though. After just two games, their play-off hopes were gone, and then, in what turned out to be a miserable week for the Wiltshire side, so were their main sponsors, EA Sports. The loss of EA's input threatened to put an end to hockey at the Link centre, and although the final outcome isn't clear at the time of writing, it seems likely to result in the break-up of the best side Swindon has ever had, a real shame for everyone involved. The mood in Blackburn wasn't much better. After a calamitous loss of form towards the end of the season, it was no surprise to see the Hawks lose both their opening play-off games. They went down 6–3 at home to Bracknell – a game watched by just 850, which suggested that the crowds had disappeared as mysteriously as the club's form – and then they were thumped 13–4 in Milton Keynes, who topped the group after winning in Guildford the night before. Joining them at the top were Bracknell, who followed the win in Blackburn with a thriller against the Flames, scoring the winner with just three minutes to go to snatch it 5–4 in front of their biggest home crowd of the season, over 2,300.

The following Saturday was rematch day, as everyone played the team they had just played once again, and obviously there were some scores to settle. The Flames owed the Bees one, for starters, and duly obliged their supporters with a 6–3 home win. Swindon followed suit, avenging that defeat in Scotland by beating Dumfries 11–9 – although not before they gave their fans coronaries by allowing the Vikings to come back from 10–5 to 10–9. Most surprisingly, though, in this litany of revenge victories, was Blackburn's shock 8–5 win over Milton Keynes. The Hawks led through a superb piece of netminding by Horatio Schlinger and rediscovered their lost form to the delight of their fans. The two play-off groups now looked very tight, and if Slough followed everyone else's lead and overturned their loss to the Storm, it would be tighter still. Manchester were determined that would not happen.

It's fair to say that I was a jumble of nerves in the run-up to that game. Work commitments meant that I would miss just one of the Storm's play-off games, and it looked as though it would be the one that mattered the most. After such a narrow win in the first game, I was fearful about the outcome of the second one. 'Don't worry about it, we'll take care of it,' Martin Smith told me as some of the players dropped into the shop that week. I wasn't convinced. After all, Alan Hough had said something similar before they had lost 22–3 in Humberside. This time, though, I should have believed them. Impatient for news, I phoned the Storm hotline, despite the fact that the game would still be going on. What I heard astounded me. The Storm were winning 6–0! In a game littered with niggly penalties, it later transpired, they had been awarded eight powerplays, and cashed in on four of them. With Finnie once again outstanding, Slough had grown frustrated, only managing to score in the final period. The final score of 7–2 to the Storm all but guaranteed promotion. Considering they had only beaten Slough by one goal at home, I asked John Lawless how they had managed to win by five in Slough.

'When Slough got back to 3–2 in that first game it was a blessing in disguise. If we'd gone down there after winning 4–1 we'd have thought, "This is a walk in the park – we can afford to lose by two goals." We went down knowing that a 3–2 scoreline meant absolutely nothing. We realised that this game was it. They came out trying to be very physical, but we were so focused on just doing a job and not retaliating whatever happened. We scored a couple of powerplay goals early on and it just set the tone. After that game it was a great feeling. Tremendous – just, "We've done it!"' Indeed they had. Assuming they won in Dumfries, promotion would be clinched with two games to spare; assuming they won in Dumfries.

# *16*

# THE GOAD TO WEMBLEY

The draw for the 1995–96 British Championship play-offs was made in Cardiff, immediately after the Devils' demolition of the Steelers in that final Premier Division meeting, and if the Steelers had been out of luck in that game, they more than made up for it when the draw was made. The system was that the team finishing first in the league was placed in a different group from the runners-up. From then on, the draw would separate the third- and fourth-placed teams, then the fifth and sixth, and finally, the seventh and eighth. As the draw took shape it became apparent that the Steelers had in each case avoided the higher-placed team, with one notable exception. The only team thought to be stronger than the side placed above it was Newcastle, whose current form made them appear a more dangerous side than the seventh-placed Basingstoke Bison. The Steelers were on a roll with this draw malarky, though, and neatly broke the sequence of drawing the lower-placed team to bag the lesser-feared Bison for themselves. This, then, is how the draw looked:

| Group A | Group B |
|---|---|
| Sheffield Steelers | Cardiff Devils |
| Nottingham Panthers | Durham Wasps |
| Fife Flyers | Humberside Hawks |
| Basingstoke Bison | Newcastle Warriors |

If everything went according to plan, we could look forward to the spectacle of a Steelers versus Devils final and what a game that would be; but it was no use trying to be Mystic Meg, it was impossible to predict that far. The play-offs are a volatile setting for hockey, and this year, as it turned out, we were in store for greater quantities of intrigue, intensity and insubordination than usual. If fact, somewhat unusually, two of the biggest stories to emerge during the campaign actually occurred before a puck was struck in anger – although by way of compensation, plenty of other things did get struck in anger.

First off, Humberside sacked their coach John Griffith – a bit of a surprise, this one. Coming just four days before the play-offs were due to begin, and two days after the Hawks had faced third-placed Durham and impressively won 6–1 in Sunderland, it took almost everyone unawares, not least Griffith himself.

'It came out of the blue,' he confessed. 'After winning the last league game, the boys were fired up. I was looking forward to the play-offs – suddenly I found myself out.'

The official explanation was that Griffith was sacked for failing to secure the Hawks a top-four spot – they had missed it by one place – and in his place they appointed Keith Milhench. With the threat of closure hanging over the club it seemed a bizarre move to change coaches when they were looking at possibly the last three weeks of the club's life. The rumour was that player unrest had had some bearing on the decision, but even so, it seemed rough on Griffith. 'I must have stepped on someone's toes,' he concluded. Still, if the players thought that all the fuss surrounding the club would now die down then they were hideously wrong.

Seven days after winning in Sunderland, the Hawks returned to face the Wasps in their opening play-off fixture. During the pre-match warm-up there was an exchange of words between Durham's player-coach Rick Brebant and the Hawks' Bruce Bell – the two had had some kind of feud running for some time, and after this incident Bell was allegedly attacked by Ross Lambert, suffering concussion, a broken nose and some lost teeth. Immediately, there was chaos. All 36 players became involved and the mêlée was, in the end, broken up by the Sunderland rink's security staff. Bell was taken to hospital, and the police were called. The game got under way, but was only 58 seconds old when it was abandoned by the referee as the police appeared on the ice in order to arrest two players, the Wasps' Ross Lambert and Jon Weaver, and question a further four players. It was total chaos, and made the news the next day in the national press and as far afield as Italy and Canada.

It was a shocking incident. Bell had, in fact, been a Wasps player himself at the start of the season, but had joined the Hawks after apparently falling out with Brebant. Since then, the two had clashed several times on the ice, and it did little to cool tempers when the

Wasps' Todd Bidner sustained three cracked ribs and a collapsed lung after being checked by Bell the week before. This, though, was even more alarming. It was the third serious incident involving the Wasps that season, after Brebant's altercation with Gary Stefan and Lambert's eye injury in the Sheffield game. The BIHA were understandably mortified, and fined both clubs, with the threat of further suspended fines. It was not the kind of publicity that anyone wanted, and served only to enhance the bad reputation the sport has to endure. The legal ramifications were not clear at the time, but everyone involved hoped that the dust would settle and everyone would be able to return to the business of playing hockey. That's what all the other teams were doing while the nonsense at Sunderland had been going on, and although these other games were overshadowed somewhat, it was not to say they weren't without incident of their own.

The best game was at Nottingham who faced Fife, a team they hadn't manage to beat all season. It seemed as though this jinx would continue when the Panthers, who were still missing the injured duo of Kelham and Tait, trailed 1–3 to a lively Flyers, but they started to get a charge together and eventually edged the game 5–4. Up in Newcastle, the Warriors, widely tipped to extend their remarkable league renaissance to the play-offs, came unstuck at home to the Devils who opened their play-off campaign in an ominously composed manner, winning 4–0. The real shock, though, came at Basingstoke. After all the Steelers' satisfaction at landing the 'easy' group, they ran into trouble away to the unfancied Bison. It seemed innocuous enough to begin with, Nemeth scoring whilst shorthanded to put the Steelers ahead early in the first, but then the Bison fought back.

Within a minute, Merv Priest had equalised, and a few minutes later he put the home side ahead. Luck still seemed to be leaning Sheffield's way, though, when an apparent two-line pass was overlooked and Tony Hand cashed in on the subsequent goalmouth scramble. That, though, was where the Steelers' luck ran out. Roared on by a full house, amazed that the Bison were playing so well, Richard Little put Basingstoke back on top and to the disbelief of the Steelers, the Bison shut out Sheffield for the last 42 minutes of the game with netminder Bill Morrison in inspired form. After Little had collected his hat-trick, the Bison were heading for a shock 5–2 win when, with just over a minute to go, Morrison caught a hefty slapshot full on the face mask. Even then, despite bleeding profusely, he refused to let the Steelers past, and returned to the ice to see out the last few seconds. Insane bravery on his part? 'Not really,' he explained. 'When you get hit like that you don't want to think about it all night long – you want to face a puck again as soon as you can.' If the Bison were to make it to Wembley for the first time in their history, they needed Morrison full of confidence.

The Steelers were stunned by the loss, their first in the last 12 meetings between the teams, but responded to this wake-up call by travelling up to Fife the next night and thrashing the Flyers out of sight, 11–0. They had been taken aback by the losses in Cardiff and Basingstoke, and were now grimly determined to get back to winning ways. The only downside to the victory was when Tommy Plommer broke his collarbone as he was checked after scoring a goal, but even that couldn't cloud what had been an awesome display. Basingstoke, after their euphoria the night before, built on their fine start with another good result, escaping from Nottingham with a 1–1 tie – Morrison was again outstanding in goal, although with Nottingham hitting the post on more than one occasion during the match, luck played its part in the point. In the other group, after their false start the night before, Durham and Humberside finally got their campaigns under way. The Hawks enjoyed a comprehensive 11–3 home victory over Newcastle, who suddenly looked once more like a struggling outfit, while Durham travelled down to Cardiff to face a side that had not lost a home play-off game for four years.

The Wasps, though, were hungry for this one. They started at a furious pace, and took the first period 3–1. The Devils fought hard to claw their way back, but could manage to put only one more goal past an inspired Stephen Foster in the Wasps net, and in the end, although the 6–2 scoreline flattered the Wasps, it didn't disguise the fact that they had been much the better side.

'You have to give credit to Durham,' conceded Devils captain Stephen Cooper, 'they were really well prepared. To be honest, we had our backs to the wall from within the first ten minutes; they put us under pressure all night.'

Now that pressure would stay with the Devils. Their next two games were on the road, and if they weren't careful, by the time they returned to Cardiff, Wembley could be beyond them.

With both teams under strict instructions to be on 'best behaviour', the following Wednesday night saw the rematch between Durham and Humberside. Any passing thoughts that it might be a more tepid contest with Bell out injured were quickly dispelled in a bruising contest that saw 126 minutes in penalties dished out. Physical though it was, however, there was no denying that the game itself was a cracker, Durham sealing a 6–4 win with an empty-netter with two seconds remaining. It had been a terrific contest, and, thankfully, free of the kind of incident that had blighted the earlier meeting. The only casualty of the night, it transpired, was Adrian Florence, the chairman of the League Management Commitee, who copped a puck on the head and needed 22 stitches. The only headlines after this game, therefore, were the ones on Florence's scalp.

The following weekend saw the play-offs reach their midway point. Durham made it three out of three with a narrow 3–2 win over Cardiff in Sunderland to complete a double over the Devils. The game itself was another penalty-filled epic; it saw Cardiff's discipline slip a few times, for which they were duly punished. The Wasps now stood just one victory away from qualification. In the other group Basingstoke were in a similar position, their 5–3 home win over Fife giving them five points out of a possible six, and they led the group. Trailing behind them were rivals Sheffield and Nottingham, who now met in Sheffield. The two sides had had some cracking encounters in recent times and the stage was set for another hard-fought battle; only it didn't happen. The Steelers took the Panthers apart, and Nottingham, unable to get anything past the outstanding Wayne Cowley, lost heart. The final scoreline of 8–0 to the Steelers was so one-sided that it was hard to tell which set of fans were more surprised. The Steelers had become the first club to rack up successive shut-outs in the play-offs and Nottingham were really going to have to pick themselves up after this one.

Twenty-four hours later, the play-off picture was a little more focused. Durham had qualified, disposing of Newcastle 5–0, and in Hull the Devils were in deep, deep trouble. They had started the game knowing that defeat would have a shattering effect on their play-off hopes, and when they recovered from a two goal deficit to make it 2–2 at the end of the first, it appeared they had turned the corner. They hadn't. The middle period was a nightmare for the Devils as Humberside, inspired by John Wolfe yet again, put four goals past them. In an effort to stem the tide, Cardiff pulled netminder Stevie Lyle and put on Jason Wood, and when that didn't work, put Lyle back on. That still didn't work, and so Wood came on again. It was a shambles. Although they rallied somewhat in the closing stages to score three times, it was too late. They lost by eight goals to six, and the Hawks, superb throughout, now held their destiny in their own hands.

In Group A there were a couple of twists. Sheffield won again, beating Fife, which wasn't a surprise, but it was only by the score of 3–1, which was. Nottingham, despondent after their mauling in Sheffield, travelled to Basingstoke knowing they had to win. In a keenly contested game the match turned on one incident where Chris

Chard drew the Bison level at 2–2, only to be cross-checked by Mark Twaite. Tempers were lost, and by the time everything was sorted out, it was Nottingham who found themselves enjoying the five-on-three advantage. They didn't waste it, and Paul Adey scored to put Nottingham back on top. From then on the Panthers raced away and the final win of 6–3 was a massive boost to their Wembley ambitions. Sheffield now led the group, with Nottingham and Basingstoke tied on five points; Fife were pointless and out of it.

Going into the final week, the only issue in Group B was whether Cardiff would still scrape through or whether Humberside could hold them off. The Devils hoped that the Hawks would slip up somewhere, and on the Wednesday they became Newcastle Warriors fans for the night as the Hawks played a midweek game there. Newcastle, though, were missing several key players and were ill-equipped to face a Hawks team determined to make it to Wembley for what might be their swansong. The Hawks won 10–4 and Cardiff were looking at the depressing prospect of missing Wembley for only the second time in seven years. They faced the Warriors themselves on the Saturday, and clocked up a 6–3 win, but could only hope that Durham had done them a favour and won in Hull. If the Hawks had lost that one, they still had to travel to Cardiff the next night and Cardiff could still overtake them. It promised to be a night of high drama in Humberside.

With Durham's place already secure there was, it was reasoned, little incentive for them to go all out and bust a gut trying to win. That took no account of the rivalry that had emerged between the two sides recently. Kip Noble put Durham ahead inside the first two minutes and Humberside looked distinctly edgy. Nerves were settled when Darcy Cahill equalised after quarter of an hour, and seconds later the match moved up a gear when David Standing put the Hawks 2–1 up; but almost immediately, Noble struck again and it was tied at two apiece. The second period was played out in a furious manner, but with both netminders on top, chances were at a premium. Finally, Brebant managed to turn a Dale Lambert slapshot past John Wolfe and, just seconds before the second period ended, he scampered clear on a breakaway and scored again to make it 4–2 to Durham.

Humberside had just 20 minutes to salvage the game, possibly the last 20 minutes they would ever play at Kingston Street, and they came out for the third period flying. Roared on by nearly 2,000 agitated fans, Barcley Pierce somehow found Graham Garden who made it 4–3, and three minutes later Pierce struck again to tie the game up at 4–4. With just over ten minutes to go now the momentum shifted back to Durham who piled the pressure on to the Hawks' goal. They couldn't find a way through, however, and the rink exploded with joy when Derek Laxdall scored against the run of play to put the Hawks ahead with just a few minutes to go. Then, as if the game hadn't provided enough incident, Wasps' netminder Stephen Foster managed to knock himself out cold when he collided with his own goal and had to be stretchered off. It was the break the Hawks needed, and after play was restarted Garden burst clear and sealed the victory with the sixth goal. The Humberside Hawks were going to Wembley.

In Group A, what had appeared straightforward a few days earlier had now been turned on its head. With Sheffield apparently cruising towards Wembley and Nottingham reeling after their 8–0 whitewash, the Panthers suddenly realised that if they could beat the Steelers at Lower Parliament Street, they would be first to qualify from the group. Amazingly, showing an enormous amount of character and spirit, they did just that, and what's more, became the first club to shut out the Steelers into the bargain. The win, by a 3–0 scoreline, was due in no small part to the heroics of Scott O'Connor in the Panthers goal. Sheffield fired 46 shots at O'Connor that night, and were stunned to see him turn every one away. The Nottingham fans were delighted. Against all the odds, they had made it to Wembley. Up in Fife, the Flyers had only pride to play for when they took on the Bison, but that was obviously motivation enough as they soared to a 6–0 first-period lead. The Bison were trailing 8–2 when they started a charge back, and, incredibly, they hauled it back to 8–7, only to see Frank Morris grab an insurance goal in the last minute, 9–7 the final score. After a terrific start, the Bison had watched their play-offs fall apart. They still had one final chance, though. If they won their final match they were still through. Trouble was, it was in Sheffield.

There was now just that final Wembley place up for grabs. In Group B Durham duly rounded things off with a win in Newcastle to make sure that the Warriors would be the only side not to gain a point in the three weeks. In the other game, Cardiff beat the Hawks 8–2, which served to highlight the fact that they had failed to do themselves justice in the play-offs. Devils' coach Paul Heavey was at a loss to explain the reason for their failure. 'Maybe we didn't gell enough,' he pondered. As for the Hawks, well, they had lost here in Cardiff, sure, but with their minds on the next weekend they honestly couldn't care less. In Fife, the Flyers shared ten goals with the Panthers, and attention now swung towards Sheffield to see if Basingstoke could do anything to stop the Steelers marching towards Wembley.

With Sheffield on course for a Grand Slam, and indeed their fifth consecutive trophy, the remainder of their season was billed as the

'Drive for Five'. Basingstoke's only drive was the one up to Yorkshire for the match, and even that wasn't a simple one, as they got snared up in traffic and the game was delayed for over an hour. When it did finally start it was Sheffield who got motoring first. After 10 minutes, Ken Priestlay put the home side ahead, and within six minutes that had stretched to a 3–0 lead with two goals from Steve Nemeth and Tim Cranston. In the second period, the Steelers were rocked by two Basingstoke goals as the Bison fought back. Firstly, Thomas Granberg scored, and then, somewhat controversially, Kevin Conway played a one-two off the back of team-mate Merv Priest's head and as the Steelers hesitated, thinking that play would be halted with Priest lying prostrate on the ice, Conway ducked in, picked up the rebound and scored. Early in the final period, a goal from Tony Hand should have settled Steelers nerves, but Basingstoke came back again, Mike Wagstaff making it 4–3 with six minutes to go. At this point, the Steelers could have wobbled, the fans were certainly anxious, but in the final three minutes they cantered across the line with goals from Priestlay, Cranston and Neil. The nerves eased, the Steelers could now start thinking about defending their Wembley crown. They may have been the last team to clinch their place, but now they were there everyone else was going to have to watch out.

# 17

# IN A LEAGUE WITH THE DEVILS

Manchester travelled up to Scotland to take on the Vikings in a confident mood. After all, they had already beaten them four times out of four during the season, and they were enjoying a winning streak that now stood at 37 games. Mind you, they had also just had a gruelling match in Slough, and the team had compounded their weariness by staying up to watch the Tyson–Bruno fight at five in the morning. They were, to put it bluntly, knackered. When Dumfries raced into a 3–0 lead inside eight minutes it was clear that they were in for a tough night. Ruggles did his best to wake everyone up with a brace before the end of the period (one of them an absolute corker, a one-timer from Byram) but in a way this only lulled Manchester into thinking that they were capable of retrieving the situation without playing as well as they should. They did manage to equalise through Ruggles's third at the start of the second, but parity lasted only 11 seconds before Richie Lamb found plenty of time and space to put another past Colin Downie, playing in place of the resting Finnie.

Dumfries were on the up now. With Manchester unable to get themselves going, and Downie left exposed by a sluggish Storm defence, they realised that victory was theirs for the taking. Jim Lynch, the Vikings coach, had surprised everyone by playing Gordon Langford in place of Moray Hanson, and Langford had responded by playing a blinder. He could do nothing, though, when a Craig Lyons mistake let in Martin Smith to tie it up at four apiece, but from then on he stubbornly kept the Storm at bay. With three-and-a-half minutes of this pulsating match remaining, the breakthrough came and Lyons atoned for his earlier mistake to give Dumfries a deserved lead. The Dumfries crowd went berserk, and then found they had to keep on going berserk when Rob Hartnell made it 6–4 just a few seconds later. Pandemonium. With the travelling Storm fans resigned to defeat, Shawn Byram did nothing but jangle a few Viking nerves when he made it 6–5; but it was too little, too late. The hooter sounded and Dumfries were deserved winners.

One man particularly pleased with the result was John Bogie, the owner of the Vikings' main sponsors, Oakbank Services. He had wanted the win so much that he had even, somewhat foolhardily, offered each of the players a £200 bonus if they managed to pull it off. After the game, the Vikings players felt so bad about clearing him out that they went to the enormous expense of giving him the match puck by way of consolation. It was probably the most expensive puck in Britain. Bogie, though, had no regrets.

'I am so proud of these players,' he told *Powerplay*. 'I am the happiest man in the rink, even paying the bonus. The puck cost more than the wheels of Neil Armstrong's moon buggy.' A fitting point to make, for one so obviously over the moon.

For the Storm fans the defeat was not as galling as it might have been. You couldn't really criticise the players; one defeat in 38 games was hardly a crisis was it? Promotion was still well within the players' grasp. Besides, if you had to lose a game you couldn't lose to a nicer club than Dumfries. Compared to the welcome that Storm fans usually got, i.e. hostility, envy and suspicion, the Dumfries fans are a refreshingly friendly bunch. They were thrilled with the victory, but careful not to gloat. As one of them put it, 'You'll probably murder us at your place next week . . . ' The only thing they seemed at all reticent about was their mascot, a Viking-helmeted, seven foot tall, drum-banging penguin called Penny (or was it Kenny? The tannoy was muffled . . . ) During the game, this endearingly absurd figure had waddled around the rink hugging fans from both sides. He was ace. Strangely, the Dumfries fans seemed less enamoured of him than we were. One thing though – he had a belly button, prompting a heated debate about whether or not penguins have them. We could accept that he wore a Viking helmet, and was seven foot tall, and could bang a drum, but a belly button?

In the other group, the Blackburn mini-revival continued. Away to Guildford, they managed a 6–6 tie, but neither side looked likely to win the group; that honour would probably go to the winners of the Milton Keynes–Bracknell clashes. These two met at Bracknell, but with the Bees missing several key players, including Brian Wilkie who, somewhat surreally, managed to injure himself during the warm-up by skating into a team-mate, they were always going to be up against it.

Never ones to look a gift horse in the mouth, the Kings were able to produce an emphatic 8–2 victory which put them in pole position for the final weekend. The game had not been played in the most congenial atmosphere, it must be said; even the match announcer ran into trouble with the referee for announcing one of the penalties 'in a manner not suitable' and received a gross misconduct penalty for his efforts. It was one of those games.

Whilst the Bees were going down at home to the Kings, the Jets were going down fighting at home to the Wildcats. After the shattering loss to the Storm the night before, they had all but resigned themselves to relegation, but were determined to win what would be their last home game of the season. They started well enough, jumping into a three-goal lead inside the first ten minutes, and even when the Wildcats pulled a couple back they responded with a pair of their own to lead 5–2 early in the second; but then the wheels fell off the wagon. Swindon went on to score five times, while the Jets scored just one of their own, and the Wildcats left Slough with a 6–7 win. The victory had not been without cost. The inspirational Brad Rubachuk, who had had an eventful début season in Britain – scoring at a prodigious rate and breaking the Swindon club record for points in a season – had spent almost as much time in the penalty box as on the ice. It wasn't that he was a dirty player, as such, but he was competitive to the point of being seriously deranged. The smart money was on him running into some serious trouble before the season was out, and then, in the shape of the Jets' Mike Flanagan, he finally met his Nemesis. After niggling at each other all night, the two finally had their set-to in the second period. Flanagan won. Rubachuk was taken to hospital with a broken jaw. Ouch. It was as unfortunate as it was unsurprising.

Without Rubachuk, Swindon travelled to Manchester for a Wednesday night game more in hope than expectation. Their cause wasn't much helped by the fact that they were also missing the injured Bryan Larkin and three of their younger players, who had been called away to represent Great Britain Under-19s, much to the annoyance of the Wildcats. On paper, they could still win the group, but their previous experiences at the Nynex, coupled with this player shortage, had done little to suggest that they would be in luck. They started well enough; despite falling behind to a Stefan Barton goal after eight minutes they continued to battle away and were rewarded with a strike of their own to level the scores after 10 minutes. They started to fade, though, and by the end of the first period, although the sides had enjoyed a similar amount of possession, the Storm led 4–1, due in no small part to the performance of Finnie in the Storm goal, who made a string of solid saves.

Finnie's good form continued in the second period, and at the start of the third, by which time Swindon had lost heart and the Storm held a commanding 9–2 lead, Lawless elected to rest him and give Downie a run-out between the pipes. His job done, Finnie continued to entertain the crowd by looning around on the bench, periodically donning an absurd afro wig and, whenever he noticed that he had been spotted, quickly whipping it off and pretending that nothing had been amiss. The crowd, amused to see the folically-challenged Finnie (akin to a 'young Bruce Willis', he insists) suddenly looking like Jimi Hendrix, loved it. Since his arrival, he had established himself as a big favourite in Manchester, his penchant for fruit machines and casinos quickly leading to the nickname of 'Vegas', and his performances in goal had been nothing short of spellbinding. If he wasn't yet the best netminder in the country, then he was certainly one of the most popular; except with one person.

To the incredulity of most observers, Finnie had recently come under fire for his performances in one section of the hockey press. Norman de Mesquita, a venerable and outspoken observer of the British game, questioned his ability in his 'From the Shoulder' column in *Ice Hockey News Review*. 'I cannot see how or why John Finnie is playing to the exclusion of Colin Downie,' he wrote. 'Dare one ask if the only reason he is playing is because he has an American accent and that means he must be better than a British-born and trained player?' It was a staggering thing to read, quite apart from the suggestion that Lawless would sign someone only because of their accent, and something that surprised everyone else who had seen Finnie play. Although player statistics can sometimes be misleading, they are a fairly reasonable barometer of how well a player is performing and Finnie's save percentage of 91.74, and goals-against average of 3.19 were both the best in the country. Over the course of the season he had probably won half a dozen games for the Storm and it was no coincidence that they had won every single match he had played in.

Although Norman de Mesquita is a passionate supporter of the game, and genuinely knowledgeable about it, it is fair to say that he enjoys a reputation for misery and despondency that makes Franz Kafka look like Su Pollard. Never one to be accused of looking at the game through rose-tinted spectacles (more like death throes-tinted spectacles, if you ask me), his fortnightly outpourings in the *IHNR* invariably bemoan the state of the British game, and his continuous lament that the game is heading for total collapse makes for dispiriting reading. I had often wondered why his column was called 'From the Shoulder', but after reading this latest tirade I could only assume it was because that was where he kept his chips. He didn't like North Americans invading our game, that was clear. Maybe, needing something new to moan about that week, he happened to see Finnie play a below-par game and unleashed his bile accordingly. Finnie was by no means the only person to suffer such criticism from Norman's pen over the course of the season, but no one else I spoke to on the matter shared Mesquita's point of view. It was interesting to note that another writer in the very next issue of *IHNR* described Finnie as Chelmsford's 'find of the century', but there was no doubt that Finnie still had a point to prove to some people.

On this day, however, it was Ruggles who stole the show. By the end of the game, the Wildcats had been convincingly beaten 11–3 and Hilton, saving his best form of the season for these play-offs it seemed, was outstanding. He scored five goals, seemingly unstoppable, and received a standing ovation from the crowd at the end. The bigger the game, the bigger he showed up. The win left Manchester one away from promotion, and the visit of Dumfries the following Sunday promised to be a night of celebration. Before that, though, all the other teams played again on the Saturday. Bracknell, needing to win to keep. the pressure on Milton Keynes, entertained Blackburn, but what followed was a horrible and bad-tempered match. For the record, the Bees eventually won 11–3 but it is unlikely that people will remember the contest for the score. At one point in the game the Hawks even left the ice, indignant at what they saw as poor officiating. While all this nonsense was going on, a much better game was being played in Milton Keynes, where the Kings eventually won a thriller over Guildford, 7–6. The result, greeted with a collective sigh of relief from the Kings fans, meant that in order for Bracknell to overtake the Kings and clinch promotion, they would have to come to Milton Keynes and win by seven clear goals. This was unlikely, given the fact that they had lost the first one 8–2 at home. The Kings safe, then? Not so fast.

When the Milton Keynes fans looked up at the scoreboard the next night and saw that the Bees were ahead 4–1, with the Kings obviously tiring, missing two players through injury and a third through suspension, and that there were over 22 minutes still to play, they must have experienced a kind of creeping dread; the kind of creeping dread you would always see on the face of some jobbing BBC actor towards the end of an episode of 'Doctor Who' just as the slithering lizard man crawled towards them as they lay powerless to resist. What would happen in the next episode, of course, was that the lizard man would become distracted by something or other and the helpless captive would be rescued by the Doctor in the nick of time. It was a similarly unsatisfying conclusion here. In the final period nobody scored and the Kings won the group. They were worried for a moment, though.

The other games in the promotion/relegation play-offs saw a Blackburn side short of bodies go down 9–12 at home to Guildford, and Swindon and Slough share 10 goals in a game that was overshadowed by some emotional scenes as the Swindon fans turned out in force to back their team in what threatened to be the last professional game played at the Link Centre. After the game, EA Sports' Bob Dewar, a man who had done a great deal to keep the sport running in Swindon, announced that the fight to continue playing would go on. Hopefully, he will be successful. The only remaining issue was whether the Storm would win their place in the élite or whether, against all the odds, little Dumfries could poop the party and take the spoils for themselves. To do that, they would have to beat the Storm at the Nynex and, before that, beat Slough at home. Unfortunately, Dumfries got the jitters, and lost 4–7 to the Jets. For the second time in their short history, the Storm were denied the opportunity to clinch the prize they sought in front of their own fans.

This disappointment was assuaged somewhat, however, when the players skated out for the final game of the season and saw how many people had turned out to see them conclude their début season. It hadn't taken a genius to work out that there was a good chance that the British record attendance might fall again. With very few vacant seats to be spotted in the arena the only surprise was that the announced attendance of 16,344 wasn't even higher. This monstrous crowd was, in truth, a greater accomplishment than winning promotion. Over the course of the B&H Cup, the league and the play-offs, the Storm had played to an accumulated crowd of 241,375 (not including the 5,275 who turned up for the 'away' Solihull game), which was more in 32 games than the entire First Division campaign of 311 games had managed the season before. The Storm could now boast the six biggest crowds in British ice hockey history, and the gate for the Blackburn game had been verified as the largest crowd for a league fixture anywhere in Europe. Before Christmas the average crowd had been 5,464, but since then the average had nearly doubled to 9,501. A remarkable figure for what, we should all remember, was a 'minority' sport.

The near-capacity crowd buzzed with anticipation as face-off approached. Apart from the thousands of Storm supporters in attendance, there was also a healthy contingent from Dumfries, including, marvellously, Penny the Penguin (or Lenny? Missed it again.) Aware that it is deemed self-indulgent to contemplate your own navel, let alone a penguin's, this time those of us watching speculated on who would win if there was ever a fight between Lightning Jack and the penguin. Dumfries may have the better mascot, we reasoned, but he wasn't as hard as Lightning Jack.

With promotion now a certainty, all that remained was for Manchester to put on a show. They didn't disappoint. The Storm, sparked by the excitement of the crowd, launched themselves at Dumfries. After ten minutes of frantic near-misses and half-chances, the crowd bursting with pent-up energy, waiting to explode at the first goal, the tension was finally released. The Storm swarmed around the Vikings goal, the crowd urging the puck in, a half-chance fell to Ruggles – 1–0. The crowd rose as one, roared their approval and the Storm were away. Jago scored with what I swear must have been the fastest shot ever taken, certainly the fastest I have ever seen – or to be more accurate, didn't see – as he put a screamer in from the blueline. David Smith, obviously intending to enjoy the night, weaved in and out of the Dumfries defence and made it 3–0; everything was going exactly to plan.

At this point, Dumfries were feeling left out of things, and so rather than mope all alone in the kitchen, they joined in the party with a couple of goals of their own from Rob Hartnell, one of which Finnie certainly should have stopped. (Was de Mesquita in the audience, I wondered?) The second period, though, had the Storm back on track as Ruggles collected his second, and then third goals of the night. In the six play-off games so far, he had scored four hat-tricks, and got a brace in one of the other games. He wasn't finished here yet, either. In the third period he made it 6–2 with his fourth of the night and then Jago popped up to make it 7–2. The final word went to Dumfries, as Ritchie Lamb scored a deserved third for the Vikings near the end. The goal was all but forgotten, however, when the final hooter sounded and the Storm celebrations began in earnest. There was no doubt about it now. The Storm were bound for top-flight hockey.

# 18

# IF YOU ALL HATE STEELERS, CLAP YOUR HANDS

Since its opening in 1934, Wembley Arena has enjoyed a reputation as the Mecca of British ice hockey, and has been home to the British ice hockey championships since 1984. The question in 1996 was, for how much longer? Although it has the advantage of being a neutral venue, it has a capacity of just 9,000 and has been overtaken, in technical terms at least, by the new arenas in Sheffield and Manchester. I wondered if its days were numbered, and I wasn't the only one. With the uncertainties of the impending Super League lurking around the corner, there was widespread speculation that this might be the last championship to be held there. There was, therefore, a distinct possibility that my first visit to the Wembley weekend might also be my last, and having heard so much about the 'magic' of the place, I wanted to find out why it was revered so much by hockey aficionados.

With the finalists not usually determined until the weekend before, and all tickets sold weeks in advance, the Wembley championships are made special because they are played in front of fans from all over the country and the whole weekend becomes a genuine celebration of hockey and the brotherhood of fan. I made my way to the arena having heard all about this but, being a cynical sort, I was somewhat sceptical about it all. How can an old building, packed full of fans whose teams have already been knocked out, possibly live up to its billing as the Mecca of hockey? By the end of the weekend, I knew. Once inside the arena, it became clear that Wembley really was a gathering place for fans from all over Britain, regardless of whether or not their team was participating. Walking around the building, I was confronted with a plethora of club jerseys from Fife to Guildford. By the time I had spotted someone wearing an Ayr Bruins shirt (the Bruins went out of business a few years ago), I decided the best game to play might be to try to spot which teams weren't represented. The atmosphere was fantastic, a babbling cauldron of anticipation and excitement – and that was only on the concourse.

Apart from the spectacle of the games themselves, one of the main attractions of Wembley is the chance to splash out all your money on hockey memorabilia at one of the many stalls that are on view. Even when the games themselves are not taking place, Wembley is alive with a bustling throng of people. Here the fans gather to swap stories and mementos, to peruse the stalls and cheerfully to fight their way through the crowds to buy food and drink. Where else in the world can you chat to some Romford Raiders fans and then buy a Berliner SC Preussen shirt? It was the nearest I've ever been to hockey heaven. It seemed as if everyone connected with British ice hockey was there. I managed to spot the GB coach, Peter Woods, Norman de Mesquita, Ken Taggart, Bob Korol and Gia Milonovich from Sky, Dave Simms the Steelers announcer, Frank Dempster and all the big cheeses from the BIHA, Sir John Hall (unhappy with his seat amongst some less-than-welcoming Durham fans, apparently), John Lawless and even Shannon Hope, although I'm sure his original plan was to be there as a player rather than just working on a stall selling his 'Shine Dog Ice Gear' (thanks for the free badge, Shannon).

Unsurprisingly, given that it seemed as if every hockey fan in Britain had taken the place over, the Wembley weekend is renowned for being a hotbed of rumour and gossip at the best of times, but with still no official announcements regarding the format for the next season, it was especially rife this year. The usual sensational claims about the pre-season movements of players – 'Ken Priestlay's signed for Manchester !' – were augmented by feverish whispers about the shape of the next season – 'The Super League is definitely going to be scrapped!', 'It's definitely going ahead!', 'Guildford have pulled out!' (True, as it turned out, although somewhat alarmingly, the only person not to hear the rumour in time was John Lord, the Super League Chief Executive, who popped up on Sky to claim that they were still in it, and made a fool of himself in the process.)

'The best thing is to start your own rumour and see how long it takes to come back to you,' *Powerplay's* Simon Potter suggested to me. 'The Super League is decided,' I began to tell everyone. 'Manchester and Sheffield play each other 42 times next season. At the end of that, the top two go through to the play-offs.' People only half-disbelieved me.

By virtue of my press pass I was able to navigate the crowds via the network of corridors under the stands, and make my way to the press room. After pigging out on the free buffet, my thoughts turned to the games themselves. Nottingham's failure to beat Fife the previous Sunday meant that Sheffield had won the qualifying group, and it was they who now enjoyed the advantage of playing in the earlier semi-final, against Humberside. Written off by many before the play-offs, and facing an uncertain future with Humberside Council due to be dissolved at the stroke of midnight on the Sunday, the Hawks arrived at Wembley determined to give it their best shot. They didn't have the flair of the Steelers, they would be the first to admit, but it was true that in a one-off hockey game, a hard-working team always has a chance if the talented team doesn't work hard as well. Besides, they were still buoyed up from the win over Durham that got them there in the first place. Who was to say they couldn't carry that sort of form on for just a little longer?

As face-off time approached the atmosphere in the arena began to build. After taking my place in the press-box, I could see that the contingent of fans from Sheffield was by far the biggest in the building, something like 2,500 in the crowd of over 8,000, and what a noise they were making. Looking elsewhere around the arena I was able to spot pockets of support for all the other clubs. Behind me were some Swindon fans, to my left, followers of Milton Keynes and Fife. Each group of fans were doing their best to make their presence felt, except one. Over on the far side there appeared to be a large group of fans gathered in the corner who were strangely subdued. Only when a 50/50 draw winner was announced as being from Wales and they all started to cheer, did I realise that they must be Devils fans.

The lights dimmed, and two glitterballs suspended from the rafters were picked out by spotlights, sending shards of light dancing around the arena. Surprisingly, the effect was a good one, and a roar went up from the Sheffield fans as a Steelers logo appeared on the ice, projected from above. This provoked boos from the Panthers fans sat behind me, which in turn, stirred the Steelers fans up even more. A group of Humberside Hawks fans in front of me started to bang their drums vigorously and you couldn't hear yourself think. The atmosphere was brilliant.

After the player introductions were over – a tumultuous roar greeting every Steeler name, and a defiant, Panthers-boosted cheer adding power to the Humberside ones – the national anthem was played. By now everyone just wanted the game to get under way, and moments later, it was. To start with, it was predictably frenetic stuff. Humberside started marginally the brighter, and when David Longstaff received a two-minute tripping penalty inside the first minute, they were presented with the first powerplay of the weekend. Although they worked hard on this powerplay, the Hawks couldn't open the Steelers up, and as if to compound this failing just as Longstaff clambered back on to the ice, the Steelers scored.

It wasn't what you would call a pretty goal. Tim Cranston picked up the puck and drove in from the left towards the goal, but with Ian Pound doing enough to hold Cranston back, he lost control and the puck slid towards John Wolfe. Wolfe quickly took the chance to poke the puck clear but, somewhat outlandishly, only managed to deflect it back over his own shoulder into the net via Ian Pound's face, breaking his stick in the process. There was a split-second delay before anyone in the building realised what had happened and then Cranston, who hadn't even managed to get a shot away, threw up his arms in celebration as the Steelers fans went wild. It was a horrible slice of luck for the Hawks, and although they tried to battle away as before, there was no doubt that it lifted the Steelers. Humberside battled hard to get some momentum going, and as the game became increasingly physical, they were unlucky when what appeared to be a blatant trip on Barcley Pierce went uncalled. The focus of interest fell on the referees when linesman Alan Craig was cut by a flying puck. As Craig started to bleed profusely the game was delayed whilst a replacement was sought. After this delay, during which the more uncharitable fans in the building made crass jokes about 'bleeding referees', the replacement official, Paul Staniforth, was thrown into the thick of things just as the game suddenly boiled over.

Phil Huber, narrowly called offside on a Hawks play, incensed the Steelers players by putting the puck past Cowley anyway (frowned upon, as it sometimes takes a psychological edge off the netminder), and as he skated by the boards the Steelers closed in on him by way of warning not to do it again. Huber, now pushed into a corner, struck out at one of them, and suddenly everyone piled in, much to the approval of the baying spectators. Although not a serious incident – it was more that both sides were asserting themselves – it did lead to a flurry of penalties and threatened to disrupt the game further when it became clear that a piece of the plexi-glass had become dislodged during the incident. As the game came to a standstill and everyone scratched their heads and wondered how to fix it, Ron Shudra, impatient to get things going again, inserted the handle of his stick through the barrier and, rather stylishly, pulled it back and watched the plexi-glass fall neatly back into place. It had probably been the niftiest bit of stick work we had seen, but not for much longer, because a few minutes later Sheffield scored again. This time it was a beauty.

Steve Nemeth, picking up his own rebound, circled back towards the blueline. As the Hawks defence trailed him he found André Malo with a neat back-hander. Malo swung round, found some space, saw Priestlay drifting into the slot, and sent in a lovely, sweeping pass that Priestlay one-timed past Wolfe: 2–0. Going into the second period, Humberside realised that it was vital not to allow Sheffield any more chances or else the Steelers could quickly put the game beyond them. That game plan looked somewhat fragile, however, when it took Sheffield all of 10 seconds to score from the restart. From the face-off, the Hawks gave the puck away to Rob Wilson, he sent it across the ice to the boards on the far side, and while everyone else seemed to stand back and watch, Steve Nemeth dived in, picked up the rebound, homed in on the goal and had plenty of time to put the puck high into the roof of the net – 3–0 and the Steelers in complete command.

After 24 minutes it was 4–0 as Nemeth, once again, took the Hawks apart. The Hawks had been reeling from the earlier goal, almost falling further behind to strikes from Hand and Priestlay, but when Rob Wilson sent an incisive pass up centre ice to find Nemeth in the clear, they had no chance as the ex-NHLer comfortably beat Wolfe in front of the delighted Steelers fans. With such a commanding lead, the Steelers took their foot off the pedal and the Hawks, with nothing to lose at this stage, started to move the puck around a little better – not that they looked any more like scoring, though. A look at the shots-on-goal figures at this stage showed that the Hawks had managed a paltry three shots on Wayne Cowley in this middle period. Imagine their surprise, then, when they scored on one of them.

They had enjoyed a good spell of possession, without looking overtly dangerous, when a long shot from Ian Pound went wide and rebounded off the boards. As Cowley lay sprawling on the ice, David Standing was able to pick up the loose puck and turn it into the net. The goal, a soft one from a Sheffield point of view, seemed to inspire the Hawks. They swarmed around the Sheffield net, putting the Steelers out of their rhythm, and a couple of minutes into the final period they cashed in again. Darcy Cahill, guilty of wasting a good chance earlier, drove in a shot from the left wing that Cowley was unable to smother. The rebound fell to Huber who made no mistake. Suddenly it was all Humberside as, with a spring in their step, they terrorised the Steelers goal. Derek Laxdall had a good effort which went close, and then a Pierce wraparound almost came off. The Steelers fans, massed behind Cowley's net, got an awful fright when Phil Huber clanged one off the post. No doubt about it, Sheffield were wobbling. As the Hawks piled on the pressure it became clear that the next goal would be a big one. To their fans' immense relief, it went to Sheffield.

It is a sign of a good side if you are able to score while under the cosh, and the Steelers showed that they are just that, when a move stemming from Wayne Cowley went all the way to the other end to make it 5–2. Rob Wilson picked up on a pass from Cowley, and found Nemeth, who in turn fed Tony Hand. Hand, who had been having a quiet game, simply one-timed it to Priestlay and the Hawks were suddenly exposed as Priestlay charged away and rounded Wolfe. That should have been the killer blow to the Hawks but, to their credit, they kept on plugging away and when Cowley could only deflect a Pierce shot into the air Derek Laxdall showed off his baseball-batting prowess by whipping the puck into the net: 5–3. Humberside threw everything at the Steelers and Cam Plante missed a glorious chance on a late powerplay. With the game again in the balance, the massed Steelers support showed their worth by getting behind their side and doing their best to sing the Steelers home. Only when Tony Hand powered a shot past Wolfe with a couple of minutes remaining could they finally relax.

For the Hawks there was no way back, and as the clock ticked away they realised that their Wembley adventure was coming to an end. They could be proud of the hard work they had put into the game, but with all the uncertainty surrounding the club, their attention would now have to turn to the fight to keep top-class hockey in Hull. The Steelers, although pushed further by the Hawks than they would have liked, were deserving winners. At the post-match press conference, Ron Shudra was asked if it had been a problem playing under the pressure of being favourites. Not really, he had felt, 'I think our fans were under more pressure than us. There's a lot of people out there wanting us to lose, and I think it's tougher for them, sometimes.' He had a point. There was an intense rivalry in the arena between the Steelers fans and just about everyone else, and most of the people watching seemed happy to support the Steelers' opponents. The Panthers fans, especially, seemed to enjoy goading the Sheffield contingent, their moving rendition of 'You're sad, and you know you are' was, for me, a particular highlight. I couldn't help hoping that the two clubs would meet in the final.

For the Steelers players, it was time to leave Wembley in order to get as much rest as possible before the final the next day. When asked after the game if he would prefer a particular opponent for the final, Ron Shudra simply wished that the other semi-final was 'as tough a game as possible' so that whoever won would be too drained to pick themselves up and do it all again. The clash between the Wasps and the

Panthers promised to be just that. The Wasps were starting to look a formidable side, and after recovering from a miserable end to the regular season, the Panthers had finally got a healthy squad back together and looked like their old selves. Whoever was going to win this one was going to have to work really hard, I thought.

The game started ferociously. With Wembley this year boasting a slightly smaller ice surface than previously, the challenges inevitably came in thick and fast. Neil Morgan got everyone in the mood with a massive hit on Dale Lambert, and team-mate Doc Durdle wasted no time in letting Brebant know he was in for a rough night too. If it carries on like this they'll kill each other, I thought. The first powerplay opportunity fell to Durham, but Scott O'Connor made a couple of outstanding saves and Nottingham survived. After seven and a half minutes it was the Wasps' turn to go shorthanded when Ross Lambert was given 2 + 10 for checking from behind, but this time, the man advantage was to prove significant. Darren Durdle picked the puck up inside his own half, and as the Wasps backpedalled, he skated past the blueline, spotted Neil Morgan, and found him in space with a pass. Morgan quickly sent the puck towards Stephen Foster in the Durham goal, and just as the puck was about to reach Foster, Paul Adey flashed in front of him and got enough of his stick on the puck to turn it in.

With a goal on the scoreboard, the Panthers enjoyed a good spell, but could not find their way past Foster again, and once they had weathered this spell, Durham took advantage of their next powerplay to level the scores. Picking up the puck by his own net, Kip Noble weaved his way the entire length of the ice to tee up Janne Seva who flipped the puck in from close range. With the sides level again, the game became increasingly tight. A series of minor penalties from Nottingham gave Durham the territorial advantage for much of the second period, but with O'Connor superb in the Panthers goal the score remained tied. For the latter part of the second, and much of the third, it was Nottingham's turn to enjoy greater possession of the puck, but with Foster in fine form they were also unable to convert their chances.

There was a slight hold-up when yet another official managed to come off worse from a close encounter with a flying puck, this time referee John Moore getting smacked on the jaw – leading to those uncharitable fans in the building this time making crass jokes about referees needing to 'take it on the chin'. When the game restarted it became clear that the next goal would probably decide who was going through to the final. After playing out of his skin, Scott O'Connor was finally beaten by a Wasps shot, but was relieved to see Kim Issel's shot come back off the post. Spurred on by this slice of luck, Nottingham pressed forward, and when Mike Blaisdell set up Simon Hunt, the winger gleefully blasted the puck past Foster. (When asked after the game what had gone through his mind as he took the shot, Hunt revealed a Zen-like composure – 'Just, go in, please . . . ') The Wasps were crestfallen. Any hopes they had of grabbing what would have been a dramatic equaliser all but vanished when Kristian Fagerstrom took a 2 + 2 for high sticks. Adey had a good chance to finish it, but Foster pulled off an unbelievable save to deny him. With time running out for the Wasps, they had to take the gamble of pulling Stephen Foster, who had been their outstanding player, but when Brebant immediately coughed up the puck to Paul Adey at centre ice the move backfired and Adey, probably relieved to see a net without Foster standing in front of it, calmly slotted the empty-netter home to seal the win.

It had been a fantastic match and a Herculean effort from both sides, but as we looked forward to the final the next day we wondered how the Panthers could possibly have enough left to take on the Steelers. Historically, the Wembley final had favoured the team playing in the earlier semi-final, with eight of the 12 Wembley winners enjoying the advantage of a longer rest. This year, it was felt that the advantage would be even greater than usual because the final was played 45 minutes earlier than was the tradition, so as to accommodate live coverage on Sky. On top of all that, the clocks were due to go forward that night. Mike Blaisdell promised everyone that they would make it a good game, but the rest of us wondered if they could just avoid a repeat of their 8–0 drubbing in Sheffield.

If I had thought that the atmosphere was good for the games the day before, I wasn't fully prepared for the noise made by the fans for the final. At times like this, commentators invariably describe it as 'electric', which is a description that had never meant much to me before. Then I noticed that the hairs on my arm were standing up, as if charged by the atmosphere and, grinning to myself, I suddenly knew what they meant. After the game, someone asked me if the atmosphere was better than at the Nynex, and seemed impressed, though surprised, when I told them it was. Great though 16,000 cheering fans are, if they're all supporting the same side you can never get the kind of edge you get when you mix screaming fans from different sides. This, I thought, was what made Wembley special. The sports commentator Barry Davies had once said that the atmosphere at Wembley was the equal of any other sporting event in the world, and what's fine by Baz is fine by me.

Sheffield began the final as clear favourites, but they didn't have the best warm-up. As the players practised shooting at Wayne Cowley, André Malo took a slapshot that broke one of Cowley's fingers. As medics treated the injury, Dampier had to consider whether or not to stick with his netminder. Although Martin McKay was an excellent replacement, Dampier was wary of putting him in at such a late stage.

'We've all got confidence in Marty, but it's a psychological thing with goalies – they get so psyched up the night before. At that point in time it might not have been fair to say "Okay Marty, you go," so the doctor strapped Wayne up and he toughed it out.'

The injury was on Cowley's stick hand, which played a big part in his game, but Cowley felt he could manage, and adrenalin did the rest. It was his opposite number, Scott O'Connor, who started the busier.

Carrying his good form into the final, O'Connor quickly came up with a couple of solid saves from Shudra and Priestlay. After surviving a couple of minutes shorthanded, the Panthers managed to create a couple of good chances themselves, but even when they enjoyed a couple of powerplays they could not get past Cowley. There was no doubt that Nottingham looked a little sluggish, and after 14 minutes the Steelers decided to step up a gear. Working a bit of space for himself, Tim Cranston managed to fire in a shot, but it sailed wide of the net. The puck whipped round the boards and fell into the path of Malo who let fly with a screamer that tore into the net past O'Connor. As the Steelers fans went wild in celebration, the goal appeared to take Nottingham aback, and exactly 60 seconds later it was 2–0. After some neat passing between Ron Shudra and Scott Neil, Chris Kelland found himself alone in a one-on-one with O'Connor; although his shot was saved, the rebound drifted invitingly across the open goal and with the Panthers defence nowhere to be seen, Scott Neil had plenty of time to score.

The Steelers threatened to bury Nottingham now, and the Panthers did themselves no favours by failing to count to five properly and playing a brief spell with six skaters on the ice. As a result, they faced the start of the second period a man short – a two-minute bench penalty the result of this lack of concentration. The Steelers took full advantage. David Longstaff managed to work the puck free of the boards and popped it across to Tim Cranston, who darted in to take a lightning shot that O'Connor barely had a chance to see; 3–0 to the Steelers and Sheffield in total command. Ecstatic though the Steelers fans were, there was no doubt that everyone else felt that the final had gone a little flat now. The Panthers fans urged their side on, fearful of what might happen if the Steelers scored again, and the neutrals in the crowd were undoubtedly ready to give the Panthers their backing. In the press-box, the goal was greeted with mutters of 'that's it, game over'. Professional detachment aside, most of us would have enjoyed seeing the Panthers stuff the Steelers. It didn't look likely.

Nottingham toiled away, though, making up for their lack of spark with stubborn defiance. When Tim Cranston took a two-minute penalty for slashing, the Panthers were given an opportunity to get back into the game, but when the goal never materialised it looked like it was starting to drift away. What they needed was a goal, a flash of inspiration, or a defensive turnover, heck, if one of the referees bagged one it would do, anything. With four minutes of the period remaining, without warning, it happened. The Panthers had dumped the puck behind Cowley's net, and as Rob Wilson collected the puck, Randall Weber set off in dogged pursuit of the defenceman. As Wilson came round in front of the net, Weber did enough to throw him off balance, and as the puck went loose, Anthony Kelham stepped up to fire it in from close range. Now everything changed.

Even as the Nottingham fans celebrated, and I was thinking that at least they would be spared the ignominy of a shut-out defeat, the Panthers struck again. From almost the same spot that Malo had scored, Graham Waghorn fired in a shot that Randall Weber managed to get a stick on, and the puck flipped over Cowley's pads to make it 3–2. Two goals in 41 seconds and the place was going absolutely wild. Unbelievably, there was more to come. Neil Morgan made his way along the boards on a breakaway and slid a pass along to Ashley Tait. Tait dropped his shoulder, feinted one way and put the shot the other, but Cowley spread his pads well and blocked the puck. As everything on the ice seemed to move in slow motion, the puck idled its way into the clear and as Morgan lunged towards it, Jamie Van Der Horst flung himself on to the ice to try and block the shot. As 9,000 people watched agape, Morgan batted the puck and though it seemed to take an age, it crept over the line. Absolute mayhem followed. It was the loudest noise I've ever heard at a sporting venue. Looking around me, I could see people roaring their astonished approval, shaking clenched fists. 'Yes! Come on!' And that was just in the press-box. The Panthers fans were going mental.

The place was wild, widespread delirium evident on every non-Steeler face. The Steelers were stunned. In just 94 seconds it seemed as if the sky had fallen in on them. They desperately needed to calm things down, to steady the ship. Somehow, though visibly shaken, they managed to scramble their way to the interval, but now, as the Panthers fans led the arena in a chorus of 'If you all hate Steelers, clap your hands', they knew they had a real battle on their hands. The end of the period was a significant moment for the Steelers. 'That was our timeout,' Clive Tuyl later conceded. The 15-minute break allowed Sheffield to calm their nerves, and they started the third period in a more confident frame of mind. Gradually, they were able to assert themselves more, but with the Panthers' supposed fatigue no longer an issue, they were pushed all the way. Although exciting – Nicky Chinn had a shot that pinged off the bar – the last period provided no more goals and, for the first time since 1990, the final was heading for sudden-death overtime.

Anyone who didn't enjoy this one had better check their pulse to see if they were dead. There is nothing in sport to compare with sudden-death. It's the finality of it all. Even if you concede a late goal in a normal game, there is always the thought at the back of your mind that you might somehow be able to force a way back. In overtime, that's it. One mistake and you've lost. There's no way back. The ten minutes of overtime in this match were the most heart-thumping ones I've ever seen. With nerves jangling in the crowd and on the ice, every chance was greeted with frantic screaming from the audience. It was wonderful, exhilarating, end-to-end stuff. With neither defence taking any chances, clear-cut scoring opportunities were at a premium.

The best chance fell to Blaisdell in the early moments, when he broke clear with Simon Hunt in a good position on his left. With everyone around me urging him to pass, he elected to shoot, but unfortunately for him it wasn't a good one and Cowley beat it away. They had agreed beforehand, Blaisdell later explained, that the man in possession should go for the shot and the supporting player would look for the rebound; Shudra had done well to cut the pass off anyway. At the other end, Sheffield had their chances, too. O'Connor made a couple of saves to deny Cranston and Chinn, and towards the end, he made yet another big save to deny Cranston again, but by then there was the distinct suspicion that we were heading for penalties.

Indeed we were. After all that had gone before, it came down to this. In contrast to the sudden-death period, which had seemed a slow-building, stomach-churning rollercoaster, this promised to be a brutally short conclusion. Nottingham went first. Paul Adey closed in on Cowley but saw his shot deflected over the bar. Then it was the turn of André Malo, only taking the shot because Nemeth had been injured in overtime. He elected to shoot early, and to the delight of the Steelers fans behind the net, the puck found a way past O'Connor. 1–0. Blaisdell now for the Panthers. He decked, and swept past Cowley to score easily. 1–1. Now it was Tim Cranston's turn. He tried to draw

O'Connor the wrong way, but at the last moment, the puck drifted away from him and the chance was gone. Still 1–1. Simon Hunt now, for the Panthers. He closed in, tried the shot, but Cowley snapped his pads shut and blocked it. Still 1–1. There was barely time to catch your breath before Ken Priestlay stepped up. He tried to jink the puck past O'Connor but ran out of room and the puck came away from the post. Still 1-1. The tension was unbelievable.

Back to the Panthers. Randall Weber tried to copy what Blaisdell had done, and seemed to have done enough, but, somehow, Cowley managed to spreadeagle himself acrobatically and slap his stick down across the gap. The puck was blocked and it was still tied. Rob Wilson's turn. Skating slower than the others, seemingly more composed, he closed in on O'Connor. The netminder was forced to shuffle across the ice to close the angle and, for a split second, there was an opening. Wilson took it. 2–1. There was brief pandemonium at the Steelers end but it was tempered by the knowledge that it wasn't over just yet. The Panthers had one more shot to take. Doc Durdle stood up now, tried to take the puck around Cowley, but the puck bobbled loose and Cowley got his stick to it. It was over. The Steelers had won.

As the Steelers players piled on to the ice to celebrate, cavorting wildly with massive grins on their faces, and the Steelers fans danced in their seats, you had to feel desperately sorry for the Panthers. They had played their hearts out, played much better than they had any right to do, but in the end, lost out by the smallest possible margin. The Steelers, though, were deserving grand slam winners, and could now start to enjoy their success. In the press conference after the game, I asked Alex Dampier if it was any less satisfying to win a final on penalties than in the usual way.

'No, I don't think so. I've been in both situations and it's certainly a bad way to lose it. But overall I think it worked out very well for the crowd, I think they enjoyed it.' Coach Clive Tuyl agreed.

'It's unfortunate that we had to go to the shoot-out situation, but I think that other than that short spell in the second period, it was a fairly solid match for us throughout.'

The hero of the hour was Wayne Cowley who, broken finger and all, had performed heroics in the Sheffield goal. He hadn't been in too much pain during the game, he said, but had started to feel it during the shoot-out. That clumsy André Malo nearly had a lot to answer for.

'He had a good game, though, he had two goals, so I can't hold it against him,' Cowley laughed.

I asked Scott O'Connor if it had been tough to lose the game like that.

'Losing this way is very hard,' he conceded. 'I'd rather have lost the game 9–0.'

After coming so close, it had been an agonising defeat. One of the ironies of the shoot-out had been that it had been two defencemen who had scored for Sheffield. O'Connor felt that in some ways they were harder to make the save from than the recognised forwards.

'If you've got Ken Priestlay, maybe you've had him [on a breakaway] two or three times during the year and you know what he does, but the other ones, the defencemen, sometimes maybe they don't know what they're going to do . . . It makes it difficult, but such is life.'

Mike Blaisdell wasn't too disappointed. After the gruelling semi-final win, he hadn't done too much to pump his players up.

'We didn't talk about Sheffield – we've played them so many times this year. Basically, we just relaxed until game time, which maybe hurt us a little because next thing we knew we were 3–0 down . . . but we battled back, and I'm certainly proud of the boys. They never quit, and I didn't expect them to.'

The much predicted fatigue factor, in the end, didn't prove as significant as had been thought, as the Panthers' adrenalin had carried them through.

'Tomorrow's gonna be a tough one, though,' laughed Blaisdell. It would be tough for the Steelers fans too; most of them were going to wake up with gruesome hangovers.

# 19

# A NEW ICE AGE

At the end of the 1995–96 season there was no doubt that it was the fans of the Sheffield Steelers and the Manchester Storm who had reasons to be most smug. The Steelers' grand slam was emphatic evidence, were any more proof needed, that they had taken the sport to the next level in Britain, and now Manchester, in attendance terms at least, were poised to take the sport even further. When the season was over, I interviewed John Lawless to find out how he thought the Storm's first year had gone. I remembered he had set out with two goals in mind: to win promotion, and to fill the building. Now both had been achieved, I asked him which he had considered the more important.

'They go hand in hand, but I guess, if you only had the one, I would take promotion because you still have time to build on the fan base. I would have hated to have had all these fans and not get promoted.'

Indeed, there was no doubt that he had been under pressure to get results, but I wondered how much of the pressure had come from himself.

'Almost all. If I don't put pressure on myself then I shouldn't be here. As soon as you do that, you relieve the pressure from outside, "Holy shit, look at the size of this arena!" It's not pressure – it's a challenge.'

Looking back on the season, it seemed that the luck had run with the Storm all the way. They had missed out on a few signings – McKay, Cadieux and Hope, for example – but that meant they now had Finnie, Byram and Pallister. When new players were needed they seemed to pop up at the right time, and when they started playing, they were invariably the right ones for the club. Lawless suggested that one of the keys to this was flexibility.

'My time in Cardiff has helped me here. When you're running a team you can get blinkered in everything you do – "I gotta get this guy" etc. – and you could be missing some other opportunity. So you do have to have an open mind. Don't get too upset if you don't sign a player.'

There were some people who argued that the Storm's success was a fad. Next season would be different, the games would be much harder and the team would lose a lot more. 'Let's see how many people turn up when they aren't winning 18–1 every week,' the critics said. Would the fans stick with them? Lawless was confident they would.

'In a sports-orientated city like Manchester, it's great to have a sport like this at an affordable price. They deserve it. I'm not having a go at football, because it's proved itself. It's the number one sport. But the marketplace is big enough for us to survive alongside a sport like that. I'm not that concerned that people are saying our fans are not knowledgeable about the sport, that they're not connoisseurs. There's plenty of time for that. Let them learn the fun way. To be honest, some of the hockey we played this season was poor. But because we were still winning – "Hey! Dale Jago slapshot! Top shelf! Whoo" – the fans had fun. But fans soon get bored of that. We had that at Cardiff. They don't want to see walkovers every week. When the games are more competitive, it gets better. If Dale Jago does it against a top European side, I think they'll appreciate it more.'

And Dale would get his chance. Towards the end of the season it was confirmed that a new European competition would start in the 1996–97 season, to run alongside the domestic programme, and by dint of their facilities and fan base, the Storm had been invited to participate. (Sheffield would play again in the European cup, as before.) Once the draw was made it was revealed that the Storm would play in a group alongside teams from Germany, Finland and Sweden. These were very good sides, no doubt about it. The Storm would be doing well if they even got a point. It was a scary prospect, but Lawless couldn't wait.

'Hey, it was scary to come and play in this building in the first place. I just look at it and say, "Hey guys. Let's go." I love the fact we'll be underdogs and should finish last. There's three ways we as a club can look at these games. Firstly, we can say, "Who the hell do these guys think they are? We're as good as them," – but we'd get killed. Secondly we can say, "Wow! Aren't these guys good? Oh my God." Go in there with our tails between our legs – and get killed. Or thirdly, we could say, "Hey, these guys are good. But let's raise our game. Respect them, but not too much." Then we'll compete and surprise a lot of people. We won't beat them, but we'll get a lot of recognition. It'll be a great experience.'

If the prospect of European competition was a step into the unknown, the same could almost be said about the domestic situation. When I started this book I thought I would be chronicling the start of a new era in British ice hockey, but as the season progressed and talk of a Super League emerged, it seemed I was also recording the last season of an old one. The modern era had begun in 1983, with the advent of the Heineken League, but the 1995–96 season would be the last one played under the Premier and First Division system. From next season we would have a different division – that of the haves and have-nots. An élite Super League was taking shape, and the smaller clubs were planning to form their own league. At the time of writing, just how everything will shape up is unclear, so forgive me if anything you now read turns out to be utter drivel, but, pulling on a loathsome woolly jumper, let me do my best Russell Grant impression and look into the future of the sport.

Even as the Wembley weekend closed, there remained uncertainty over what format would be used the next season. Finally, it emerged that the Super League would definitely go ahead in time for the 1996–97 season. The league would start with eight teams: Manchester, Sheffield, Cardiff, Nottingham, Basingstoke, Bracknell, Newcastle and Ayr. The inclusion of Ayr was a surprise to many. In what may finally prove to be the end of one of the longest running sagas in British ice hockey, the Ayr Centrum was finally due for completion in time for the new season. Work had originally started on the building in 1986, when it would have been the largest arena in Britain, but a succession of financial problems had delayed its opening – leading some wags to suggest that it was called the Centrum because it had taken a century to build. Now, finally, it seemed it was ready. The inclusion of Nottingham was also a late one, but the Panthers had announced plans for a new arena which it was hoped would be up and running soon. Cardiff were another side entering the league with plans afoot for a new facility.

No such problems at Newcastle where the arena was already in place. However, the team due to play there was not the Newcastle Warriors, but the Durham Wasps. The Super League was based on a franchise system; that is to say, teams would apply for membership and once accepted, be given exclusive rights to a particular catchment area. It surprised no one that Hall's Wasps, having been one of the prime movers in the whole scheme, should be awarded the Newcastle area franchise, but that is not to say it wasn't harsh on the Warriors, who had applied for membership to the league, but been turned down. The Warriors, it transpired, were to be kicked out of the Newcastle arena and the Wasps installed in their place. You had to feel sympathy for them, but only the most naive observer could have been surprised. Politics, in the end, would mean the Warriors would have to pack their bags and return to Whitley Bay.

Although the Guildford Flames had decided to delay their entry to the new league, feeling the jump in playing standards might be too big to manage in one year, they still intended to join in the second year, as was the case with Solihull, who announced plans to move into the Birmingham NEC. Speculation continued that either the London Docklands Arena or Wembley, perhaps both, might also be persuaded to join, but for the time being there would be eight teams. The league would be governed by the clubs themselves, rather than by the BIHA, a move the BIHA seemed to welcome – a self-governed, professional body seemed the way forward. There would be changes too to the play-off system – although exactly what these were to be was unclear at the time of writing – and drawn games would be followed by ten minutes of sudden-death overtime. The league also announced that they intended to place no restrictions on the nationalities of the players, a move possibly prompted by the daunting European challenges faced by the Steelers and the Storm, which nevertheless drew criticism from John Lawless.

'I think they should still have three imports. There are so many players available right now why should you open it up? You've got so many options – North Americans, dual-nationals, Europeans, British players, etc. Jeeze, if you can't get a half-decent team from all those . . . The concerns must also be heard from the players' union and the Department of Employment regarding displacement of resident labour, all these things.'

Another worry regarding this brave new world was its timing. It was clear that arena-based teams opened up new possibilities for the sport, but all too few teams had them. Wasn't a Super League starting too soon, a case of running before we could walk?

'That was one of my concerns,' concedes Lawless. 'The answer I got was,"Well, what is the right time?" Maybe when we've got more facilities, I thought. The answer I got then was, "In order for that to happen, we've got to take it forward. There are going to be teething problems, sure. But we've really got to take it forward now. Then, get Birmingham on board. Get a London team going, maybe Glasgow, and then we're well on our way. But if we wait another year, then another year, and so on, Birmingham are going to say, 'Hey, you guys don't believe it, so why should we?' It's all facility-led. Get the facilities, get the fan base, get the sponsorship, the television coverage . . . and hopefully a higher standard of hockey. So yes. It is the right time."'

There were other issues that perturbed hockey fans. Super League aside, the gap between the wealthy clubs and the rest was growing. Wasn't there a danger that the likes of Sheffield and Manchester could in fact damage the rest of the sport? Mike Blaisdell, by no means alone in his opinions, voiced his concerns.

'I'm convinced that Johnny Lawless, Alex Dampier and Rick Brebant, and maybe some of the other clubs, have got to sit around a table and really discuss the future of this game. Maybe Johnny Lawless has got to say, "It's not in the best interests of hockey right now for me to go out and buy every damn good hockey player in the country, pack my arena, and stuff it up the ass of every team that I play – just because I can." And maybe it's best for Sheffield to do the same – but human nature doesn't work that way. Everyone looks out for themselves. Can you imagine in the NHL if one club said we're buying all the best players in the country – Lemieux, Gretzky etc. Some sheikh could come in with all the oil money and just make a farce of the league. And it could happen in this country if we don't watch it. Some of the head honchos who are making the decisions are going to have to make some smart ones.'

I put this argument to Lawless. It was one he recognised.

'I don't see it being a major threat – but it is a concern. Everyone likes to win, true, but what are we here for? We're also here to develop the sport, help it grow, but if we go out and kill it it's no good for us or for anybody. Potentially, Newcastle, Manchester and Sheffield, probably in that order, have the biggest budgets. Sir John Hall could throw money at the Wasps that doesn't even relate to what he spends on football, and probably wouldn't be concerned about a return. But at the same time, he knows it's no good for the sport. Ogden know it too. They could throw money at it but where's the return? We've got a nice facility but it's no guarantee that we'll fill it. If we start walking every game, the fans aren't going to come. Anyway, I don't think that just spending money is going to guarantee anything at this level now because even if you had double the budget we had that doesn't mean you'll get double the team.' In many cases, where finance was concerned, it simply didn't add up.

After Wembley, Blaisdell had made the point that the Steelers' budget was something like three times that of the Panthers. On the one hand this showed how well he and the Panthers had done for taking the Steelers all the way, only losing on penalty shots, but on the other hand, it also backed what Lawless was saying. With that kind of spending power the Steelers should have walked it, but were still pushed all the way. The Devils, with a similarly large wallet, hadn't even got that far. Throwing money at a team was no assurance of success. Once you reached a certain point you had to spend considerably more just to improve your team by a slight amount. It was always going to be harder for teams on smaller budgets, obviously, but when Blaisdell promised that even though the Panthers didn't have the financial clout of others, they would 'still compete and be a thorn in the side', no one doubted him for an instant. Although money has always courted success it has never guaranteed it.

What about all the other teams, the Milton Keynes, Sloughs and Blackburns of this world, how do they all fit in? Well, it has long been argued that a club like Slough can never compete with the likes of Sheffield, so why even try? If a team is only going to bankrupt itself trying to keep up it is probably better off not even attempting to. As the Super League took shape, a new league called the National Ice Hockey League (NIHL) was formed. With the exception of Billingham, who seemed to be confining their ambitions to English League hockey, and Paisley, whose entire future seemed in doubt when their local council reduced their backing, all the remaining teams from the Premier and First Divisions agreed to take part. They were to be augmented by the Durham City Wasps, Belfast's Castlereagh Flames and the reborn Streatham Redskins. The Humberside Hawks, hopefully, would re-emerge in this league in one guise or another, and it was hoped a Swindon side would also take part.

The plan seemed to be to have two conferences, North and South, but possibly with differing salary caps in force in each. With the role of the British player looking distinctly vulnerable in the Super League, it was hoped that the NIHL would act as a sanctuary for domestic talent. There would still be imports, but perhaps a voluntary restraint on the number, and this would allow junior players to develop their skills sufficiently to make the leap up to the big league. Like the Super League, the NIHL was looking for sponsorship, and considering a re-vamp of the play-off system, possibly with some system of profit-sharing in place so as to cushion the blow on sides that missed the play-offs. It all sounded commendable enough. Sure, there was a long way to go, but with the right noises being made, there was a chance that the sport was finally getting its act together in time for the next century. There were reasons to be cheerful.

See you at the rink.

# APPENDIX

## BRITISH LEAGUE 1995–96: FINAL STANDINGS

### PREMIER DIVISION

|  | P | W | L | D | GF | GA | Pts |
|---|---|---|---|---|---|---|---|
| **Sheffield Steelers** | 36 | 27 | 4 | 5 | 268 | 122 | 59 |
| Cardiff Devils | 36 | 26 | 7 | 3 | 271 | 140 | 55 |
| Durham Wasps | 36 | 22 | 10 | 4 | 213 | 158 | 48 |
| Nottingham Panthers | 36 | 19 | 12 | 5 | 214 | 174 | 43 |
| Humberside Hawks | 36 | 16 | 16 | 4 | 202 | 235 | 36 |
| Fife Flyers | 36 | 14 | 16 | 6 | 209 | 238 | 34 |
| Basingstoke Bison | 36 | 11 | 20 | 5 | 146 | 190 | 27 |
| Newcastle Warriors | 36 | 10 | 22 | 4 | 167 | 256 | 24 |
| Milton Keynes Kings | 36 | 7 | 22 | 7 | 186 | 237 | 21 |
| Slough Jets | 36 | 5 | 28 | 3 | 172 | 298 | 13 |

### CHAMPIONSHIP PLAY-OFFS

| Group A | P | W | L | D | GF | GA | Pts |
|---|---|---|---|---|---|---|---|
| Sheffield Steelers | 6 | 4 | 2 | 0 | 31 | 12 | 8 |
| Nottingham Panthers | 6 | 3 | 1 | 2 | 20 | 21 | 8 |
| Basingstoke Bison | 6 | 2 | 3 | 1 | 24 | 28 | 5 |
| Fife Flyers | 6 | 1 | 4 | 1 | 22 | 36 | 3 |

| Group B | P | W | L | D | GF | GA | Pts |
|---|---|---|---|---|---|---|---|
| Durham Wasps | 6 | 5 | 1 | 0 | 30 | 18 | 10 |
| Humberside Hawks | 6 | 4 | 2 | 0 | 41 | 31 | 8 |

| | | | | | | |
|---|---|---|---|---|---|---|
| Cardiff Devils | 6 | 3 | 3 | 0 | 28 | 22 | 6 |
| Newcastle Warriors | 6 | 0 | 6 | 0 | 14 | 42 | 0 |

## Semi-finals

| | | | |
|---|---|---|---|
| Humberside Hawks | 3 | Sheffield Steelers | 6 |
| Durham Wasps | 1 | Nottingham Panthers | 3 |

## Final

| | | | |
|---|---|---|---|
| Sheffield Steelers | 3 | Nottingham Panthers | 3 | after overtime |

(Sheffield win 2–1 on penalty shots)

## FIRST DIVISION

| | P | W | L | D | GF | GA | Pts |
|---|---|---|---|---|---|---|---|
| **Manchester Storm** | 52 | 49 | 2 | 1 | 539 | 185 | 99 |
| Blackburn Hawks | 52 | 37 | 13 | 2 | 440 | 278 | 76 |
| Bracknell Bees | 52 | 35 | 13 | 4 | 420 | 233 | 74 |
| Swindon Wildcats | 52 | 35 | 15 | 2 | 472 | 280 | 72 |
| Dumfries Vikings | 52 | 34 | 16 | 2 | 395 | 243 | 70 |
| Guildford Flames | 52 | 32 | 16 | 4 | 384 | 234 | 68 |
| Paisley Pirates | 52 | 30 | 19 | 3 | 428 | 298 | 63 |
| Telford Tigers | 52 | 26 | 25 | 1 | 369 | 340 | 53 |
| Medway Bears | 52 | 18 | 30 | 4 | 296 | 373 | 40 |
| Chelmsford Chieftains | 52 | 16 | 31 | 5 | 267 | 377 | 37 |
| Peterborough Pirates | 52 | 14 | 35 | 3 | 274 | 434 | 31 |
| Solihull Barons | 52 | 10 | 39 | 3 | 276 | 504 | 23 |
| Billingham Bombers | 52 | 6 | 45 | 1 | 242 | 665 | 13 |
| Murrayfield Royals | 52 | 4 | 47 | 1 | 172 | 530 | 9 |

## PREMIER/DIVISION ONE PLAY-OFFS

| Group A | P | W | L | D | GF | GA | Pts |
|---|---|---|---|---|---|---|---|
| **Milton Keynes Kings** | 6 | 4 | 2 | 0 | 42 | 27 | 8 |
| Bracknell Bees | 6 | 4 | 2 | 0 | 31 | 25 | 8 |
| Guildford Flames | 6 | 2 | 3 | 1 | 37 | 38 | 5 |
| Blackburn Hawks | 6 | 1 | 4 | 1 | 33 | 53 | 3 |

| Group B | P | W | L | D | GF | GA | Pts |
|---|---|---|---|---|---|---|---|
| **Manchester Storm** | 6 | 5 | 1 | 0 | 41 | 20 | 10 |
| Swindon Wildcats | 6 | 2 | 3 | 1 | 36 | 46 | 5 |
| Slough Jets | 6 | 2 | 3 | 1 | 30 | 27 | 5 |
| Dumfries Vikings | 6 | 2 | 4 | 0 | 30 | 44 | 4 |

# MANCHESTER STORM 1995–96 Season
(Bold denotes home fixture)

| Date | Team | Result | Score | Att. |
|---|---|---|---|---|
| **Benson & Hedges Cup** | | | | |
| Aug 26 | Telford Tigers | L | 4-6 | 1,007 |
| Aug 27 | Milton Keynes Kings | L | 9-11 | 1,575 |
| Sept 3 | Humberside Hawks | L | 3-22 | 1,000 |
| Sept 10 | Durham Wasps | L | 1-10 | 995 |
| Sept 15 | **Telford Tigers** | D | 6-6 | 10,034 |
| Sept 17 | Durham Wasps | L | 3-5 | 4,441 |
| Sept 23 | Milton Keynes Kings | W | 9-6 | 1,791 |
| Sept 24 | **Humberside Hawks** | L | 3-9 | 3,723 |
| **British Division One** | | | | |
| Oct 1 | **Dumfries Vikings** | W | 6-2 | 4,880 |
| Oct 7 | **Billingham Bombers** | W | 18-1 | 3,796 |
| Oct 8 | Solihull Barons | W | 12-5 | 850 |
| Oct 14 | Guildford Flames | W | 8-5 | 2,039 |
| Oct 15 | **Murrayfield Royals** | W | 9-4 | 4,941 |
| Oct 21 | **Medway Bears** | W | 9-3 | 3,376 |
| Oct 22 | **Paisley Pirates** | D | 7-7 | 5,834 |
| Oct 28 | Dumfries Vikings | W | 6-3 | 988 |
| Oct 29 | Paisley Pirates | W | 6-4 | 1,200 |
| Oct 31 | **Bracknell Bees** | W | 8-3 | 6,410 |
| Nov 4 | Billingham Bombers | W | 13-2 | 220 |
| Nov 5 | **Solihull Barons** | W | 15-2 | 4,167 |
| Nov 9 | **Blackburn Hawks** | L | 9-12 | 8,974 |
| Nov 12 | **Telford Tigers** | W | 9-5 | 5,874 |
| Nov 16 | Peterborough Pirates | W | 15-6 | 3,556 |
| Nov 18 | Telford Tigers | W | 11-6 | 1,124 |
| Nov 19 | **Swindon Wildcats** | W | 8-2 | 6,499 |
| Nov 25 | Swindon Wildcats | L | 6-10 | 1,405 |
| Nov 26 | Murrayfield Royals | W | 8-2 | 460 |
| Nov 30 | Medway Bears | W | 16-7 | 610 |
| Dec 3 | Peterborough Pirates | W | 7-0 | 637 |
| Dec 5 | **Billingham Bombers** | W | 15-1 | 5,819 |
| Dec 9 | Billingham Bombers | W | 18-5 | 230 |
| Dec 10 | Bracknell Bees | W | 9-8 | 1,482 |
| Dec 17 | **Peterborough Pirates** | W | 18-1 | 8,367 |

| Dec 23 | Dumfries Vikings | W | 9-1 | 355 |
|--------|------------------|---|-----|-----|
| Dec 30 | **Murrayfield Royals** | W | 16-0 | 8,173 |
| Dec 31 | Peterborough Pirates | W | 11-4 | 590 |
| | | | | |
| Jan 2 | **Telford Tigers** | W | 8-4 | 5,863 |
| Jan 5 | **Guildford Flames** | W | 8-5 | 6,344 |
| Jan 7 | **Paisley Pirates** | W | 9-1 | 6,210 |
| Jan 9 | Telford Tigers | W | 5-4 | 907 |
| Jan 13 | Paisley Pirates | W | 6-3 | 1,250 |
| Jan 14 | Murrayfield Royals | W | 10-1 | 377 |
| Jan 16 | **Chelmsford Chieftains** | W | 9-1 | 3,687 |
| Jan 21 | Blackburn Hawks | W | 9-3 | 3,500 |
| Jan 27 | Chelmsford Chieftains | W | 12-3 | 675 |
| Jan 28 | **Solihull Barons** | W | 26-3 | 8,256 |
| | | | | |
| Feb 3 | Medway Bears | W | 8-4 | 618 |
| Feb 4 | **Bracknell Bees** | W | 4-2 | 12,386 |
| Feb 8 | Solihull Barons | W | 13-3 | 5,275* |
| Feb 10 | Guildford Flames | W | 6-2 | 1,966 |
| Feb 11 | **Swindon Wildcats** | W | 8-2 | 11,356 |
| Feb 14 | Bracknell Bees | W | 8-5 | 1,750 |
| Feb 17 | Swindon Wildcats | W | 7-3 | 1,406 |
| Feb 18 | **Chelmsford Chieftains** | W | 14-5 | 9,075 |
| Feb 21 | **Blackburn Hawks** | W | 11-3 | 16,280 |
| Feb 24 | **Medway Bears** | W | 9-3 | 10,487 |
| Feb 25 | **Dumfries Vikings** | W | 10-1 | 11,580 |
| Feb 28 | **Guildford Flames** | W | 11-2 | 7,315 |
| | | | | |
| Mar 2 | Blackburn Hawks | W | 17-4 | 2,950 |
| Mar 3 | Chelmsford Chieftains | W | 11-7 | 800 |

## PREMIER/DIVISION ONE PLAY-OFFS

| Mar 9 | Swindon Wildcats | W | 8-4 | 1,743 |
|-------|------------------|---|-----|-------|
| Mar 10 | Slough Jets | W | 3-2 | 9,940 |
| Mar 16 | Slough Jets | W | 7-2 | 1,500 |
| Mar 17 | Dumfries Vikings | L | 5-6 | 1,074 |
| Mar 20 | **Swindon Wildcats** | W | 11-3 | 7,298 |
| Mar 24 | **Dumfries Vikings** | W | 7-3 | 16,344 |

*Played at Nynex arena, Manchester